PAUL SILLS'

STORY
THEATER
FOUR SHOWS

Paul Sills

Cover Photo: Rachel MacKinnon and Paul Dooley in The Indian Parrot, *RUMI*, Los Angeles, 1999 Photo by Jophie Olmsted

PAUL SILLS'

STORY THEATER

FOUR SHOWS

THE BLUE LIGHT AND OTHER STORIES
A CHRISTMAS CAROL BY CHARLES DICKENS
STORIES OF GOD BY RAINER MARIA RILKE
RUMI, TRANSLATED BY COLEMAN BARKS

ADAPTED FOR THE STAGE BY PAUL SILLS

WITH THEATER GAMES
FOR STORY THEATER
BY VIOLA SPOLIN

NEW YORK • LONDON

AN APPLAUSE ORIGINAL

Paul Sills' Story Theater Four Shows

© Copyright 2000 by Paul Sills

Library of Congress Cataloging-In-Publication Data

Library of Congress Catalog Card Number 99-067983

British Library Catalogue in Publication Data

A catalogue record for this book is available from the British Library.

APPLAUSE BOOKS

1841 Broadway Suite 1100
New York, NY 10023
Phone (212) 765-7880
Fax: (212) 765-7875

Combined Book Services Ltd.
Units I/K Paddock Wood Dist. Ctr.
Paddock Wood,
Tonbridge Kent TN12 6UU
Phone 0189 283-7171
Fax 0189 283-7272

PRINTED IN CANADA

Table of Contents

Todd Cazaux

First Story Theater company, August 1968, from left to right: Paul Sills, Joseph Bell, Cordis Heard, Thomas Erhart, Eugenie Ross, Warren Leming and Joyce Piven. Missing: Bernard Beck, Jeffrey Court and Peter Gorwin

Todd Cazaux

July, 1968. Audience outside The Theater at 1848 N. Wells Street, Chicago.

PREFACE

Story Theater evolved at the Game Theater in Chicago. After the assassination of John F. Kennedy in 1963, my wife, Carol, and I returned from New York to Chicago in search of community. We played traditional games in Lincoln Park with a group of friends, moving indoors when winter came to play Viola Spolin's theater games[1] . This activity led me to leave Second City and with the help of the community group open The Game Theater[2].

For several years we played theater games there in public on Friday and Saturday nights, taking suggestions from the audience. Viola Spolin often ran the game nights. During the week we played theater games in workshop to see where this would lead. One afternoon in 1967 the breakthrough into story theater occurred when I coached players to tell the story of *Snow White* while acting the roles, thus eliminating the need for a separate narrator. I began to read seriously the great traditional stories.

Shortly after this, another story helped me see how theater could respond to what was happening in the larger world. The Democratic Party Convention was scheduled in Chicago for August 1968. The Game Theater had closed so some of us thought of opening a bar and doing a show that put the politicians on trial for getting us into Vietnam, but this battle for the soul of the people was beyond satire. Martin Luther King was assassinated in the Spring and the black community was on fire. In June Bobby Kennedy was assassinated. Thousands of students were com-

---

[1] We played the games found in Neva Boyd's *Handbook of Recreational Games*, Dover Press, which is still available. When Viola Spolin was a young woman, Neva Boyd was her teacher for three years in group work with emphasis on traditional games, folk dances and fairy stories. Spolin's *Improvisation for the Theater*, Northwestern University Press, now in its third edition, was first published in 1963.

[2] The Game Theater at 1935 N. Sedgwick opened in May, 1965. The original group included Mona Mellis, Dennis Cunningham, my wife Carol Bleackley, Joanne Shapiro, Mel Spiegel, Jacqueline Kronberg, Mickey Leglaire, Margaret Cunningham, Richard Slowinski, Robert Auerbach, Jeffey Court, Gloria Monroe, Bob Perry and Todd Cazaux . On occasion Betty and James Shiflett, John and Ann Schultz and other community members came to play.

ing to the convention to protest the Vietnam war. We knew Mayor Daley was ready to use city, state, and even national power to keep order. What could theater do or say in the face of these events? Then I read *The Blue Light*,[3] and saw the story happening in stage space just as it was told.

Second City had moved and we could rent the deserted space for four or five months, before a highrise would break ground. We raised some money and transformed the old night club into a theater, built benches, hung lights, rehearsed six stories and opened in July. We charged no admission, but asked for a donation at the end. When Convention Week started and "the whole world was watching," the police chased demonstrators out of Lincoln Park right to our gate but did not enter. Like the churches of the neighborhood, the theater was somehow a sanctuary, off-limits to police. Convention Week has been called 'a turning point in American History' [4] and when our audiences saw an old soldier defeat all authority in *The Blue Light*, the ones most deeply touched by the spirit of liberty shouted "Right on!"

Scheherazade tells stories in the *The Thousand and One Nights* to fascinate her husband and thereby save her life. Often in the story she tells, a fisherman or other character[5] must tell the story of his life or be executed. The stories we must tell, like Scheherazade's, have hidden in them something of the story of our own life. What is hidden according to Viola Spolin, is awareness of the inner self. "Story and games" she said, "bring out self rather than ego." Story tells of the coming forth of the self from hiddenness.

The hiddenness of the true king, king being a metaphor for self, is a major theme for Shakespeare. Hamlet, Malcolm in *Macbeth*, Prince Hal in *Henry IV*, Lear, the Duke in *Measure for Measure*, Prospero in *The Tempest* and even the banished Duke Senior in *As You Like It* come to mind. If in his plays he was intuitively telling the story of his life, Shakespeare was and knew he was a hidden king.

---

[3]. #116 in the Grimm Brothers collection of stories. A Story Theater version appears in this edition.

[4]. Chicago Historical Society Magazine, a few years later.

[5]. In *The Porter and the Ladies of Baghdad*, told on the ninth night, three one-eyed men in succession must each tell the story of his life or lose his head.

Why is my verse so barren of new pride,
So far from variation or quick change?
Why with the time do I not glance aside
To new-found methods and to compounds strange?
Why write I still all one, ever the same,
And keep invention in a noted weed,
That every word doth almost tell my name,
Showing their birth, and where they did proceed?
Oh, know, sweet love, I always write of you,
And you and love are still my argument.
So all my best is dressing old words new
Spending again what is already spent.
For as the sun is daily new and old,
So is my love still telling what is told.

Sonnet 76

This is the way of the storyteller: still telling what is told.

Paul Sills, 1999

THE BLUE LIGHT

AND OTHER STORIES

Adapted for the stage by

Paul Sills

THE BLUE LIGHT AND OTHER STORIES

Copyright © Paul Sills, 2000

Copyright for *The Wedding of Sir Gawain and Dame Ragnelle* by Arnold Weinstein and Paul Sills, 1999

INTRODUCTION

THE BLUE LIGHT AND OTHER STORIES

The first show in story theater form was done in Chicago, July, 1968.[1]

The stories staged in this first production were *The Bremen Town Musicians*, Grimm #27, *The Goose Girl*, #89, *Godfather Death*, #44, *The Fisherman and His Wife*, #197, *The Blue Light*, #116, and *The Wedding of Sir Gawain*, a 14th century poem by Anonymous, discovered for me by Heinrich Zimmer in '*The King and the Corpse*'. [2] I read the old English poem in the Newberry Library and adapted it for our production. It was later rewritten by Arnold Weinstein, the poet/playwright who has since done many shows with me in story theater form, some soon to be published in a companion volume.

The Blue Light was done without a script; we referred to the story but rarely told it in the storyteller's words. We did the actions, accompanied by blues music and said the necessary dialogue, as if it were a movie. I still see Tom Erhart dangling on a rope being lowered by the Witch into the fatal space of her well (his feet never leaving the stage floor) and Joyce Piven on a higher level laboriously turning the winch on which his life depended. It must be remembered that story theater is done without scenery or properties in their material form; all is invisible until brought into existence by the players who shape the space. This space is the place of 'the unfolding of the unpredictable', as Viola Spolin said, where the invisible can become visible, the space of vision. The combination of this sense of space, nurtured by Spolin theater games, with the space of story, on an open stage with no obstructing scenery or furniture, helps the audience see the invisible.

Clever Gretel, #77 in Grimm, was scripted for Mildred Dunnock, at the time a member of the acting company of the Yale Repertory

---

[1] A discussion of this theater and the year 1968 may be found in the preface. The cast included Tom Erhart and Joyce Piven who had worked with me at Playwrights Theater in the 50's doing classic plays, Joseph Bell, Bernard Beck, Jeffrey Court, Warren Leming and Eugenie Ross who had played Spolin Theater Games at the Game Theater and young players Peter Gorwin and Cordis Heard. I directed and played some roles. The renovation of the old Second City at 1848 N. Wells was by Hugh Ralley, the stage design by Carol Bleackley.

[2] The Bollingen Series, XI, Pantheon Books.

Theater for whom I did a story theater show in the Fall of 1968. Robert
Brustein had invited me to teach a class in improvisation at the drama
school and when students complained of racism in the production scheduled for his repertory company, Brustein needed another show. Larry
Arrick, who directed the Compass [3] in the 50's for a time, had heard about
story theater and told Brustein, who asked me to do the show with his
company[4] . Besides *Clever Gretel* [5] I added *The Golden Goose*, #64, to my
collection of stories. We had only two weeks to opening so Larry Arrick
helped direct two of the stories after I laid out the way they were to be
told. Story Theater was a hit at Yale and a television show of the performance was made by PBS.

Mike Nichols, a friend from university days and The Compass,
donated seed money and I returned to Chicago, gathered a young company, [6] and rented and renovated space on Lincoln Avenue[7]. My wife,
Carol, thought of naming our new theater The Body Politic.

I chose stories from Ovid's *Metamorphoses* for the opening show,
but a Penguin prose translation discouraged the players until Arnold
Weinstein took the original poem and wrote his version with me by his
side. The show opened to good reviews.

The young company did a second show, *The Master Thief* (#192)
and Other Stories, which included the folktale *Henny Penny* and *The Robber
Bridegroom*, #40. When it was time for a third show Alan Myerson called
from The Committee in San Francisco to ask if I had a place in the company for Del Close. Del returned to Chicago and played *The Little
Peasant*, #61 for its story theater debut in a show called *The Parson In The
Cupboard*.

Along with *The Fisherman and His Wife*, *The Bremen Town
Musicians*, *The Golden Goose* and some short pieces, these stories were the

---

[3] The Compass, Chicago, the first improvisational theater, producer/director
David Shepherd.

[4] David Ackroyd, Alvin Epstein, Michael Lombard, Mildred Dunnock, David
Clennon, Joan Pape and Pamela Jones, with Barbara Damashek on the guitar and
as princess.

[5] *Clever Gretel* is an old folk tale. In the Arabian Nights it comes as *The Butcher's
Tale*, told on the 850th night. The American Indians also have a story with the
same comic idea.

[6] The Body Politic company, some of them fresh from Northwestern University
Drama School, included Charles Bartlett, Gerrit Graham, Cordis Heard,
Caroline Jones, James Keach, Molly McKasson, Bernadine Redeaux and Tom
Towles.

[7] From James Shiflett, Community Arts Foundation.

ones performed in 1970 by the professional company which presented Story Theater at the Mark Taper Forum in Los Angeles and went on to Broadway's Ambassador Theater in New York.

These events resulted from a suggestion my mother made to Mark Taper director Gordon Davidson that he see what I was doing in Chicago. Gordon, who had been stage manager for Second City on Broadway in 1961, came and invited me to do a few performances for his New Theater for Now in L.A. Then, just as happened at Yale, he lost a show; Actor's Equity refused him permission to use an English actress the author insisted on and Gordon, who had a subscription audience waiting, took a chance on Story Theater. [8]

The Los Angeles Drama Critics voted Story Theater the Best Production of the Year, honoring me as best director. Produced by Zev Bufman, we then went to New York for a nine month run, where we were nominated for Tony Awards for Best Show and Best Director and won for Best Lighting by H.R. Poindexter and Best Supporting Actor, Paul Sand. [9]

In 1971 a 26-week, half-hour television series of Story Theater was made in Vancouver with CTV, and syndicated in major US cities. The old Scottish ballad *Binnorie* was first done on this TV series. I have presented this story four times word for word from the retelling of the ballad in prose by Joseph Jacobs in his English Fairy Tales, published by Dover Press. *Lucky John*, Grimm #83, was also first done on the TV series with Alan Alda in the title role. *All Three of Us*, #120, was first played then also.

In San Francisco, 1974, I produced a story theater show in the former Committee nightclub, which we renovated. In this company John Brent of Second City/Committee and Garry Goodrow, longtime Committee member, were the first to perform *The Farmer and the Money Lender*.[10] Melinda Dillon played the title role in *Our Lady's Child*, Grimm # 3; also first performed in this production.

---

[8] The Los Angeles company of former Second City/Committee players included Hamilton Camp, Melinda Dillon, Peter Bonerz, Valerie Harper, Richard Schaal, Richard Libertini and Paul Sand, with Mary Frann and Lewis Arquette as alternates. Hamilton Camp's band, The True Brethren, with Raphael Grinage, Waquidi Falicoff, Lewis Ross and Loren Pickford provided the music. Camp and Ross sang songs by himself, Bob Dylan, George Harrison and Country Joe McDonald.

[9] The script for that production, *Paul Sills' Story Theatre* and the subsequent *More From Story Theatre* can be ordered from Samuel French Inc., 45 W. 25th St., New York, N.Y. 10010, who have amateur and professional leasing rights.

[10] The story is from the Dover edition of *East Indian Folk and Fairy Tales.*

Peter Bonerz as Bird, Hamilton Camp as Mouse, Avery Schreiber as Sausage; Grimm #23, CTV 1971.

The four very short stories in *The Blue Light and Other Stories* include one from Aesop, *The Housedog and the Wolf*, adapted for television by Arnold Weinstein, and three fables from Grimm performed at my Learning Theater, Pipers Alley, Chicago, 1980. These stories are: *The Golden Key*, #200, *The Fox and the Geese*, #86, and *The Poor Man in Heaven*, #167. This company[11] also performed *Our Lady's Child*, *Lucky John* and *The Farmer and the Money Lender* . Tapes of this show's stories were transcribed into the scripts included in this anthology's *The Blue Light and Other Stories*.

---

[11] Perry Anzilotti, Larry Coven, Frank Farrell, Rick Kuhlman, Jeannette Schwaba, Marsia Turner, and Vince Waldron; music played on guitar by Rick Mann.

Left to Right: Valerie Harper as Henny Penny, Richard Schaal as Cocky Locky, Hamilton Camp as Ducky Daddles, Melinda Dillon as Goosey Poosey with Paul Sand as Turkey Lurkey in *Paul Sills' Story Theatre*, Ambassador Theatre, New York, 1970

Richard Libertini as The Count, Paul Sand as The Clerk, Richard Schaal as The Parson and Peter Bonerz as The Master Thief, in *Paul Sills' Story Theatre*, Ambassador Theatre, New York, 1970.

THE BLUE LIGHT AND OTHER STORIES
ACT ONE

THE GOLDEN KEY
Young Person (boy or girl)

ALL THREE OF US
Three Entertainers
The Devil
Band Leader
Innkeeper
Innkeeper's Wife
Rich Man
Bailiff
Judge
Messenger

BINNORIE
Eldest Sister
Younger Sister
Sir William
Miller's Daugheter
Miller
Harper
King Queen

LUCKY JOHN
John

His Master
Horseman
Farmer's Wife
Butcher
Goose Girl
Scissors Grinder

OUR LADY'S CHILD
Announcer
Woodcutter
Wife
Mary
Little Angels (four)
The Girl
King
Courtiers (three)
Nurse Townspersons (four)
Judge
Executioners (two)

THE FOX AND THE GEESE
Fox
Geese (any number)

INTERMISSION

Act Two

The Blue Light

Soldier
King
Witch
Blue Man
Hotel Owner
Princess
King's Men
Child
Soldiers of King
Guard
Judge

A Poor Man in Heaven

Poor Man
Rich Man
Saint Peter
Angels

Clever Gretel

Gretel
Her Master
The Guest

The Farmer and the Money Lender

Farmer
Money Lender
Brahman
Yogi
Beggar (Ram)
Musician

The Housedog and the Wolf

Wolf
Housedog

The Wedding of Sir Gawain and Dame Ragnelle

Singer
King Arthur
Gromer Somer Joure
Sir Gawain
Women (up to ten)
Dame Ragnelle
Queen Guenevere
Knights

THE BLUE LIGHT AND OTHER STORIES

ACT ONE

THE GOLDEN KEY

YOUNG PERSON: One winter's day, when the ground lay deep in snow, a poor boy went into the forest with a sled to bring back wood. Because he was so cold, he decided to make a fire and warm himself a bit. He cleared a space, and as he was scraping away the snow, he found a tiny golden key. 'Where there's a key, there's sure to be a lock'. So he dug down into the ground and found an iron box. 'There must be precious things in it! If only the key fits!' At first there seemed to be no keyhole, but then at last he found one, so small he could hardly see it. He tried the key and it fit perfectly. He began to turn it . Now we'll have to wait until he turns it all the way and opens the lid. Then we shall know what wonderful things were in the box.

ALL THREE OF US

FIRST PLAYER: There were once three traveling players.

SECOND PLAYER: They swore they'd always stay together on the road.

THIRD PLAYER: And work together as long as possible.

FIRST PLAYER: One time they found themselves stranded, out of town, and out of work.

SECOND PLAYER: They were practically in rags.

THIRD PLAYER: They had nothing to live on.

FIRST PLAYER: They decided they'd better split up the act.

SECOND PLAYER: We can keep in touch through the mail.

THIRD PLAYER: And work together as soon as one of us finds a gig.

FIRST PLAYER: Don't forget to write, okay?

MAN: (*enters*) I wouldn't do that if I were you.

SECOND PLAYER: A sharply dressed dude approached them

THIRD PLAYER: through the fog and mist.

MAN: Hey, I've seen your act. You're pretty good. Better stick together.

First Player: We can't find any work.

Man: Maybe I can help you with that. It so happens that I have a job for you.

Third Player: Oh yeah, what kind of job?

Man: One where you can make a lot of money.

Second Player: As long as we don't have to sell our souls or nothing.

(all laugh)

Man: No, it's not your souls that I'm interested in.

(the three suddenly realize who the man is)

Three: Agh! A cloven hoof!

(all scream in fright)

Devil: Hold it! Didn't you hear what I said? It's not your souls that I'm interested in. Souls I want are other people's souls. Souls already half mine. All I need you for is to give them a little nudge, know what I mean? Listen, I tell you what. Why don't I give you a little money in advance. For on the road expenses. Call it a per diem. Talk it over. Let me know what you decide.

(all three make sounds of agreement)

First: So, feeling themselves safe,

Second: they agreed,

Third: to listen.

Devil: Good! Now listen, here's the script. Whenever anybody asks you a question I want you *(indicating to them in order)* to reply 'all three of us.'

First: All three of us.

Devil: Right. And then you come in and say, 'For the money.'

Second: For the money.

Devil: Yeah. And then you have the big topper: 'That's right.'

Third: That's right.

Devil: Right! Now as long as you answer with exactly these replies to every question put to you, your pockets will always be filled with money. *(the three murmur in excitement)* But, if you depart by even one syllable from the answers I have given you, that money will disappear. Is that clear?

FIRST: Clear as a bell.

SECOND: Sure, you bet.

THIRD: No problem.

(they realize the money has vanished)

DEVIL: I mean, do you understand?

FIRST: All three of us.

SECOND: For the money.

THIRD: That's right.

DEVIL: Now we're cooking with gas.

(the three find their money again)

DEVIL: Now listen, I want you to go down the street to the hotel. Check in. Eat and drink, have a good time, spend the night. But most importantly, I want you to see everything and hear everything that goes on there. You got that?

FIRST: All three of us.

SECOND: For the money.

THIRD: That's right.

DEVIL: You're beautiful. You're going to be terrific. *(exits)*

FIRST: So, they went to the hotel. *(music is playing)*

MUSICIAN: Thank you and welcome to the Flamingo Room here at the Hotel Up the Road. And now here's your host for this evening, Johnny Domino.

INNKEEPER: Thank you, what a crowd here tonight! Here are three wayfarers I have not met. Have you been traveling a long time?

FIRST: All three of us.

INNKEEPER: Well you won't get a group discount. *(laughs)*

SECOND: For the money.

INNKEEPER: You gotta make every penny you can these days.

THIRD: That's right.

INNKEEPER: This one agrees. Sweet! *(scat sings)*

INNKEEPER'S WIFE: Johnny, Johnny, come here a second.

INNKEEPER: The little lady has called a short break. *(to her)* What do you want?

WIFE: Johnny, get the money up front.

INNKEEPER: Yes. (*to the players*) There's the little matter of a check. Who's going to pay?

FIRST: All three of us.

SECOND: For the money.

THIRD: That's right.

INNKEEPER: Thank you. (*takes cash*) Ruby, they paid even more than was due.

WIFE: They must be mad.

INNKEEPER: All the better for us, snookums. (*scat sings under the following*)

FIRST: So for a time,

SECOND: they stayed at the hotel,

THIRD: and said nothing but,

FIRST: All three of us.

SECOND: For the money.

THIRD: That's right.

FIRST: But they saw everything,

SECOND: and they knew everything

THIRD: that went on there.

(*knock on the door, music stops*)

WIFE: That night a rich man arrived at the inn.

INNKEEPER: Welcome, welcome, sir.

RICH MAN: Take my bag, will you son.

INNKEEPER: It's heavy. You must be a big reader.

RICH MAN: That's not books, son, that's gold. Twenty four carat gold. (*to wife*) Listen, cutie, just a second, who might these people be?

WIFE: These are just three traveling players.

RICH MAN: (*to the three*) Actors, huh?

FIRST: All three of us.

SECOND: For the money.

THIRD: That's right.

RICH MAN: I don't trust them a bit. Bring that gold up and I'll keep it under my bed where it's safe.

INNKEEPER: As you wish, sir. Ruby, put him in the special suite. And you traveling players, you're going to have to camp down here for tonight. Ciao. (*exeunt*)

(*Clock bells ring. Innkeeper and Wife enter. Players sleepily see them.*)

INNKEEPER: And late that night

WIFE: when everybody was asleep,

INNKEEPER: the innkeeper

WIFE: and his wife, crept downstairs to the fireplace,

INNKEEPER: where they took an ax

WIFE: and went to the rich man's room, (*exits*)

INNKEEPER: to chop him to bits. (*exits*)

(*the wife screams off, three players waken, innkeeper and wife enter*)

WIFE: Oh, murder! The rich man is dead! He's covered in blood! Oh, I need a drink!

INNKEEPER: Murder in my hotel! I think I know who did it, and I can prove it. You there, who killed the rich man? Spit it out, sweetheart!

FIRST: All three of us.

INNKEEPER: Why did you want to do something like that?

SECOND: For the money.

INNKEEPER: And what do *you* say?

THIRD: That's right.

INNKEEPER: This one agrees. Ruby, call the cops. (*exeunt*)

(*Scene transforms to a prison cell. They hold the space bars.*)

FIRST: So they were thrown in prison. And were to be tried.

SECOND: And when they saw that everything had taken a turn for the worse,

THIRD: they got really frightened.

DEVIL: (*enters*) Sweethearts! Over here. I know this is seeming like a bummer gig to you guys now, but I want you to hang in there. Remember, an oral contract is just as valid as a written one. And besides, we're troopers, we're in the business. Hey, do you agree the show must go on?

FIRST: All three of us.

SECOND: For the money.

THIRD: That's right.

DEVIL: Aw, you're beautiful!

> *(Scene transforms to the court.)*

BAILIFF: Hear ye, hear ye, court's now in session.

JUDGE: Who killed the rich man?

FIRST: All three of us.

JUDGE: Why did you do it?

SECOND: For the money.

JUDGE: And you have no remorse for this deed?

THIRD: That's right.

JUDGE: Off with their heads!

BAILIFF: So they were taken to the executioner's circle.

INNKEEPER: The Innkeeper

WIFE: and his wife

INNKEEPER: had front row seats.

> *(The ax is raised above them and the three fall to their knees shaking with fear. Sounds of arrival.)*

MESSENGER*: *(enters)* Stop! I bring a message from the governor. His excellency states that the three traveling players are to be given full and complete pardon. And now, they are to speak the truth about what they saw and heard the night of the murder.

FIRST: We didn't kill the rich man, they did.

INNKEEPER: Hold on here.

SECOND: It was the Innkeeper and his wife.

INNKEEPER: That's right, she was there too.

THIRD: And there's more bodies in the basement. Look for yourself.

INNKEEPER: And so the judge sent his men to the basement of the hotel.

WIFE: Where everything they said was found to be true.

JUDGE: Off with their heads!

INNKEEPER: Thanks a lot, guys! Next time make reservations.

DEVIL: Should have been sent to hell for his jokes alone. Now I've got the souls I wanted and you've got all the money you need for the rest of your lives. Maybe I'll catch your act some day. Break a leg, you understand? (*exits*)

FIRST: And so the three traveling players went off into the world.

SECOND: And for all we know, they're traveling still.

THIRD: That's right.

(*They walk in place as lights fade.*)

The Rich Man and the Messenger can be played by the actor who plays the Devil.

BINNORIE

(*The song is played*.*)

ELDEST SISTER: Once upon a time there were two king's daughters who lived in a bower

YOUNGER SISTER: near the bonny mill-dams of Binnorie.

SIR WILLIAM: And Sir William came wooing the eldest

ELDEST SISTER: and won her love

SIR WILLIAM: and plighted troth with glove and ring. (*they dance*)

YOUNGER SISTER: But after a time he looked upon the youngest,

SIR WILLIAM: with her cherry cheeks and shining hair, and his love went out to her

YOUNGER SISTER: 'til he cared no longer for the eldest one.

ELDEST SISTER: So she hated her sister for taking away Sir William's love, and day by day her hate grew and grew and she plotted and planned how to be rid of her. So one fine morning, fair and clear, she said to her sister, 'Let's go and see our father's boats come in at the bonnie mill-stream of Binnorie.'

YOUNGER SISTER: So they went there hand in hand.

ELDEST SISTER: And when they came to the river's bank

YOUNGER SISTER: the youngest got upon a stone to watch for the beaching of the boats.

* Music on Page 56

ELDEST SISTER: And her sister, coming behind her, caught her round the waist and dashed her into the rushing mill-stream of Binnorie.

YOUNGER SISTER: O sister, O sister, reach me your glove! And you shall have Sir William's love.

ELDEST SISTER: Sink on! Your sweet William will be all mine when you are drowned beneath the bonny mill-stream of Binnorie. *(exits)*

YOUNGER SISTER: And the princess floated down the mill-stream, sometimes swimming and sometimes sinking, till she came near the mill.

MILLER'S DAUGHTER: Now the miller's daughter was cooking that day, and needed water for her cooking. And as she went to draw it from the stream, she saw something floating towards the mill-dam. Father! Draw your dam! There's something white - a mermaid or a milk-white swan - coming down the stream.

MILLER: So the miller hastened to the dam and stopped the heavy cruel mill-wheels. And then they took out the princess and laid her on the bank. Fair and beautiful she looked as she lay there. In her shining hair were pearls and precious stones;

MILLER'S DAUGHTER: you could not see her waist for her golden girdle, and the golden fringe of her white dress came down over her lily feet.

MILLER: But she was drowned,

MILLER'S DAUGHTER: drowned!

HARPER: And as she lay there in her beauty, a famous harper passed by the mill-dam of Binnorie, and saw her sweet pale face. *(She is carried off.)* And though he traveled on far away he never forgot that face, and after many days he came back to the bonny mill-stream of Binnorie. But then all he could find of her where they had put her to rest were her bones and her shining hair. So he made a harp out of her breast-bone and her hair, whose sounds would melt a heart of stone, and traveled on up the hill from the mill-dam of Binnorie, till he came to the castle of the king her father.

SIR WILLIAM: That night they were all gathered in the castle hall to hear the great harper -

KING: King

QUEEN: and Queen,

ELDEST SISTER: their daughter, the eldest sister,

SIR WILLIAM: Sir William and all their Court.

HARPER: And first the harper sang to his old harp, making them joy and be glad, or sorrow and weep just as he liked. But while he sang he put the harp he had made that day on a stone in the hall. And first the harp sang low and clear

YOUNGER SISTER: *(her voice) Binnorie, O Binnorie!*

Farewell, my father and mother dear,

By the bonnie mill dams of Binnorie.

SIR WILLIAM: Next when the harp began to sing

YOUNGER SISTER: *(her voice)* Binnorie, O Binnorie

Farewell William,

SIR WILLIAM: said the string

YOUNGER SISTER: *(her voice)* By the bonnie mill dams of Binnorie.

KING: Then they all wondered,

HARPER: and the harper told them how he had seen the princess lying drowned on the bank near the bonnie mill dams of Binnorie, and how he had afterwards made this harp out of her hair and breast bone.

QUEEN: Just then the harp began singing again,

ELDEST SISTER: and then as plain as plain could be:

YOUNGER SISTER: *(her voice)*   Binnorie, O Binnorie!

There sits my sister, who drowned me,

By the bonnie mill dams of Binnorie.

(The Eldest Sister kneels and bows her head.)

HARPER: And the harp snapped and broke,

ELDEST SISTER: and never sang more.

LUCKY JOHN

JOHN: John had worked for his master seven years and his time was up. I want to go back to my mother. Give me my wages.

MASTER: You served us loyally and honestly. Like service, like wage. *(opens safe)* Here, John, is a piece of gold as big as your head.

JOHN: John wrapped the gold in his pocket handkerchief, put it on his shoulder and started for home. On the road he saw a man on a horse.

HORSEMAN: *(entering, riding)* The horseman was trotting along on a lively chestnut mare. *(See instruction/advice on riding a horse onstage, page 211.)*

JOHN: Ah! How fine! It's like sitting in a chair. You spare your shoes, and you get there in no time.

HORSEMAN: Right you are, John! But why are you walking so slowly?

JOHN: I have to get home with this nugget of gold. It weighs me down.

HORSEMAN: It's as big as your head!

JOHN: Yeah, but the lump makes it impossible to hold my head straight. And it hurts my shoulder like crazy.

HORSEMAN: I'll tell you what; let's exchange. I'll give you my horse, and you give me your lump.

JOHN: What a deal! But I warn you, it's a heavy son-of-a-gun.

HORSEMAN: *(exchanging horse for gold)* Here. *(helping John on to the saddle)* Now if you want to go fast, just click your tongue and call 'giddup! giddup!' *(Horseman exits carrying the gold as best he can.)*

JOHN: Look at me! *(trots around)* I bet I can ride faster than this. Giddup! *(Horse bucks and John is thrown.)*

FARMER: *(Enters, grabs reins, and calms the horse. He is leading a cow.)* What happened, John?

JOHN: *(groans)* Riding is a bad joke - especially with this sort of horse. I could have broken my neck. I'm through with riding. Now your cow is different. She's nice and slow. She gives milk and cheese every day. What I wouldn't give to have such a cow!

FARMER: Well, if it would make you so happy, I'll trade you.

JOHN: My horse for your cow?

FARMER: Yes.

JOHN: A deal! *(They exchange. Farmer exits with horse.)* John was truly happy. As long as I have a piece of bread I'll have cheese sandwiches and milk to drink. *(Feels noon sun.)* It'll take an hour to cross this heath. My tongue is sticking to the roof of my mouth. I need something to drink. *(Takes off cap and tries to milk the cow.)* Not a drop came. On top of it, he was clumsy and the cow got irritated. *(She kicks him in the head.)* Where am I?

BUTCHER: Along came a butcher with a pig in a wheel barrow. *(He helps John up.)* What's the game?

JOHN: John told him the whole story.

BUTCHER: Have a drink of this. *(Hands him a flask.)* The cow probably won't give milk because it's an old creature fit only to be butchered.

JOHN: *(Stroking back his hair.)* Who'd have thought of that! What a lot of meat one could get! Of course, I'm not fond of cow meat. Too dry. Now a young pig like that is juicy! And there are sausages, too!

BUTCHER: Listen, John, as a favor I'll give you my pig for the cow.

JOHN: May God reward your kindness. *(They exchange, Butcher exits.)* How everything works out! I get anything I want. The least trouble is immediately set right.

GOOSE GIRL: A girl came by with a goose. Good day, John.

JOHN: Good day to you. Nice goose you got there.

GOOSE GIRL: Just heft it for the weight of it. They've been fattening it eight weeks for a party. Anyone who takes a bite of it once it's roasted will have to wipe the fat from both sides of his mouth.

JOHN: *(Hefting the goose.)* She's heavy enough, but my pig is bigger yet. And he told her the whole story, about all the trades he'd made.

GOOSE GIRL: *(Looking around with a worried look.)* Listen, there may be something wrong with your pig. In the village back there someone just stole one from the mayor's sty. The police are on the alert. If they catch you with that pig it means the black hole.

JOHN: Help me get out of this! You know the way around these parts. Take my pig and leave me your goose.

GOOSE GIRL: It's risky. But I don't want to be blamed for your getting into trouble. *(They exchange animals, she exits.)*

JOHN: Bless you! *(alone)* Thinking it over, I have the best of the bargain again. First there's the taste of the goose! Then there's three month's goose fat. And last but not least, there's the feathers for my mother's pillow. How glad she'll be! *(Walks along, the goose honks. A grinder enters and turns his wheel.)*

GRINDER: *(sings)* I grind the scissors and turn the wheel. Who can tell how good I feel.

JOHN: You must be the happy man I've heard so much about.

GRINDER: Because a scissors grinder always finds money in his pockets. But where did you buy that fine goose?

JOHN: I didn't buy it, I traded it for a pig.

GRINDER: And the pig?

JOHN: I got that for a cow.

GRINDER: And the cow?

JOHN: I got that for a horse.

GRINDER: And the horse?

JOHN: For that I gave a lump of gold as big as my head.

GRINDER: And the gold?

JOHN: That was my wages for seven year's service.

GRINDER: You sure know how to look out for yourself. If only you knew how to hear money jingle in your pocket, you'd make your fortune.

JOHN: How can I do that?

GRINDER: You've got to be a scissors grinder like me. All you need is a grindstone. Here! *(holding out his stone)* It's a little worn on the edge, but you don't have to give me anything for it except your goose. What do you say?

JOHN: How can you ask? I'll be the luckiest fellow on earth. If I find money every time I feel in my pocket, what have I got to worry about?

GRINDER: *(picking up field stone)* Here's another good stone in the bargain. You hit your old bent nails on it, you straighten them out. Take good care of it. *(Exits with the goose.)*

JOHN: *(carries grindstone, shoulders field stone, walks)* I'm a lucky boy! Everything I want I get. He had been on his feet all day and was tired. The weight of the stones was killing him. Wish I didn't have to carry these stones. Water! There was a well by the roadside. He carefully set the stones on the edge of the well. But when he bent over to drink he made a false move, and both of the stones went into the well. *(plop, plop)* When he saw them disappear into the water, John jumped for joy! *(he kneels)* With tears in his eyes he thanked God for relieving him of those heavy stones. No one under the sun can be as happy as I! *(rises)* So with a light heart and free from every burden, he skipped along until he reached his mother and home.

OUR LADY'S CHILD

(When this story was done to gospel music, the following introduction was used:)

- And now brothers and sisters, I want you to sit back and relax, give your eyes and your ears to us, because we are about to tell you the most beautiful and serene story of Our Lady's Child.

WOODCUTTER: On the edge of a large forest lived a woodcutter and his wife.

WIFE: *(holding baby)* And they had an only child, an infant in arms.

WOODCUTTER: They were so poor that they no longer had their daily bread.

WIFE: The mother's milk dried up.

WOODCUTTER: The child grew sickly,

WIFE: and they looked for her to die.

WOODCUTTER: One morning as the woodcutter sadly set out to work

WIFE: a tall and beautiful woman approached,

WOODCUTTER: a crown of shining stars on her head.

MARY: I am the Virgin Mary, mother of the child Jesus. You are poor and needy and your child will surely die. Give her to me. I will take her with me and be her mother, and care for her.

WOODCUTTER: Not knowing what else to do

WIFE: they gave her the child.

MARY: The Virgin Mary took the child and brought her up to heaven.

ANGEL ONE: The little angels took good care of her.

ANGEL TWO: They fed her sweet cakes

ANGEL THREE: and fresh milk.

ANGEL FOUR: The child grew and was happy,

ANGEL ONE: and the little angels played with her.

MARY: One day, when she was fourteen, the Virgin Mary called to her. Child!

GIRL: What do you want?

MARY: Dear child, I am about to make a long journey. Take charge of the keys to the Thirteen Doors of Heaven. *(Little Angels and Girl ooh and aah over the keys.)* Twelve of these you may open, and behold the glory that is within them, but the thirteenth door, which this little key opens, is forbidden to you.

GIRL: All right!

MARY: Be careful not to unlock it or you will be unhappy.

GIRL: Okay!

ANGELS: Goodbye Virgin Mary. Have a nice trip.

MARY: Goodbye children. *(exits)*

GIRL: When the Virgin was gone the girl began to open the doors of the Heavenly Kingdom,

ANGELS: always accompanied by the little angels.

GIRL: Each day she unlocked one door,

ANGEL TWO: until she made a round of the twelve.

GIRL: In each dwelling sat one of the twelve apostles in the midst of a glorious light.

ANGELS: Look, there's Peter / or is it Paul? / He's hanging upside down.

GIRL: She was delighted by all the pomp and splendor.

ANGELS: And the little angels rejoiced with her.

ANGEL THREE: Until finally only the forbidden door was left.

GIRL: I won't open it wide or go in or nothing, but I'll unlock it so we can get a tiny peek through the crack.

ANGEL FOUR: O no! that would be a sin.

ANGEL ONE: The Virgin Mary has forbidden it. It might cause your misfortune.

GIRL: Come on, you babies.

ANGEL TWO: Better not, you'll go to hell. *(exeunt Angels)*

GIRL: Then she kept still, but the desire in her heart gnawed at her and tormented her, and gave her no peace. Until at last, when she was all alone, and sure no one would ever know, *(puts key in lock)* she took the thirteenth key and opened the forbidden door. There sat the Trinity in fire and light. She reached in to touch the light and immediately her finger was golden. *(In fear, slams door and runs away.)* And no matter how much she washed it and rubbed it, the gold stayed on, and would not go away.

ANGELS: *(chanting)* Gold on your finger! Gold on your finger!

MARY: *(off)* Hello, I'm home!

ANGELS: It's the Virgin Mary. Welcome back, Mary!

MARY: *(School bell rings. Mary enters and writes on blackboard.)* What a trip!

ANGEL THREE: Where did you go?

MARY: _____. *(any appropriate local spot)* Pass your assignments to the right, please. Child, may I have the Keys of Heaven back. *(Girl hands them over.)* You didn't open the Thirteenth Door, did you?

GIRL: *(indignant)* No!

MARY: Then the Virgin Mary put her hand on the girl's beating heart.

ANGELS: Uh oh!

MARY: Are you sure you didn't do it?

GIRL: Yes.

MARY: All right everyone, show me your hands.

ANGELS: Here's mine! Here!

MARY: Then the Virgin Mary touched the girl's golden finger. O child, you lied to me, and disobeyed me as well. You are no longer worthy to be in Heaven. Be off with you. *(Pushes her, Girl spins and falls.)*

GIRL: Then the girl sank into a deep sleep. She awoke in a wilderness. She tried to cry out but found she could make no sound. And wherever she turned she was held back by thick hedges of brambles and thorns. An old hollow tree had to be her dwelling place, at night and in storm and rain. *(rain and wind sounds heard)* And how bitterly she did weep when she thought how fine it had been in Heaven, and how the little angels played with her. Roots and berries were her only food, and nuts in autumn, and fallen leaves to creep among when snow came, and ice. Soon her clothes were torn, and bit by bit they fell away. But when the sun shone warm again, her long hair covered her sides like a cloak. She would go out and sit in front of the hollow tree, and there she sat year after year, and felt the woe and misery of the world.

KING: *(entering)* One day when the trees again were fresh and green, the King was hunting in the forest. Following a deer into a thicket, he saw a beautiful maiden covered with her long golden hair. Who are you? Why are you sitting here in the wilderness?

GIRL: She tried to speak, but could make no reply.

KING: Will you come with me to my palace? *(She nods her head. He helps her mount beside him and they trot off.)*

GIRL: She said not a word but mounted the horse,

KING: and they rode till they reached his courtyard.

COURTIER ONE: At the castle everyone came out to greet them.

(*All call out their greetings.*)

KING: The King ordered the finest clothes be brought to her.

COURTIER TWO: An abundance of everything was given to her.

KING: And though she could not speak, the King began to love her with all of his heart.

COURTIER THREE: It was not long before he married her.

(*All perform and celebrate wedding. Exeunt omnes. A nurse enters, carrying an infant.*)

NURSE: After a year she gave birth to a little boy.

GIRL: (*alone*) And in the night the Virgin Mary appeared to her.

MARY: (*enters*) If you will tell the truth and confess that you unlocked the forbidden door, I will unseal your lips and give you back your power of speech. But if you are still obstinate, I must take your newborn child away with me. Then the Queen was permitted to answer.

GIRL: No! I did not open the forbidden door. (*Virgin Mary exits, infant in her arms.*)

NURSE: The next morning, when the baby was discovered missing

TOWNSPERSON ONE: it was whispered among the people

TOWNSPERSON TWO: that the Queen was an ogress

TOWNSPERSON THREE: and had eaten her own baby.

GIRL: (*helplessly trying to speak*) She heard all this but could not deny it.

KING: The King would not believe it, out of love for her.

NURSE: A year later the Queen gave birth to another son. (*gives infant to Queen and exits*)

MARY: (*appearing*) If you will confess that you opened the forbidden door, I will give you back your child and free your tongue.

GIRL: No! I did not open the forbidden door.

MARY: Then I must take this infant as well.

TOWNSPERSON FOUR: The next morning, when the second child was discovered missing,

TOWNSPERSON THREE: there were cries in the street:

TOWNSPERSON TWO: The Queen is an ogress!

TOWNSPERSON ONE: She has eaten her children!

KING: The next one to speak will die! The King still loved her with all of his heart. (*Pause. He embraces her.*)

NURSE: (*entering*) And after the third year she gave birth to a baby

(*Girl exits*)

(*The Queen is alone with the baby, rocking it in her arms.*)

MARY: (*appearing*) Follow me. (*She holds out her hand.*) Mary took the Queen by the hand and led her to Heaven.

(*Sound of angel voices singing 'ooh - ooh' to the tune of Shortening Bread.*)

GIRL: (*looking over the audience*) And there she saw her two sons who greeted her with joy. They were playing with the ball of the world. (*She looks back and forth as the ball flies.*)

MARY: Is your heart not softened yet? If it is, I will give you back your two sons.

GIRL: (*almost weeping*) I didn't open the forbidden door.

MARY: (*taking the infant*) Then the Virgin Mary let her sink back down to earth.

TOWNSPEOPLE: Next morning all the people cried out for judgement.

KING: This time there was nothing the King could do.

JUDGE: Accordingly, a trial was held.

GIRL: And because she could not speak or defend herself

JUDGE: she was condemned to be burnt at the stake.

TOWNSPERSON: The wood was gathered,

EXECUTIONER ONE: her hands were tied behind her,

EXECUTIONER TWO: and the fire was lit.

GIRL: When the fire began to burn around her, the hard ice of her pride melted, and she was moved by repentance. If only I could confess before I die that I opened that door. Then, suddenly, the power of speech was restored to her, and she cried out in a loud voice: Yes, Mary, I did do it!

TOWNSPERSON: And straightaway the rain began to fall.

TOWNSPERSON: And the rain put our the fire.

TOWNSPERSON: A light broke forth above her,

MARY: and the Virgin Mary came down from Heaven, her two little boys by her side, the new-born daughter in her arms. *(giving her the infant)* Whoever repents a sin and confesses it will be forgiven. *(Makes a sign over the girl's lips.)*

ALL: Hallelujah!

GIRL: The power of speech was restored to her, and she was given happiness for the rest of her life.

ALL: *(singing)* Amen!

(LIGHTS OUT)

THE FOX AND THE GEESE

(Geese are walking about, honking.)

FOX: This is the story of the fox and the geese. *(more honking)* The fox was crossing a meadow when he saw a fine flock of fat geese. *(Taps one on shoulder from behind.)* Pardon me, do you know what time it is?

GOOSE ONE: Why yes, it's about quarter to - Fox! Fox!

FOX: Lunch time! *(All honk and run wildly about.)* Do not beg. I will eat you one by one. Starting with this one here.

GOOSE TWO: Please! Please, have mercy on us. Please, just let us say our prayers before we die.

GOOSE THREE: Then we'll line up and you can pick the fattest one to eat first.

(All honk pitiably.)

FOX: I like your suggestion. It is a reasonable and pious request. Go ahead and pray.

(All honk into place, then piously honk out a hymnal; the tune, not the words.)

FOX: The story shall be resumed when they have finished praying. *(Geese continue in full voice.)* But from that day to this, the geese are praying incessantly. *(The lights go down.)*

INTERMISSION

ACT TWO

THE BLUE LIGHT

SOLDIER: There was once a soldier who fought many years and had so many battle wounds that when the war was over, he went before his King.

KING: The King said to him, I don't need you. You have done your service. Of course you are not getting any more pay. I only pay wages to those who are fit to work for me.

SOLDIER: Well now, the soldier had no knowledge of anything but soldiering and didn't know how to make even a bare living. So he walked and walked and walked away very worried and definitely displeased. When night came he was in a dark forest. But he saw a light. He approached it and saw it was a house.

WITCH: And in the house lived a witch.

SOLDIER: And he called out in the night - Oh please! And he said, Oh Please! let me in. Let me in. Give me a place to sleep and something to eat or I swear I'll die!

WITCH: Now who gives anything to a runaway soldier? Look at you. I'll open my heart just a little bit and take you in, if you do just what I want you to do.

SOLDIER: I'll do anything. What do you ask me to do?

WITCH: I want you to dig my garden and chop my wood.

SOLDIER: Tomorrow came, you see, and he went out in the garden for that witch - and he dug and he dug but he could not finish by evening.

WITCH: I see you can do no more today. But I will keep you one more night if you chop me a cord of wood tomorrow.

SOLDIER: It took the soldier all day to do the job.

WITCH: Tomorrow I'll give you the easiest task. You're gonna go down into my old dry well and find me a light that has fallen into it. The light burns blue, and never goes out.

SOLDIER: So the next day the witch took him to a well and let him down in a basket. Down, down and down the well he went and found the blue light and signalled her to draw him up again.

WITCH: The witch pulled

SOLDIER: and pulled

WITCH: and pulled, but when he was almost to the top, she stretched out her hand to take the blue light away from him.

SOLDIER: Oh no you don't. You don't get the lamp till I'm up there with you, with both of these feet on the ground.

WITCH: Give me the lamp!

SOLDIER: Let me up! Let me up!

WITCH: Give me the lamp!

SOLDIER: Let me up! Let me up!

WITCH: The witch flew into such a rage that she dropped the rope and let him fall to the bottom of the well. 'Bye, bye boy.'

SOLDIER: He wasn't hurt because the ground was soft. The blue light was burning strong but what could it do for him? Now he saw that he could not escape death. He sat a while, a very sad soldier. Then he pulled out a pipe half full of tobacco. This was to be his last little pleasure. He lit the pipe with the blue light and began to smoke. You know what? As the smoke began to cloud around him,

BLUE MAN: a little blue man appeared. Master, what are your commands?

SOLDIER: What can you do for me?

BLUE MAN: I must do anything you want.

SOLDIER: Get me out of this well.

BLUE MAN: The blue man took him by the hand and led him through a tunnel.

SOLDIER: The soldier did not forget to take the blue light.

BLUE MAN: And by the light of the lamp he was shown a treasure which the witch had hidden.

SOLDIER: The soldier took as much of the gold as he could carry. Then he was out on the earth again. There is one more thing I want you to do. You know that witch? Tie her up and take her before the judge. And the next thing he knew,

BLUE MAN: the witch was flying on the back of a tom cat.

WITCH: Screaming!

BLUE MAN: Is there anything else you need?

SOLDIER: At the moment, nothing. You can go home but be ready for me to call you.

BLUE MAN: Remember: anytime you want me all you have to do is light your pipe on that blue light and I will appear. Then he vanished from sight.

SOLDIER: So, the soldier went back to his home town and bought himself some beautiful clothes and went into the finest hotel.

HOTEL OWNER: The owner arranged the most magnificent room he had available.

SOLDIER: And when he was alone, the soldier took out his pipe and sat down for a smoke. Smoke rings began to rise around him...and

BLUE MAN: here was the blue man.

SOLDIER: You know what? I worked hard for the King, then he sent me away to starve and now I want revenge.

BLUE MAN: What do you need me to do?

SOLDIER: I know it's bad stuff but I can't help it. Late at night when the king's daughter is asleep I want you to bring her to me. I want you to bring her to me asleep, and then I want her to be my cleaning maid.

BLUE MAN: That's an easy thing for me; for you it's dangerous.

(The clock tower strikes twelve midnight.)

SOLDIER: I think you'd better go.

BLUE MAN: At midnight the door sprang open and the blue man led the princess into the soldier's chamber.

SOLDIER: You're here, huh, fresh and ready to go! Here's soap and water. Now scrub the floor!

(The princess drops on her knees and scrubs the floor, without resisting.)

SOLDIER: Get the corners! Come over here! Now pull off my boots! *(When she has done this, he throws them at her.)* Pick them up and polish them!

PRINCESS: So she polished his boots without a word of resistance and with half closed eyes. This went on all night long. *(a cock crows)*

BLUE MAN: At the first crow of the cock the little blue man took her back to the castle.

PRINCESS: Father, I had the strangest dream last night. I dreamed I was taken through the streets as fast as lightening and brought to a room where a soldier made me do all manner of menial work; cleaning his room, polishing his shoes. It was only a dream and yet I'm as tired as though I worked all night.

KING: The dream might have been true. Take my advice: fill your pockets full of peas and make a tiny hole in the pocket and if you are taken away again you will leave a trail through the streets.

BLUE MAN: The blue man was standing invisibly by and heard all. NIGHT! And he took the sleeping princess through the town once again, slyly spreading sweet peas all over the streets so she could not leave a trail. And he took her back to the soldier's chambers. *(Exeunt)*

KING: Next morning the King sent his people out looking for the trail.

SOLDIERS: But all they found were poor children picking up peas.

POOR CHILD: It must have rained peas in the night! *(Exeunt)*

KING: *(enters)* We must think up something else. Tonight when you go to sleep, keep one shoe on and one shoe off, and if you are taken away again, somehow contrive to hide it there. I will find it soon enough.

BLUE MAN: The little blue man was listening again, and this time urged the soldier not to send for the princess for the king might find the shoe and things would go bad for the soldier.

(Bells toll midnight.)

SOLDIER: Do what I tell you.

BLUE MAN: But...but...things will go bad!

SOLDIER: Go on. Go on!

(The Blue Man brings the Princess to the soldier's room. She cleans his shoes and then the cock crows. The Blue Man comes to take her back.)

PRINCESS: But she hid her shoe before she was taken home. *(Exeunt)*

KING: The next morning the King had the whole town searching for that shoe!

KING'S SOLDIER: It was found by the King's men.

SOLDIER: They arrested the soldier and they beat him and put him in jail. His two best things were hung on the wall out of reach: the pipe and all the gold except for one coin in his pocket.

GUARD: A soldier stood guard by his cell.

SOLDIER: Pssst! You. Come here. Well, how's it goin'? Hey, be a good man and hand me my little pack there.

GUARD: What? Are you kidding?

SOLDIER: I'll give you this gold coin.

GUARD: So his brother soldier did him a favor.

SOLDIER: Thank you. Thank you. And when the soldier was alone he took out his pipe and had himself a smoke and as the smoke rings began to rise...

BLUE MAN'S VOICE: *(whispering)* Anything you need?

SOLDIER: What do I do now?

BLUE MAN'S VOICE: *(whisper)* Don't fear a thing. Go where they take you, only don't forget to take that blue light with you.

JUDGE: The next day he was put on trial.

SOLDIER: And although his crime was not so grave,

JUDGE: he was condemned to death.

SOLDIER: King, I have one last request.

KING: Only one.

SOLDIER: I wonder if I could smoke one last pipeful before I go.

KING: You can smoke three, but don't think I shall grant you your life.

SOLDIER: Then the soldier pulled out his pipe and lit it with the blue lantern and as a pair of smoke rings rose in the air...

BLUE MAN: the blue man appeared. Anything you need?

SOLDIER: As a matter of fact, yes, there is. I want you to beat that lying judge for me and knock his bloodhounds to the ground and don't spare the King either, who treated me the rotten way he did.

BLUE MAN: Yes sir. And away went the blue man - zick zock - and he knocked the King down hard. And the judge, and the rest of them.

KING: Soldier, I tell you what I'll do: Spare my life and I'll give you your life. You can have my kingdom and my daughter will be your wife!

SOLDIER: I accept!

(LIGHTS OUT)

A POOR MAN IN HEAVEN

(Angel voices singing)

POOR MAN: Once upon a time a poor man died and arrived before the Gates of Heaven.

RICH MAN: *(arriving)* At about the same time a very rich man died and he wanted to get in as well. Waiting a long time?

POOR MAN: No, not at all.

ST. PETER: Then St. Peter came to open the Pearly Gates, and invited the rich man in. Hey, gang, look who's here.

ANGELS: *(celebrating)* Ta ra ra boom de ay, Ta ra ra boom de ay! Welcome to Heaven! *(They toss confetti, kiss him on the cheek, dance him around, etc.)*

ST. PETER: And St. Peter closed the Gate not seeing the Poor Man standing behind.

POOR MAN: *(knocking frantically)* You forgot me! St. Peter!

ST. PETER: Just a second, I'm coming. Who's there? Oh! I'm sorry, I didn't see you before. Come on in. Hey, gang, look who's here.

ANGELS: Hello there. Welcome to Heaven. Hi. Have a seat.

POOR MAN: Hey, wait a second. St. Peter, how come the angels didn't sing and dance for me like they did for the rich man? Oh, I get it, Heaven is just like earth. The rich get everything and the poor get nothing.

ST. PETER: Hold on there, my good man. I don't think you understand. You see, we get poor men like you every day, but a rich man? Not one in a hundred years.

(Angel voices sing harmoniously to a close)

CLEVER GRETEL

GRETEL: There was once a cook named Gretel who wore shoes with red knots, and when she went out with them she used to turn about this way and that way. 'Ah, you are a very pretty girl!' And when she came home she drank a glass of wine for joy. And as the wine made her want to eat, she used to taste the best she had. 'A cook ought to know how her cooking tastes.'

MASTER: One day it happened that her master said to her, 'Gretel, this evening a guest is coming. So cook me two chickens very nicely.'

GRETEL: I will do it directly, master. She soon killed the chickens, plucked, dressed, and spitted them, and as evening came she put them before the fire to roast. They began to turn brown and to cook through, but still the guest had not come. 'If your guest does not come soon I shall have to take the chickens from the fire, but it will be a great shame not to eat them soon, while they are juicy.'

MASTER: I will run out myself and bring the guest home. *(exits)*

GRETEL: *(taking spit off the fire)* Ah, I have stood so long before the fire that I am quite hot and thirsty. Who knows when he will come? Meanwhile I will run down into the cellar and have a drink. *(running down stairs, setting down jug)* God bless you, Gretel! *(takes a good pull at the beer)* And when that was down she had another. *(goes upstairs and puts spit back on the fire, spreading butter on the skins)* They had better be tasted now. *(dips finger in the gravy)* Ah, how good these chickens are. It is a sin and shame that they should not be eaten at once. *(runs to window to see if they are coming, but nobody)* Ah, one wing is burnt! I had better eat that. *(cuts it off and eats)* I had better take the other, too, or the master will see that something is missing. *(eats, goes to window again)* Who knows whether they will come or not? Maybe they stopped off at a saloon. Well, Gretel, be of good courage. The one chicken is begun. Have another drink and eat it up completely, for then you will be at rest. Why should good things be allowed to spoil? *(Eats up the chicken with pleasure. Looks out window; looks at other chicken.)* The two belong with one another. What is right for the one is right for the other. Another draft wouldn't hurt me. Where the one is the other ought to be. *(Goes toward the cellar.)*

MASTER: *(enters)* Make haste, Gretel, the guest is coming directly.

GRETEL: Yes, master. It will soon be ready.

MASTER: I'll sharpen the carving knife. *(Takes space knife and exits. Knife sharpening is heard.)*

(The guest politely knocks on the door.)

GRETEL: *(finger to lips to enjoin silence)* Go away, please, go away! If my master finds you here you are lost. He certainly did invite you here to supper, but he has it in his mind to cut your ears off. Just listen how he is sharpening his knife!

GUEST: *(The guest listens, then hurries away. Gretel runs screaming to her master.)*

Gretel: A fine guest you have invited!

Master: What? What do you mean?

Gretel: Why, just as I was about to serve them up, your guest took the two chickens off the dish and bolted away with them.

Master: What was he thinking! He might have left me one of them at least, so I had something to eat. *(Calling after guest, who pretends not to hear him)* Stop! *(runs after him, knife in hand)* Just one! Just one! You have two! Give me one! *(exeunt running)*

Gretel: God bless you, Gretel.

(LIGHTS OUT)

The Farmer & The Money Lender

Musician: This story is from India. It's called: The Farmer and the Money Lender. *(music: sitar style)*

Farmer: There was once a farmer who suffered much at the hands of a money lender. Good harvest or bad, the farmer was always poor and the money lender rich. At last, when he hadn't a penny left, he went to the money lender's house.

Money Lender: *(Enters, playing with coins, singing.)* 'The best things in life are free...'*(Farmer knocks.)* Just a second! *(Puts money away.)* Come in!

Farmer: Here's your money, Money Lender.

Money Lender: There is yet more to be given me.

Farmer: But I don't have any more. You can't squeeze water from a stone. And well, since you can't get anything from me now, you might at least tell me the secret of becoming rich.

Money Lender: Rich? Riches come from Ram. Ask him. *(exits)*

Farmer: Ram! Thank you, I will. And so the farmer ran home and made three griddle cakes to last him on his journey, and set off to find Ram. *(walks in a big circle)*

Braham: The first man coming down the road was a Braham.

Farmer: To him he gave one of his cakes. Could you please point me in the direction of Ram?

BRAHAM: *(Braham exits gobbling down cake.)* But the Braham couldn't talk with his mouth full so off he went.

FARMER: The farmer continued on. *(Walks, music continues as well.)* Next he came to a Yogi. *(The yogi is in one of his postures.)*

YOGI: To him he gave the second of his cakes.

FARMER: Oh, great one, could you please show me the best way to get to Ram?

YOGI: *(eating)* No fried foods. *(exits)*

FARMER: So the farmer continued onwards. *(Sounds of struggle off.)* At last he came to an old beggar thrown out on the street.

BEGGER: *(Cursing off.)* A curse on you and your family! May your sacred cow make a mess on your carpet! Excuse me, sir. Might you have a drachma or two to spare for an old codger down on his luck?

FARMER: No, no. I'm very sorry. I don't have any money at all. But wait, I do have one last griddle cake.

BEGGER: A griddle cake! Yum!

FARMER: Yes, you may take it if you like.

BEGGER: Thank you! Why don't you sit down and join me for lunch.

FARMER: I can't, you see. I have a long journey ahead of me.

BEGGER: Where are you going?

FARMER: I'm going to find Ram. *(Beggar chokes.)* I don't suppose you could tell me where he is.

BEGGER: I just might be able to help you. I am Ram.

FARMER: P'shaw! You're not Ram! You are an old beggar in the street.

BEGGER: I am Ram! *(Harmonious sounds heard as Beggar assumes finger and foot positions of Ram.)*

FARMER: Oh, my Ram! Oh my!

BEGGER: Take it easy. I put my tunic on one leg at a time, just like you. Well, what can I do for you?

FARMER: Then the farmer told Ram the whole story.

BEGGER: Oh, the money lender. I have just the thing for you. Here is a magical conch shell. When you blow into it every thing your heart desires will be yours. Go ahead and try it. *(No luck.)* Here is the trick of it. *(Shows him how; the conch sounds as farmer blows.)* But beware of the money lender. Not even magic is proof against his wiles.

FARMER: Thank you, Ram. I will be careful.

BEGGER: Good luck to you. *(Exits)*

FARMER: *(Music starts again.)* So the farmer went back to his village rejoicing! *(Laughs in pleasure.)*

MONEY LENDER: The money lender saw the farmer returning. The idiot must have had some very good fortune to make him so happy. So he went over to the farmer's house and congratulated him, using such clever words, pretending to have heard all about it,

FARMER: that before long the farmer found himself telling the whole story of Ram and the conch, all except the secret of blowing the conch, for with all his simplicity, the farmer was not quite such a fool as to tell that. *(He pushes money lender out.)* Come back for tea sometime. Thanks very much, goodbye. *(Puts conch on space table.)*

MONEY LENDER: But the money lender was determined to get hold of the conch by hook or crook. And he waited for a favorable opportunity, *(At night, he creeps in through window.)* and stole the conch.

(Makes off with it, as farmer returns, sees it missing and loudly laments as he goes off looking for it.)

MONEY LENDER: I want a goat! *(Tries to blow conch in futility.)* And after trying every conceivable way to blow the conch, he had to give it up as a bad job. So he went back to the farmer's house. Oh, farmer, look what I have! *(Waves it.)*

FARMER: *(Tries to grasp it.)* Oh, you have it! *(Is made to miss.)*

MONEY LENDER: No, you don't. Stop screeching. Now listen! I cannot use this conch because I don't know how to blow it. And you cannot use it because you do not have it. So we must make a deal.

FARMER: *(Tearfully.)* Yes, let's make a deal.

MONEY LENDER: Good. Now I will give you back this conch and promise never to interfere with your playing it, on one condition.

FARMER: What condition?

MONEY LENDER: That whatever you get, I am to get double.

FARMER: *(Gasps)* No, no! That would be the same unfair business all over again.

MONEY LENDER: *(Holding conch high.)* Oh, well, then I'll just have to break the conch.

FARMER: *(Screaming)* No! No!

MONEY LENDER: Maybe I'll throw it in the air and catch it. *(Farmer is in agony.)* What do you care what I get as long as you get what you want? Don't be such a spoil sport.

FARMER: *(Lamenting to the last.)* No! Yes! Oh, I agree, oh yes, of course, I agree.

MONEY LENDER: Very good, I'm glad you do. *(Exits)*

FARMER: And from that time on, no matter what the farmer gained by the power of the conch *(blows and it sounds)*, ice cream cone,

MONEY LENDER: *(Enters with a cone in each hand.)* the money lender got *(Exits licking cones.)* twice as much.

FARMER: This so preyed on the mind of the farmer that he got no satisfaction out of anything. And then, at last, there came a dry season. *(Sounds of whistling winds.)* So dry that all the crops withered for want of rain. He blew into his conch *(Sound)* and asked for a new well to water them. And lo! there was a new well!

MONEY LENDER: *(Enters)* But the money lender got two! *(Giggles)*

FARMER: This was too much for any farmer to stand. He brooded over it, and brooded over it, until, suddenly, an idea came into his head. He took his conch...

MONEY LENDER: Wonder what he's going to give me this time?

FARMER: *(Blowing)* Oh, Ram, I wish to be made blind in one eye. Oh! And he was.

MONEY LENDER: *(Cries out)* I can't see! Who turned out the light? I can't see!

FARMER: But the money lender was blind in both. And in trying to steer his way between his two new wells *(Exits; splashing heard.)* he fell into one of them and was drowned. Now, this true story goes to show that even a simple farmer can get the better of a money lender.

MUSICIAN: But only at the cost of an eye.

FARMER: That's right. Unfortunately, yes.

The Housedog And The Wolf

Wolf: One night a wolf was roaming in the middle of the woods,

Dog: when a housedog came barking by.

Wolf: How sleek and well fed that fine fat dog seemed to the lean and lonely wolf. *You* seem to have done very well for yourself, especially in the food department. Me, I can hardly keep from starving.

Dog: Listen, if you'd like to get in on this with me, help me guard my master's house, you'll eat as well as I!

Wolf: I'm with you! *(howls in delight)* But as they approached the housedog's house, the wolf noticed something around the housedog's neck. What is that? I've never seen the like of it before.

Dog: This is my collar.

Wolf: What is the collar for?

Dog: And the dog told him. But before he could even finish explaining how his master tied him up by the collar...

Wolf: The wolf said: 'Good bye!' and parted company with the housedog. I prefer the lean long life I lead in liberty, to having plenty but with strings attached. *(howls)*

The Wedding Of Sir Gawain And Dame Ragnelle

Arthur: King Arthur hunting in the wood
drew his bow, and let his arrow fly.
And killed a deer.
But a knight did appear -

Knight: with Arthur's death in his eye!
(a sword to Arthur's throat)

Arthur, my lord! Do not resist -
drop the weapon from your regal fist,
fill your royal mouth with prayer.
Prepare! Your time has come!

Arthur: You, sir, are in a most foul mood.

Knight: Arthur, my lord,

you have wronged me year upon year,
taken my lands, put them in your favorite's hands.
Therefore, a sword for your reward,
my most privileged profiteer!

ARTHUR: But who are you?

KNIGHT: My name is Gromer Somer Joure. I own this land.

ARTHUR: Gromer Somer Joure?
I know no Gromer Somer Joure.

GROMER: I know you don't and you won't. *(playing with the sword at Arthur's throat)*

ARTHUR: But I plainly see
you are a noble knight
in the fight for right - like me.
We are of the self-same family.

GROMER: No man, even unknowingly, harms his brother.

ARTHUR: But think of what the other knights would say
if you killed me this cowardly way.
You have a fighting sword and I this little knife.

GROMER: Words will not avail to save your life!

ARTHUR: What will you take to make amends?

GROMER: I take nothing if not from friends.

ARTHUR: I will give you anything you need.

GROMER: Anything?

ARTHUR: Anything.

GROMER: I will let you go if you come back
bearing the one answer all men lack.

ARTHUR: My hand upon your sword I shall be back
bearing the answer that we lack.

GROMER: Vow to meet me here a year from now
with an answer to the deepest mystery in all of history -
what do women most desire!

SONG: Unless the sovereign, son and sire discovered woman's chief desire
his life would end.
So to Sir Gawain, his dearest friend,
he rode past moor and mire.

(Before the castle..)

GAWAIN: Share your heaviness of heart with me,
          have no more fear, make no more moan.
          This quest for the answer to what women
          love best you shall not bear alone.
          Now ride to the western counties
          and ask the women there,
          I'll ride the opposite way
          to hear what eastern women say.

(In town and country they talk to women.)

SONG: A twelve month time both men inquired
          what womenkind most desired
          They did listen and they did look,
          but in their book
          both wrote answers uninspired:
WOMAN ONE: There were those who wanted wisdom,
WOMAN TWO: and there were those who wanted clothes.
WOMAN THREE: Some wanted to be treated nicer.
WOMAN FOUR: Some wanted a nicer nose.
WOMAN FIVE: Some loved to have a loaf in the oven.
WOMAN SIX: Some loved nothin' else but lovin'.
WOMAN SEVEN: Some longed to be a widow so they could be rewed.
WOMAN EIGHT: Others never muss the bed.
WOMAN NINE: Some were not about
WOMAN TEN: to let the slightest hint slip out.
          (Arthur and Gawain meet again on horseback.)

GAWAIN: I inquired of woman and man, sir,
          enough to fill this book with answer.
          (They exchange books.)

ARTHUR: Our answer books are full.
          But leave us look a little more.
          My soul is sick and sore.
          (They ride off on separate paths.)

SONG: Sir Gawain riding in the wood
          came across a creature,
          a monstrous hideosity
          in form and fume and feature.

GAWAIN: Her nose was red and snotted,
          and jutted forth.
          From her mouth one tusk came north,

and one hung South.

DAME RAGNELLE: Her eyes were bleary,
    blubbery her lips...

GAWAIN: Hips as wide as hippos' hips.

DAME RAGNELLE: Her breasts were a load for a horse to bear.

GAWAIN: She had a belly like a barrel.

DAME RAGNELLE: And a nose full of hair.
    Godspeed, Sir Knight, I am well pleased to meet thee.
    Speak with me, I advise, before thou go. The king's
    life is in my hand, without me he is dead.

GAWAIN: Why, Lady, are you saying you have the answer?

DAME RAGNELLE: Yes, and with it he won't lose his head.
    I know what women most desire.

GAWAIN: I will give you what you will and give
    you more and then more still. What is
    it women most desire?

DAME RAGNELLE: That is only for the ear of our sire.

GAWAIN: Come, I will give you anything,
    if your answer saves the king.

DAME RAGNELLE: If my answer save his life,
    I, my lord, must be your wife.

GAWAIN: Woman, I will tell you true
    never have I seen one as ugly as you.

DAME RAGNELLE: I may be a gross and gruesome lump.
    There may be a hump upon my back,
    but I have the answer that you lack.
    My nostrils are hairy and flaring wide,
    my nose is red and my eyes are bleary,
    but deary, I must be your bride.

GAWAIN: To save my king
    I would wed you and wed you again.

DAME RAGNELLE: Take me to your king.
    I will give the answer then.

(She jumps onto the horse's back, behind him.)

SONG: Back he rode with his ugly prize.
    All the court turned its eyes aside.

The men turned white, the women gray
gazing upon Sir Gawain's fiance.

ARTHUR: No! I cannot let you make this haggish bag your bride!

GAWAIN: When a knight gives his word, he does not backslide.
I will have her and the fangs above her flapping lips;
these hands will hold her endless hips,
for love of thee, my king.

ARTHUR: For love of me? Then for love of thee,
I cannot refuse.
This loathsome lady
wins the knight.
The lovelies lose.

DAME RAGNELLE: Now, king, shalt thou know
what every woman high and low
desires above all other desires.
Above her desire to be fresh and fair,
or to share the loving bed;
or to be wed and be rewed,
her highest desire past all flattery,
is to have her sovereignty.
For when she has power all belongs to her.
Though her man be most manly still she'll prefer
to have the mastery over her sir.
So now thou know, in certainty,
women desire sovereignty.

SONG: On the last dawn of the appointed year,
King Arthur to his fate drew near.

GROMER: Sir King, you near dead mere man,
you cannot answer what no man can.
What does woman most desire?

ARTHUR: The king took out book after book -

GROMER: and Gromer Somer there did look.
And when he read, said,
now your majesty will bleed,
no answer in here do I read.

ARTHUR: Then I answer this -
in certainty women desire sovereignity over manly man.
To rule you, too, is their heart's plan.
Female desire, the answer you lack

is to hold you down though they be on their back.

GROMER: You, sir, have been talking with my sister.

ARTHUR: A certain Dame Ragnelle.

GROMER: That blot of shame upon our family name!
            That hulk hurled out of hell!
            Well, all I can say, King Arthur,
            is farewell!

SONG: I'm glad to sing and happy to report
          a joyous King Arthur rode back to court.

(The court enters.)

DAME RAGNELLE: Now keep the promise, no tarrying.
            It's time for marrying and giving of the ring
            and over threshold carrying
            and doing the nuptial thing.

ARTHUR: Gawain, it needn't end this way.
            There's no amount I would not pay.

GAWAIN: My king, I have a solemn promise made.
            I'll keep my word and marry me this maid.

DAME RAGNELLE: Courteous knight of such goodwill,
            would I were a prettier promise to fulfill.

QUEEN: Alas, alas, said Dame Guenevere
            O dear, O dear, O dear, O dear!
            Let us make the marriage very early in the day
            as privately as we possibly may.

DAME RAGNELLE: Nay, by heaven's king I'll be married in the proper
      way,
            wedded in white and in mid day.
            And in the public hall I'll dine
            and low and high will drink my wine.
            Or don't you know this day is mine?

SONG: *(Chorus comes in and sets out dishes and drinks for all.)*

            And she was wed and all were fed
            And all did marvel at Sir Gawain's lady foul:
            for at the feast she ate at least
             one hen, two capons and three geese, four grouse
            five ducks, six turkeys and an owl.

DAME RAGNELLE: Then said the bride, quite satisfied,

'If you'll all excuse me we have obligations to abide
and our work cut out inside.'

(All exit throwing confetti and rice)

BEDCHAMBER

DAME RAGNELLE: Sir Gawain, since I have you wed,
show me your chivalry in bed.
By right tonight it may not be denied,
for husband, to one bed both our souls are tied.
Love me a little if you love your king.
Kiss me a kiss, do do me this thing.

GAWAIN: I will do more before God than kiss!
And for my king - how like you this!? *(Kisses her.)* And this! *(Presses her tight.)*

DAME RAGNELLE: I like it!

GAWAIN: Suddenly he saw the sweetest features
ever seen on female creatures.
Her dribbling lips were roses to his fingertips.
Where once were pimples joyous little dimples grew - Jesu!
Her beauty was endless, deep.
That vast behind became the tender kind
you lay your head against and weep.
What are you?

DAME RAGNELLE: Your wife, sir.

SONG: And marvelous to tell
her hair was now arboreal.
Her bosom was marmoreal.
Corporeally speaking they were doing very well.

GAWAIN: Was I blind or not in my mind!
Now you're a lady, fair in my sight.
Today you were a most foul fright.

DAME RAGNELLE: Yes - but you must choose, my love.
My beauty will keep only half the day.
Either you have me fair at night
and foul to see in early light.
Or fair by day, and foul in sleep.

GAWAIN: The choice is hard, how can I choose?
To win at night, by day to lose.
I will not choose.

DAME RAGNELLE: Who will?

GAWAIN: You will,

DAME RAGNELLE: Me? A woman choose?

GAWAIN: *(kisses her palm)* Sealed and kissed
I put my soul in your control.

DAME RAGNELLE: If you insist.
Of earthly knights you most blessed be
whose love hath given me my sovereignty.
You shall have me fair, day and night, at your side.
For it was magic deformed me
till the most manly man should make me his monarch
taking me as bride.

GAWAIN: Thank God and Mary mild, for we are blessed!
The test is past and we have passed the test.

SONG: So they made joy, joy out of mind
Till the king came by to find
the lovely bride and loving groom
in each other intertwined.
And in glory and in glee
blessed them in the name of the trinity.

Music for *BINNORIE*, p. 26

A

CHRISTMAS

CAROL

BY

CHARLES DICKENS

Adapted for for the stage by

Paul Sills

A CHRISTMAS CAROL

Copyright © Paul Sills, 2000

CHARLES DICKENS'

A CHRISTMAS CAROL

Stave one:
Marley's Ghost

Stave Two: Christmas Past
The First of the Three Spirits

Stave Three: Christmas Present
The Second of the Three Spirits

Intermission

Stave Four: Christmas Past
The Last of the Great Spirits

Stave Five:
The End of It

Characters

Bob Cratchit
Ebenezer Scrooge
Fred
Solicitor
Solicitor
Marley's Ghost
The Waiter
The Ghost of Christmas Past
Youngest Scrooge
Young Scrooge
Little Fan
Schoolmaster
Servant
Postboy
Dick Wilkins
Fezziwig
Mrs. Fezziwig
Miss Fezziwig
Belle
Ghost of Christmas Present
Six Shipmates
Mrs. Cratchit
Belinda Cratchit
Peter Cratchit
Martha Cratchit
Boy Cratchit
Girl Cratchit
Tiny Tim

(Twenty-two players, including four under the age of twelve.)

INTRODUCTION TO A CHRISTMAS CAROL

Carol and I found a century-old farm in Door County, Wisconsin in 1970, when the Broadway show was running at the Ambassador Theater. Leaving this home base from time to time we went and did story theater in the cities.

It was years before I began to direct community theater shows in Door County. Not until asked to direct a production of Charles Dickens' *A Christmas Carol* did I know what it was to work with kids and teenagers and local people with no theatrical experience.[1] Rehearsing three times a week, two hours a session, with a little extra time as performance neared, even though over a two month period, did not leave time for training the players. What helped were a few Spolin theater games.

To warm up, besides playing traditional games to bring everyone happily into the same place, I coached the troupe, children and adults together, in playing Viola Spolin's Feeling Self With Self and in her Space Walks, which take very little time. For speech I did Vowels and Consonants on the text or in small group conversations, and Extended Sound, where players send sound through space to fellow players, and let it land, then begin to focus on the sound in words.

These and other theater games are in the section of this anthology titled Theater Games for Story Theater, written by Viola Spolin when she was special consultant for my production of Ovid's Metamophoses[2] at the Mark Taper Forum in Los Angeles.

In editing A Christmas Carol for the theater, I tried to stay with

---

[1] In my December 1994 production at the Door Community Auditorium in Fish Creek, Gerald Pelrine was Producer and Scrooge. The other adults in the cast were Richard Engberg, Martha Garvey, John Redmann, Bruce McKeefry, Jeanne Aurelius, Leif Erickson, Valerie Murre, Debbra Mahlzahn, Rich Higdon, Dan Beck, David Hatch; teenagers: Claude Cote, Ali Rericha, Neva Sills, Adrian Murre, Alisson Burda; children: Kate Fordney, Nathan Hatch, Martha Aurelius, and Christina Fordney as Tiny Tim. Music was by Fred Kaz, longtime pianist for Second City; stage design by Carol Bleackley; costumes by Joan Kelly and Polly Sills; stage manager, Barbara Fordney.

[2] *Ovid's Metamorphoses,* adapted with Arnold Weinstein, will be published by Applause Books in a companion volume, along with *The Wind in the Willows* by Kenneth Grahame, *Monkey* by Wu Cheng En, and *The American Revolution, Part One.*

what Dickens the storyteller wanted us to hear. At no time did I drama-
tize a scene but always kept to his narrative, only eliminating the occasional digression. For Dickens has something to say to us but knows that
before we can hear him we must come to heartbreak, and he brings it
about. By narrative means he helps us to experience the joy of repentance.
A Scottish philosopher, Thomas Carlyle, who did not keep Christmas, on
reading A Christmas Carol sent out for a turkey and asked two friends to
dine. Jane Welsh Carlyle wrote that her husband "was seized with a perfect convulsion of hospitality" and "actually insisted on improvising two
dinner parties with only a day in between."

ACT I

STAVE ONE: MARLEY'S GHOST

SLIDE No. 1, FOGGY LONDON. (Fog machine is on, black traveller is open to the width of the projection. Stave sign is brought on and hung, s.r.or s.l.)

(A Young Person's chorus sing 'God Rest Ye Merry Gentlemen' and hold out the hat before the door, which is space, to Scrooge's office, downstage center. Cratchit comes to work and gives them a coin; Scrooge comes and gestures them to 'Go away!')

CHORUS ONE: Once upon a time - of all the good days in the year, on Christmas Eve - it was cold, bleak, biting weather: foggy withal.

CHORUS TWO: The people went wheezing up and down, beating their hands upon their breasts,

CHORUS THREE: and stamping their feet upon the pavement stones to warm them.

CHORUS FOUR: The fog came pouring in at every chink and keyhole,

CHORUS FIVE: the houses opposite were mere phantoms.

SCROOGE: The door of Scrooge's counting-house was open that he might keep his eye upon his clerk,

CRATCHIT: who in a dismal little cell beyond, a sort of tank, was copying letters.

SCROOGE: Scrooge had a very small fire,

CRATCHIT: but the clerk's fire was so very much smaller that it looked like one coal. But he couldn't replenish it,

SCROOGE: for Scrooge kept the coal-box in his own room.

CRATCHIT: Wherefore the clerk *(puts on long scarf)* tried to warm himself at the candle. *(he fails)*

CHORUS ONE: Oh! but he was a tight-fisted hand at the grindstone, Scrooge!

CHORUS TWO: A squeezing, wrenching, grasping,

CHORUS THREE: scraping, clutching,

CHORUS FOUR: covetous old sinner!

CHORUS FIVE: Hard and sharp as flint;

CHORUS THREE: secret and self-contained,

CHORUS ONE: and solitary as an oyster.

FRED: *(entering)* A merry Christmas, Uncle! God save you! It was Scrooge's nephew, Fred.

SCROOGE: *(startled)* Bah! Humbug!

FRED: Christmas as humbug, Uncle! You don't mean that, I am sure?

SCROOGE: I do. Merry Christmas! What right have you to be merry? What reason have you to be merry? You're poor enough.

FRED: *(gaily)* Come then. What right have you to be dismal? What reason have you to be morose? You're rich enough.

SCROOGE: Bah! Humbug!

FRED: Don't be cross, Uncle.

SCROOGE: What else can I be when I live in such a world of fools as this? Merry Christmas! Out upon Merry Christmas! What's Christmas time to you but a time for paying bills without money; a time for finding yourself a year older, and not an hour richer. If I could work my will, every idiot who goes about with 'Merry Christmas' on his lips should be boiled with his own pudding, and buried with a stake of holly through his heart.

FRED: *(pleading)* Uncle!

SCROOGE: Nephew! Keep Christmas in your own way, and let me keep it in mine.

FRED: Keep it! But you don't keep it.

SCROOGE: Let me leave it alone then. Much good may it do you! Much good it has ever done you.

FRED: There are many things, by which I have not profited, I dare say, Christmas among the rest. But I am sure I have always thought of Christmas time, when it has come round, as a good time: the only time I know of, in the long calendar of the year, when men and women seem to open their shut-up hearts freely, and to think of other people as if they really were fellow-passengers to the grave, and not another race of creatures bound on other journeys. And therefore, Uncle, though it has never put a scrap of gold or silver in my pocket, I believe that it *has* done me good, and *will* do me good; and I say, God bless it!

(Cratchit involuntarily applauds; then aware of the impropriety, pokes the fire, extinguishing it.)

SCROOGE: Let me hear another sound from *you*, and you'll keep your Christmas by losing your situation. *(turning to Fred)* You're quite a powerful speaker, sir. I wonder you don't go into Parliament.

FRED: Don't be angry, Uncle. Come! Dine with us tomorrow.

SCROOGE: I'll see you in hell first.

FRED: But why? Why?

SCROOGE: Why did you get married?

FRED: Because I fell in love.

SCROOGE: Because you fell in love. Good afternoon!

FRED: Nay, Uncle, but you never came to see me before that happened. Why give it as a reason for not coming now?

SCROOGE: Good afternoon.

FRED: I am sorry, with all my heart, to find you so resolute. But I'll keep my Christmas humor to the last. So A Merry Christmas, Uncle!

SCROOGE: Good afternoon!

FRED: And a Happy New Year!

SCROOGE: Good afternoon!

(Fred leaves the room, stops to bestow season's greetings on the clerk, who, cold as he is, returns them cordially.)

SCROOGE: There's another fellow, my clerk, with fifteen shillings a week, and a wife and family, talking about a merry Christmas. I'll retire to Bedlam.

(As Fred exits, he lets in two pleasant looking people who carry books and papers, and bow to Scrooge.)

ONE: At this festive season of the year, Mr. Scrooge, *(taking up a pen)* it is more than usually desirable to make some slight provision for the poor and destitute, who suffer greatly at the present time. Many thousands are in want of common necessaries;

TWO: Hundreds of thousands are in want of common comforts, sir.

SCROOGE: Are there no prisons?

TWO: Plenty of prisons.

SCROOGE: And the Union workhouses? Are they still in operation?

ONE: They are. Still, I wish I could say they were not.

SCROOGE: The Treadmill and the Poor Law are in full vigor, then?

ONE: Both very busy, sir.

SCROOGE: Oh! I was afraid from what you said at first that something had stopped them. I'm very glad to hear it.

TWO: They scarcely furnish Christian cheer of mind or body. A few of us are raising a fund to buy the Poor some meat and drink, and means of warmth.

ONE: We choose this time because it is a time when Want is keenly felt, and Abundance rejoices. What shall I put you down for?

SCROOGE: Nothing!

ONE: You wish to be anonymous?

SCROOGE: I wish to be left alone. Since you ask me what I wish, that is my answer. I don't make merry myself at Christmas, and I can't afford to make idle people merry. I help to support the establishments I have mentioned: they cost enough: and those who are badly off must go there.

TWO: Many can't go there; and many would rather die.

SCROOGE: If they would rather die, they had better do it, and decrease the surplus population. Good afternoon.

(Seeing it is useless to pursue their point the two withdraw, leaving Scrooge to resume his labors in a better mood. As the two are leaving, a boy looks in and sings to him:)

BOY: 'God bless you merry gentlemen, Let nothing you dismay'...

(Scrooge seizes a ruler and attacks, the boy flees.)

CRATCHIT: *(hearing bells)* At length the hour of shutting up the counting-house arrived.

SCROOGE: With an ill-will Scrooge dismounted from his stool.

(Seeing his tacit admission of the fact, the clerk instantly snuffs his candle and puts on his hat.)

SCROOGE: You'll want all day tomorrow, I suppose.

CRATCHIT: If quite convenient, sir.

SCROOGE: It's not convenient, and it's not fair. If I was to stop half-a-crown for it, you'd think yourself ill used, I'll be bound?

CRATCHIT: The clerk smiled faintly.

SCROOGE: And yet, you don't think *me* ill used, when I pay a day's wages for no work.

CRATCHIT: The clerk observed that it was only once a year.

SCROOGE: A poor excuse for picking a man's pocket every twenty-fifth of December. *(He buttons his great-coat to the chin.)* But I suppose you must have the whole day. Be here all the earlier next morning!

CRATCHIT: The clerk promised that he would.

(Scrooge walks out with a growl. The clerk closes the office in a twinkling and, with his long comforter dangling, he has no great-coat, he rushes out.)

(A group of children run in playing, going to slide down a hill.)

CRATCHIT: In honor of its being Christmas eve, the clerk got behind a line of children, and went down a slide twenty times, and then ran home as hard as he could pelt to play at blindman's-buff. *(Exeunt omnes, projection off, traveller closes.)*

SCROOGE: *(a waiter brings out a chair and sets it as at a space table)* Scrooge took his melancholy dinner in his usual melancholy tavern; and having read all the newspapers, and beguiled the rest of the evening with his bankbook *(space objects)*, went home to bed. He lived in a house that had once belonged to his deceased partner. It was dreary enough, for nobody lived in it but Scrooge, the other rooms being all let out as offices. The yard was so dark that even Scrooge had to grope with his hands. Now, it is a fact, that there was nothing at all particular about the knocker on the door, except that it was very large. And then let anyone explain to me how it happened that Scrooge *(his key in the lock)* saw in the knocker, not a knocker but Marley's face.

MARLEY'S FACE: Marley's face. It had a dismal light about it, like a bad lobster in a dark cellar. It was not angry or ferocious, but looked at Scrooge with ghostly spectacles turned up upon its ghostly forehead. *(The hair seems to blow in a wind, the eyes are perfectly motionless)*

SCROOGE: *(As Scrooge looks fixedly)* It was a knocker again. To say that he was not startled would be untrue. *(But he puts the key in the lock, turns the door; examines back of door and sees nothing but the screws.)* Pooh, pooh! Nobody under the table, *(Bed and bed-curtains enter.)*nobody under the sofa, nobody under the bed, nobody in the closet. He double-locked himself in. There was a clanking noise deep down below, as if some person were dragging a heavy chain in the wine-merchant's cellar. *(A booming sound, then a chain on the stairs.)* It's humbug still! I won't believe it. It came on through the heavy door, and passed into the room before his eyes. The dying flame leaped up as though it cried:

FLAME: I know him! Marley's Ghost!

(The Ghost is wrapped in chains, its jaw bound with a kerchief.)

SCROOGE: *(cold and caustic, as ever)* How now! What do you want with me!

MARLEY: Much!

SCROOGE: Marley's voice, no doubt about it. Who are you?

MARLEY: Ask me who I *was.*

SCROOGE: Who *were* you then.

MARLEY: In life I was your partner, Jacob Marley.

SCROOGE: Can you - can you sit down?

MARLEY: I can.

SCROOGE: Do it then.

(The ghost sits as if he were quite used to it.)

MARLEY: You don't believe in me.

SCROOGE: I don't.

MARLEY: What evidence would you have of my reality, beyond that of your senses?

SCROOGE: I don't know.

MARLEY: Why do you doubt your senses?

SCROOGE: Because a little thing affects them. You may be an undigested bit of beef, a crumb of cheese. There's more of gravy than of grave about you. Humbug, I tell you - humbug!

(At this the Spirit raises a fearful cry, shakes its chain; Scrooge almost swoons. Then he sees with horror the phantom taking off its kerchief from its head, and the lower jaw drops to its breast. Scrooge falls to his knees and clasps his hands before his face.)

SCROOGE: Mercy! Dreadful apparition, why do you trouble me?

MARLEY: Man of the worldly mind! Do you believe in me or not?

SCROOGE: I do. I must. But why do spirits walk the earth, and why do they come to me?

MARLEY: It is required of every man, that the spirit within him should walk abroad among his fellow-men; and if that spirit goes not forth in life, it is condemned to do so after death. It is doomed to wander through the world - oh, woe is me! - and witness what it cannot share, but might have shared on earth, and turned to happiness! *(Again it cries, shakes its chains, and wrings its hands.)*

SCROOGE: *(trembling)* You are fettered. Tell me why.

MARLEY: I wear the chain I forged in life. I made it link by link, and yard by yard; I girded it on of my own free will, and of my own free will I wore it. Is its pattern strange to you?

SCROOGE: *(looking behind himself)* Jacob *(imploringly)*, Old Jacob Marley, tell me more. Speak comfort to me, Jacob.

MARLEY: I have none to give. It comes from other regions, Ebenezer Scrooge, and is conveyed by other ministers to other kinds of men. I cannot rest, I cannot stay, I cannot linger anywhere.

SCROOGE: You travel fast?

MARLEY: On the wings of the wind.

SCROOGE: You must have got over a great quantity of ground in seven years.

(The ghost sets up another cry and shakes its chains.)

MARLEY: Oh! Captive bound and double-ironed, not to know this earth must pass *(SLIDE No. 2A: Chains on bed curtain.)* into eternity before the good of which it is susceptible is all developed. Not to know any Christian spirit will find its mortal life too short for its task. Yet such was I! Oh! Such was I! *(Wash projection out with dark color till cue for slide No. 2)*

SCROOGE: But you were always a good man of business, Jacob.

MARLEY: Business! *(wringing its hands)* Mankind was my business. The common welfare was my business. The dealings of my trade were but a drop of water in the ocean of my business. *(Holds up its chain and flings it down again)* At this time of the rolling year I suffer most. Why did I walk through crowds of fellow-beings with my eyes turned down, and never raise them to that blessed Star which led the Wise Men to a poor abode? *(Scrooge begins to quake exceedingly)* Hear me! My time is nearly gone.

SCROOGE: I will. But don't be hard upon me!

MARLEY: I am here to warn you that you have yet a chance and hope of escaping my fate. A chance and hope of my procuring, Ebenezer.

SCROOGE: You were always a good friend to me. Thank'ee!

MARLEY: You will be haunted by three spirits.

SCROOGE: *(faltering)* Is that the chance and hope you mentioned, Jacob?

MARLEY: It is.

SCROOGE: I - I think I'd rather not.

MARLEY: Without their visits you cannot hope to shun the path I tread. Expect the first tomorrow, when the bell tolls one.

SCROOGE: Couldn't I take 'em all at once, and have it over?

MARLEY: Expect the second on the next night at the same hour. The third upon the next night at the stroke of midnight. Look to see me no more. *(It winds the kerchief around its head. The sound of the teeth is heard when the jaws are brought together. It goes to the window and beckons Scrooge. When he is within two paces Marley raises his hand. The sound of noises are heard: wailing, lamentations of regret, sorrow, and self-accusation. Marley's ghost joins in the wails and floats out the window. Scrooge's curiosity takes him to the window. Enter spirits.)*

SPIRITS: *(CHAIN SLIDE No. 2B appears.)* The air was filled with phantoms, / wandering hither and thither in restless haste / and moaning as they went. / Every one of them wore chains like Marley's Ghost; / Some few (they might be guilty governments) were linked together; / none were free.

SCROOGE: Scrooge had been quite familiar with one old ghost, with a monstrous iron safe attached to its ankle,

SPIRIT: who cried piteously at being unable to assist a wretched woman with an infant.

MARLEY: He had lost the power for good, for ever...

(Lights go to dark. All ghosts and Marley exeunt.)

SCROOGE: And being worn out from the emotions, Scrooge fell asleep upon the instant.

STAVE TWO: Christmas Past
The First of the Three Spirits

(Stave II sign is brought on. In the darkness the bell tolls.)

SCROOGE: Quarter past; half past; The hour itself and nothing else!

(The bell tolls ONE. Again lights flash up, and the curtain of his bed are drawn.)

SCROOGE: The curtains of his bed, were drawn aside, I tell you, by a hand.

SLIDE No. 3, *a hand, up briefly.*

(Scrooge is face to face with "the unearthly visitor who drew them, as close

to it as I am to you, and I am standing in spirit at your elbow.") It was a strange figure -

SPIRIT: like a child:

SCROOGE: yet not so like a child

SPIRIT: as like an old man.

SCROOGE: Its hair was white as if with age

(Spirit turns its back to audience)

SPIRIT: *(turning back)* and yet the face had not a wrinkle in it, and the tenderest bloom was on the skin.

SCROOGE: From the crown of its head there sprung a bright clear jet of light; it carried a great extinguisher for a cap *(which it holds under its arm and uses, cap on, cap off)*

SPIRIT: What was light one instant, at another time was dark, now a thing with one arm, now with one leg, now with twenty legs, now a pair of legs without a head, now a head without a body. *(demonstrates all this)*

SCROOGE: Are you the spirit, sir, whose coming was foretold to me?

SPIRIT: I am!

SCROOGE: Who, and what are you?

SPIRIT: I am the Ghost of Christmas Past.

SCROOGE: Long Past?

PAST: No. Your Past.

SCROOGE: Scrooge had a special desire to see the Spirit in his cap. *(gestures and begs)*

PAST: What! Would you so soon put out, with worldly hands, the light I give? Is it not enough that you are one of those whose passions made this cap, and force me to wear it low upon my brow!

SCROOGE: What business brought you here?

PAST: Your welfare.

SCROOGE: A night of sleep would be conducive to that end.

PAST: Your reclamation then. Take heed! *(puts out its hand and clasps him gently by the arm)* Rise! and walk with me!

SCROOGE: I am mortal, and liable to fall.

PAST: Bear but a touch of my hand *there, (on his heart)* and you shall be upheld in more than this! *(Bed and curtains are removed).*

SCROOGE: They passed through the wall, *(Traveller opens.)*

(SLIDE No. 4, Open road.) and stood upon an open road, with fields on either hand. The city had entirely vanished!

PAST: The darkness and the mist had vanished with it, for it was a clear, cold, winter day, with snow upon the ground.

SCROOGE: *(clasping his hands together)* I was bred in this place! I was a boy here! *(The Spirit gazes at him mildly. Scrooge still feels its gentle touch.)* He was conscious of a thousand odors floating in the air, a thousand hopes, and joys, and cares long, long forgotten!

PAST: Your lip is trembling. And what is that upon your cheek?

SCROOGE: *(hiding the tear)* Scrooge begged the Ghost to lead him where he would. *(They set off.)*

PAST: You recollect the way?

SCROOGE: *(with fervor)* Remember it! I could walk it blindfold.

PAST: Strange to have forgotten it for so many years! Let us go in.

SCROOGE: Scrooge recognized every gate, and post, and tree; until a little market town appeared with its bridge, its church, and winding river. *(Children on shaggy ponies call and sing to one another.)*

PAST: These are but shadows of the things that have been. They have no consciousness of us.

(Snow falls, Townspeople enter singing 'Joy to the World'.)

SCROOGE: *(as children and other jocund travelers come on)* Scrooge knew and named them every one. Why did his cold eye glisten, and his heart leap up as they went past! Why was he filled with gladness when he heard them give each other Merry Christmas, as they parted for their several homes! What was Merry Christmas to Scrooge? Out upon Merry Christmas! *(SLIDE out.)*

PAST: The school is not quite deserted. A solitary child, neglected by his friends, is left there still.

SCROOGE: Scrooge said he knew it. And he sobbed. *(They enter)*

SLIDE No. 5, SCHOOLROOM.

BOY: In a long, bare, melancholy room a lonely boy is reading near a feeble fire.

SCROOGE: *(Scrooge weeps to see his poor forgotten self as he used to be.)* Suddenly a man in foreign garments appears leading an ass. *(ecstatic)* Why it's Ali Baba! It's dear old honest Ali Baba! Yes, yes, I know! One Christmas time, when yonder solitary child was left here all alone, he *did* come, for the first time, just like that. Poor boy! And the Three Musketeers! *(they enter swords out and cross to exit)*

THREE MUSKETEERS: *(shouting)* All for one! And one for all!

SCROOGE: *(after drying his eyes with his cuff)* I wish, but it's too late now.

PAST: What is the matter?

SCROOGE: Nothing. Nothing. There was a boy singing a Christmas Carol at my door last night. I should like to have given him something: that's all.

PAST: *(smiling thoughtfully, waving his hand)* Let us see another Christmas!

SCROOGE: Scrooge's former self grew larger at the words, and the room became a little darker and more dirty; but how this all was brought about, Scrooge knew no more than you do. There he was, alone again, when all the other children had gone home for the jolly holidays. *(He is not reading, but walking up and down in despair. Scrooge shakes his head mournfully and glances at the door. It opens and a little girl darts in and puts her arms about his neck, often kissing him.)*

GIRL: Dear, dear brother. I have come to bring you home, dear brother! *(clapping her hands and bending down to laugh)* To bring you home, home, home!

YOUNG SCROOGE: Home, little Fan?

GIRL: *(with glee)* Yes! Home for good and all. Home, for ever and ever. Father is so much kinder than he used to be, that home's like Heaven! He spoke so gently to me one dear night when I was going to bed, that I was not afraid to ask him once more if you might come home; and he said, Yes, you should; and sent me in a coach to bring you. *(sound of horses outside)* And you're to be a man! And are never to come back here.

YOUNG SCROOGE: You are quite a woman, little Fan. *(She claps her hands and laughs, and tries to touch his head; but being too little, laughs again, and stands on tiptoe to embrace him. Then she drags him towards the door, and he follows.)*

SCHOOLMASTER: *(in a terrible voice)* Bring down Master Scrooge's box, there! *(appears and shakes hands and glares at young Scrooge with ferocious condescension.)* He then produced a decanter

YOUNG SCROOGE: of curiously light wine,

SCHOOLMASTER: and a block

FAN: of curiously heavy cake *(Schoolmaster serves them)*

SERVANT: at the same time sending out a meager servant to offer a glass of 'something' to the post boy,

POST BOY: who answered that he thanked the gentleman, but if it was the same tap as he had tasted before, he had rather not.

DRIVER: *(enters)* Master Scrooge's trunk being by this time tied on to the top of the chaise, *(a bench is brought to seat them as the space trunk is tied on)*

YOUNG SCROOGE: the children bade the schoolmaster goodbye right willingly;

FAN: and getting into it, drove gaily down the garden sweep; *(Both are aboard the chaise, with driver and footman, the whip is cracked and off they go.)*

YOUNG SCROOGE: the quick wheels dashing the hoar-frost and snow

FAN: like spray! *(exeunt from stage left removing bench. SLIDE out.)*

PAST: Always a delicate creature, whom a breath might have withered. But she had a large heart!

SCROOGE: So she had. You're right. I'll not deny it, Spirit. God forbid!

PAST: She died a woman, and had, as I think, children.

SCROOGE: One child.

PAST: True. Your nephew!

SCROOGE: *(uneasy in mind)* Yes. Suddenly they were in a city.

PAST: *(stopping at a certain door)* Do you know this place?

SCROOGE: Know it! Was I apprenticed here? *(they enter to find an old gentleman in a Welch wig)* Why, it's old Fezziwig! Bless his heart; it's Fezziwig alive again!

SLIDE No. 6, FEZZIWIG' S WAREHOUSE

FEZZIWIG: *(Fezziwig lays down his pen, looks up at the clock (seven), rubs his hands, adjusts his capacious waistcoat; laughs all over himself, from his shoes*

to his organ of benevolence; calls out in a comfortable, oily, rich, fat, jovial voice:) Yo ho, there! Ebenezar! Dick! Hang the party decorations!

(Enter the young Scrooge and his fellow apprentice with real decorations evergreens to hang on wire, center, connected by red ribbons criss -crossing the stage to four beribboned poles, are to be set into pre-positioned stands, and are brought on by Fezziwig workers and other players.)

SCROOGE: *(to Ghost)* Dick Wilkins, to be sure! Bless me, yes. There he is. He was very much attached to me, was Dick. Poor Dick! Dear, dear!

FEZZIWIG: Yo ho, my boys. No more work tonight. Christmas Eve, Dick. Christmas, Ebenezer! Let's have the shutters up *(a sharp clap of his hands)* before a man can say, Jack Robinson!

SCROOGE: You wouldn't believe how those two fellows went at it!

EBENEZER: They charged into the street with the shutters *(opening and closing space doors to the street, downstage.)* - one

DICK: two,

EBENEZER. three -

DICK: had 'em up in their places - *(on the space wall near the audience)*

EBENEZER: four,

DICK: five,

EBENEZER: six - barred 'em and pinned 'em -

DICK: seven,

EBENEZER: eight,

DICK: nine - and came back before you could have got to twelve, *(opening and closing space doors)*

EBENEZER: panting like race horses.

FEZZIWIG: Hilli-ho! Clear away, my lads, and let's have lots of room here! Hilli-ho, Dick! Chirrup, Ebenezer!

DICK: Clear away!

EBENEZER: There was nothing they wouldn't have cleared away,

DICK: or couldn't have cleared away, with old Fezziwig looking on.

EBENEZER: It was done in a minute.

DICK: Every movable was packed off, as if it were dismissed from public life for evermore;

EBENEZER: the floor was swept and watered,

DICK: the lamps trimmed,

EBENEZER: fuel was heaped upon the fire; *(Broom, lamps, firewood are all space objects)*

DICK: and the warehouse was as snug, and warm and dry,

EBENEZER: and bright a ball-room, as you would desire to see

DICK: upon a winter's night.

FIDDLER: In came a fiddler with a music-book, and tuned like fifty stomach-aches.

MRS. FEZZIWIG: In came Mrs. Fezziwig, one vast substantial smile.

MISSES FEZZIWIGS: In came the Miss Fezziwigs, beaming and lovable.

YOUTH: In came the young followers, whose hearts they broke.

MAID: In came the housemaid with her cousin,

BAKER: the baker.

COOK: In came the cook,

MILKMAN: with her brother's particular friend,

COOK: the milkman.

BOY: In came the boy from over the way,

MRS. FEZZIWIG: who was suspected of not having board enough from his master;

BOY: trying to hide himself behind the girl from next door but one,

GIRL: who was proved to have had her ears pulled by her Mistress.

>   - In they all came,
>   - one after another,
>   - some shyly,
>   - some boldly,
>   - some gracefully,
>   - some awkwardly,
>   - some pushing,
>   - some pulling,
>   - in they all came, anyhow and everyhow.

(Music for Square Dance)

>   - Away they all went, hands half round,
>   - and back again the other way;
>   - down the middle,

- and up again,
- round and round
- in various stages of affectionate grouping;
- old couple always turning up in the wrong place;
- new couple starting off again as soon as they got there,
- all top couples at last and not a bottom one to help them.

FEZZIWIG: *(clapping hands to stop dance)* Well done! *(all clap)*

FIDDLER: And the fiddler plunged his hot face into a pot of porter,

DICK: especially provided for that purpose.

FIDDLER: He instantly began again, as if the other fiddler had been carried home exhausted; and he were a brand-new man resolved to beat him out of sight.

- There were more dances,
- and there were forfeits,
- and more dances,
- and there was cake,
- and there was mulled wine,
- and there was a great piece of Cold Roast,
- and there was a great piece of Cold Boiled,
- and there were mince pies,
- and plenty of beer.

FIDDLER: But the great effect of the evening came when the fiddler (an artful dog, mind!) struck up 'Sir Roger de Coverly'!

FEZZIWIG: Then old Fezziwig stood out to dance, with Mrs. Fezziwig.

MRS. FEZZIWIG: Top couple, too; with a good stiff piece of work cut out for them;

- people who were not to be trifled with;
- people who *would* dance, and had no notion of walking.
- Bow and curtsy; and retreat,
- corkscrew; thread the needle.

FEZZIWIG: Fezziwig cut so deftly, that he appeared to wink with his legs, and came upon his feet again without a stagger.

FIDDLER: When the clock struck eleven, this domestic ball broke up.

FEZZIWIG: Mr. and Mrs. Fezziwig took their stations,

MRS. FEZZIWIG: one on either side the door, *(door is in space, downstage center.)*

FEZZIWIG: and shaking hands individually with every person as he or she went out,

MRS. FEZZIWIG: wished him or her a Merry Christmas. *(The apprentices take down the decorations, helped by Fezziwig and his family.)*

PAST: A small matter, to make these silly folks so full of gratitude.

SCROOGE: Small!

PAST: Why! Is it not? He has spent but a few pounds of your mortal money: three or four, perhaps. Is that so much that he deserves this praise?

SCROOGE: *(heated by the remark)* It isn't that, Spirit.

(Beribboned pole are removed and traveller closes; SLIDE No. 5 out.)

He has the power to render us happy or unhappy, to make our service light or burdensome; a pleasure or a toil. The happiness he gives, is quite as great as if it cost a fortune. *(Remembers)*

PAST: What is the matter?

SCROOGE: Nothing particular.

PAST: Something, I think.

SCROOGE: No. I should like to be able to say a word or two to my clerk just now! That's all.

(SLIDE OUT. Ebenezer and Dick turn down the lights as Scrooge and Spirit go through a wall into the open air.)

PAST: My time grows short. Quick!

(A young woman appears in a mourning dress.)

BELLE: It matters little, to you, very little. Another idol has displaced me, and if it can cheer and comfort you in time to come, as I would have tried to do, I have no just cause to grieve.

SCROOGE: *(made-up and costumed as he has been)* What idol has displaced you?

BELLE: A golden one.

SCROOGE: There is nothing on which the world is so hard as poverty.

BELLE: You fear the world too much. I have seen your nobler aspirations fall off one by one, until the master-passion, GAIN, engrosses you. Have I not?

SCROOGE: What then? Even if I have grown so much wiser, what then? I am not changed towards you. *(She shakes her head.)* Am I?

BELLE: Our contract is an old one. When it was made, you were another man.

SCROOGE: *(impatiently)* I was a boy.

BELLE: You were not what you are. I am. How often and how keenly I have thought of this, I will not say. It is enough that I *have* thought of it, and can release you.

SCROOGE: Have I ever sought release?

BELLE: In words. No, never.

SCROOGE: In what then?

BELLE: In an altered spirit; in another atmosphere of life. In everything that made my love of any worth or value in your sight. Tell me, would you seek me out and try to win me now? Ah, no!

SCROOGE: *(knowing she is right)* You think not.

BELLE: If you were free today, can I believe that you would choose a dowerless girl - you who weigh everything by Gain? I release you. With a full heart, for the love of him you once were. *(turns her head away)* You may - I half hope you will - have pain in this. A very, very brief time, and you will dismiss the recollection of it, gladly, as an unprofitable dream, from which you awoke. May you be happy in the life you have chosen. *(She leaves him, "and they parted.")*

SCROOGE: Spirit! Show me no more! Conduct me home. Why do you delight to torture me?

PAST: One shadow more! To see her children and whom she married, and how they celebrate Christmas.

SCROOGE: No more! I don't wish to see it. No more!

PAST: These are shadows of the things that have been. They are what they are.

SCROOGE: Remove me! I cannot bear it! Haunt me no longer! *(Wrestles with the Spirit; seizes the extinguisher cap of the Spirit and presses it down on its head. The Spirit drops so that the extinguisher covers its whole form. But the light streams out from under it. Scrooge is exhausted and falls on his own bed and is in a heavy sleep.)*

INTERMISSION

ACT II

STAVE THREE: *Christmas Present*

The Second of the Great Spirits

(STAVE III sign is brought on. A clock tower bell tolls ONE. Scrooge wakes in the middle of a snore.)

SCROOGE: No shape appeared *(he trembles violently)*; five minutes, ten minutes, a quarter of an hour went by, yet nothing came. *(a blaze of ruddy light touches his bed, he senses the source of the light to be in the next room. Gets up and shuffles in his slippers to the door.)*

VOICE: Enter, Ebenezer Scrooge! *(Traveller opens for SLIDE NO. 7: ABUNDANCE. The space transforms, slide shows walls hung with living green, with holly and mistletoe and mirrors of light. A blaze in the fireplace. A jolly giant carries a torch, like Plenty's horn.)*

GHOST: Come in! Come in! And know me better, man! I am the Ghost of Christmas Present. Look upon me! You have never seen the like of me before!

SCROOGE: Never. Spirit, conduct me where you will. I went forth last night on compulsion, and I learnt a lesson which is working now.

PRESENT: Touch my robe! *(As Scrooge does so the room, the ruddy glow, the hour of night vanishes. SLIDE No. 7 out . SLIDE No. 8 up: LONDON CHRISTMAS. Cratchit house of burlap scrim appears on wire, pulled on by a player.)*

SCROOGE: They stood in the city streets on Christmas morning. *(snow falls)*

CHORUS: The people made a rough, but brisk and not unpleasant kind of music
    - in scraping the snow from the pavement in front of their dwellings,
    - and from the tops of their houses,
CHILD: whence it was a mad delight to the children to see it come plumping down into the road below,

CHILD: and splitting into artificial little snow-storms.
    - The people shoveling away were jovial and full of glee;
    - calling out to one another from the parapets,
    - and now and then exchanging a facetious snowball -
    - laughing heartily if it went right,
    - and not less heartily if it went wrong.

POULTERER: *(carrying squawking space chickens)* The poulterers' shops were still half open,

FRUITERER: and the fruiterers were radiant in their glory and winking in wanton slyness at the girls as they went by,

GIRL: glancing demurely at the hung-up mistletoe.

OTHERS: There were pears and apples, clustered high in blooming pyramids;

- there were piles of filberts, mossy and brown,
- recalling, in their fragrance, ancient walks among the woods,
- and pleasant shufflings ankle deep through withered leaves.
(Church bells)
- But soon the steeples called good people all, to church and chapel
(Entering)- and away they came, flocking through the streets in their best clothes,
- and with their gayest faces.
- At the same time there emerged from scores of bye streets, lanes,
- and nameless turnings, innumerable poor people, carrying their dinners to the baker's shops to be cooked.

(Present takes his torch and sprinkles incense on their food; lifting a cover or two as needed.)

PRESENT: And it was a very uncommon kind of torch he waved,

SCROOGE: for once or twice when there were angry words between some dinner-carriers *(who have jostled each other)*,

PRESENT: he shed a few drops of water on them,

SCROOGE: and their good humor was restored directly.

CARRIERS: For, they said, It was a shame to quarrel upon Christmas Day.
- And so it was!
- God love it, so it was!

SCROOGE: Is there a peculiar flavor in what you sprinkle from your torch?

PRESENT: There is. My own.

SCROOGE: Would it apply to any kind of dinner on this day?

PRESENT: To any kindly given. To a poor one most.

SCROOGE: Why to a poor one most?

PRESENT: Because it needs it most. And with that, he went straight to Bob Cratchit's dwelling,

SCROOGE: Scrooge holding to his robe,

PRESENT: and on the threshold of the door blessed it with his torch

SCROOGE: Think of that! Bob had but fifteen 'Bob' a-week himself; and yet the Ghost of Christmas Present blessed his four-roomed house!

MRS. CRATCHIT: Then up rose Mrs. Cratchit, Cratchit's wife, dressed out but poorly in a twice-turned gown, but brave in ribbons, which are cheap and make a goodly show for sixpence; and she laid the cloth,

BELINDA: assisted by Belinda Cratchit, second of her daughters, also brave in ribbons;

PETER: while Master Peter Cratchit plunged a fork into the saucepan of potatoes (*space objects, from fork to stove*), and getting the corners of his monstrous shirt-collar,

BELINDA: Bob's private property,

PETER: into his mouth, rejoiced to find himself so gallantly attired,

BELINDA: and yearned to show his linen in the fashionable parks.

BOY: And now the two smaller Cratchits, boy

GIRL: and girl,

BOY: came tearing in,

GIRL: screaming that outside the baker's they had smelled the goose,

BOY: and known it for their own;

GIRL: and basking in luxurious thoughts of sage and onion,

BOY: these young Cratchits danced about the table,

GIRL: and exalted Master Peter Cratchit to the skies,

PETER: while he, not proud, although his collars nearly choked him, blew the fire,

BOY: until the slow potatoes bubbling up, knocked loudly at the saucepan lid,

GIRL: to be let out and peeled.

MRS. CRATCHIT: What has ever got your precious father then. And your brother, Tiny Tim; and Martha warn't as late last Christmas Day by half-an-hour.

MARTHA: *(entering)* Here's Martha, mother.

BOY: Here's Martha, mother! Hurrah!

GIRL: There's *such* a goose, Martha!

MRS. CRATCHIT: *(kissing her a dozen times, and taking off her shawl and bonnet with officious zeal)* Why, bless your heart alive, my dear, how late you are!

MARTHA: We'd a deal of work to finish up last night, and had to clear away this morning, mother!

MRS. CRATCHIT: Well! Never mind so long as you are come. Sit ye down before the fire, my dear, and have a warm, Lord bless ye! *(Two six foot benches can handle the family, moving them from fire to table and back, as needed.)*

GIRL: No! There's Father coming.

BOY: Hide, Martha, hide.

MARTHA: So Martha hid herself,

CRATCHIT: and in came little Bob, the father, his thread-bare clothes darned up and brushed, to look seasonable,

TINY TIM: and Tiny Tim upon his shoulder.

CRATCHIT: Alas, for Tiny Tim. *(letting him down for Boy and Girl to take him to a seat near the hearth)*

BOY: He bore a little crutch,

GIRL: and had his limbs supported by an iron frame!

CRATCHIT: Why, where's our Martha?

MRS. CRATCHIT: Not coming.

CRATCHIT: *(declension of high spirits)* Not coming! Not coming upon Christmas Day!

MARTHA: Martha didn't like to see him disappointed,

CRATCHIT: and ran into his arms,

BOY AND GIRL: while the two young Cratchits hustled Tiny Tim,

BELINDA: and bore him off into the wash-house

TINY TIM: that he might hear the pudding singing in the copper.

MRS. CRATCHIT: And how did little Tim behave?

CRATCHIT: As good as gold, and better. Somehow he gets thoughtful sitting by himself so much, and thinks the strangest things you ever heard. He told me, coming home, that he hoped the people saw him in church, because he was a cripple, and it might be pleasant to them to remember upon Christmas Day, who made the lame walk and blind men see.

MRS. CRATCHIT: His active little crutch was heard upon the floor,

TINY TIM: and back came Tiny Tim,

BOY: escorted by his brother

GIRL: and sister

BOY: to his stool,

GIRL: before the fire;

CRATCHIT: and while Bob, turning up his cuffs -

MRS. CRATCHIT: as if, poor fellow, they were capable of being made more shabby -

CRATCHIT: compounded some hot mixture in a jug with gin and lemons *(stirs it round and round and puts it on the hob to simmer)*;

PETER: Master Peter

BOY AND GIRL: and the two ubiquitous young Cratchits

PETER: went to fetch the goose,

BOY AND GIRL: with which they soon returned in high procession.

BELINDA: Such a bustle ensued that you might have thought a goose the rarest of all birds:

CRATCHIT: a feathered phenomenon,

MARTHA: to which a black swan was a matter of course;

BELINDA: and in truth it was something very like it in that house.

MRS. CRATCHIT: Mrs. Cratchit made the gravy hissing hot.

PETER: Master Peter mashed the potatoes with incredible vigor.

BELINDA: Miss Belinda sweetened up the apple sauce;

MARTHA: Martha dusted the hot plates;

CRATCHIT: Bob took Tiny Tim beside him in a tiny corner at the table

BOY AND GIRL: the two young Cratchits set silverware for everybody,

BELINDA: not forgetting themselves,

BOY: and crammed spoons into their mouths,

GIRL: lest they should shriek before their turn came to be helped.

MARTHA: At last the dishes were set on, and grace was said.

BELINDA: It was succeeded by a breathless pause,

MRS. CRATCHIT: *(looking slowly along the knife) as* Mrs. Cratchit prepared to plunge the knife in the breast. *(She does.)*

(A murmur of delight from all. Tiny Tim beats on the table with his knife.)

TINY TIM: Hurrah!

(The meal is eaten within the next seven or eight lines.)

CRATCHIT: There never was such a goose.

PETER: It's tenderness

MARTHA: and flavor,

BELINDA: size

MRS. CRATCHIT: and cheapness,

CRATCHIT: were the themes of universal admiration.

MRS. CRATCHIT: Indeed, as Mrs. Cratchit said with great delight

BELINDA: surveying one small atom of a bone upon the dish

MRS. CRATCHIT: they hadn't ate it all at last!

PETER: Yet everyone had had enough,

BOY: and the youngest Cratchits in particular

GIRL: were steeped in sage and onions to the eyebrows!

BELINDA: But now, the plates being changed by Miss Belinda,

MRS. CRATCHIT: Mrs. Cratchit left the room alone -

MARTHA: too nervous to bear witnesses -

CRATCHIT: to take the pudding up, and bring it in.

GIRL: Suppose it should not be done enough!

BELINDA: Suppose it should break in turning out!

BOY: Suppose somebody should have got over the wall of the backyard and stolen it.

CRATCHIT: All sorts of horrors were supposed.

MRS. CRATCHIT: Hallo!

PETER: A great deal of steam!

MRS. CRATCHIT: *(off)* The pudding is out of the copper.

PETER: A smell like washing day!

MARTHA: That was the cloth.

BELINDA: A smell like an eating house and a pastry cook's.

CRATCHIT: That was the pudding.

MRS. CRATCHIT: In half a minute Mrs. Cratchit entered: flushed, but smiling proudly: with the pudding,

BOY: like a speckled cannon ball,

GIRL: so hard and firm,

PETER. *(lighting the flame)* blazing in half of half-a-quartern of ignited brandy,

TINY TIM: with Christmas holly stuck into the top.

CRATCHIT: Oh, a wonderful pudding! He regarded it as the greatest success achieved by Mrs. Cratchit since their marriage.

MRS. CRATCHIT: Now that the weight was off her mind, she confessed she had her doubts about the quantity of flour.

GIRL: Everybody had something to say about it,

BELINDA: but nobody said or thought it was at all a small pudding for a large family.

CRATCHIT: It would have been flat heresy to do so.

PETER: Any Cratchit would have blushed to hint at such a thing.

BOY: At last the dinner was all done,

BELINDA: the cloth was cleared,

MARTHA: the hearth swept,

CRATCHIT: and the fire made up.

PETER: The compound in the jug being tasted, and considered perfect,

GIRL: apples and oranges were put upon the table,

BOY: and a shovel-full of chestnuts on the fire.

CRATCHIT: Then all the Cratchit family drew round the hearth,

MRS. CRATCHIT: in what Bob Cratchit called a circle,

MARTHA: meaning half a one;

CRATCHIT: and brought out the family display of glass;

BELINDA: two tumblers, and a custard-cup without a handle.

MRS. CRATCHIT: These held the hot stuff from the jug, however, as well as golden goblets would have done;

CRATCHIT: A Merry Christmas to us all, my dears. God bless us!

ALL: God bless us!

TINY TIM: God bless us every one!

(Bob takes Tiny Tim's withered hand and puts him by his side, as if he dreads Tim will be taken from him.)

SCROOGE: Spirit, tell me if Tiny Tim will live.

PRESENT: I see a vacant seat in the poor chimney corner, and a crutch without an owner, carefully preserved. If these shadows remain unaltered by the future, the child will die.

SCROOGE: No, no, oh no, kind Spirit! Say he will be spared.

PRESENT: What then? If he be like to die, he had better do it, and decrease the surplus population.

(Scrooge hangs his head in penitence and grief.)

MRS. CRATCHIT: All this time the chestnuts and the jug went round and round,

MARTHA: and bye and bye they had a song from Tiny Tim.

(Dickens did not write the words for this song, but perhaps Yeats did in The Stolen Child, whose refrain runs: 'Come away, O human child! To the waters and the wild - With a faery, hand in hand, For the world is more full of weeping than you can understand.')

PRESENT: There was nothing of high mark in this. They were not a handsome family, they were not well dressed;

MARTHA: their shoes were far from being water-proof;

BELINDA: their clothes were scanty;

PETER: and Peter might have known,

BELINDA: and very likely did -

PETER: the inside of a pawnbroker's,

MRS. CRATCHIT: but they were happy,

BOY: grateful,

MARTHA: pleased with one another,

GIRL: and contented with the time. *(The family rise, remove the benches, exeunt.)*

PRESENT: And when they faded in the bright sprinklings of the Spirit's torch at parting,

SCROOGE: Scrooge had his eye upon them, and especially on Tiny Tim, until the last. *(LONDON CHRISTMAS SLIDE No. 8 out and house scrim off at exit.)*

PRESENT: And now without a word of warning from the Ghost, they stood upon a bleak and desert moor,

SCROOGE: where monstrous masses of rude stone were cast about, as though it were the burial place of giants.

PRESENT: Down in the west the setting sun had left a streak of fiery red, which glared upon the desolation like a sullen eye.

SCROOGE: What place is this?

PRESENT: A place where Miners live, who labor in the bowels of the earth. But they know me. See!

(A cheerful company assembles round an old, old man and woman. He is singing them a Christmas song, 'Deck the Halls With Boughs of Holly'; all join in the chorus and dance. The howling wind competes with them. When they raise their voices, the old couple sing blithe and loud. Exeunt omnes.)

PRESENT: Hold my robe! (They sail aloft.)

SCROOGE: Whereto? Not to sea?

PRESENT: *(A thundering of water, much to Scrooge's horror.)* To sea.

SCROOGE: Some league or two from shore, there stood a solitary light-house, and storm birds

(SLIDE No. 9, LIGHTHOUSE)

PRESENT: born of the wind one might suppose, rose and fell like the waves they skimmed!

LIGHTHOUSE KEEPER: But even here two men had lit the fire

HIS PARTNER: that shed out a ray of brightness on the awful sea.

(The two men join hands and wish each other Merry Christmas, as they exeunt.)

PRESENT: Again the Ghost sped on, above the black and heaving sea - on, on, -

SCROOGE: until, being far away from any shore, they lighted on a ship,

PRESENT: by the helmsman at the wheel, the officers who had the watch;

SCROOGE: the lookout in the bow; dark, ghostly figures in their several stations.

PRESENT: But every man among them hummed a Christmas tune, or had a Christmas thought,

SAILOR ONE: or spoke below his breath to his companion of some bygone Christmas Day,

SAILOR TWO: with homeward hopes belonging to it.

SAILOR ONE: And every man on board, good or bad, had a kinder word for another on that day,

SAILOR TWO: and had remembered those he cared for at a distance,

SAILOR ONE: and had known that they delighted to remember him.

SCROOGE: It was a great surprise to Scrooge, while listening to the moaning of the wind, to hear a hearty laugh.

(SLIDE No. 9 out; traveller closes and players entering bring on white curtain.)

It was a much greater surprise to recognize it as his own nephew's, and to find himself in a bright, dry, gleaming room,

PRESENT: with the Spirit standing smiling by his side.

FRED: Ha, ha! Ha, ha, ha!

(Fred's wife and friends all laugh as lustily.)

FRED: He said that Christmas was a humbug, as I live. He believed it too!

WIFE: More shame for him, Fred!

PRESENT: Bless those women: they never do anything by halves. They're always in earnest.

FRED: He's a comical old fellow, that's the truth: and not so pleasant as he might be. However, his offenses carry their own punishment.

WIFE: I have no patience with him.*(Her sisters and the others express the same opinion. All pour tea and eat cake.)*

FRED: I am sorry for him; I couldn't be angry with him if I tried. Who suffers by his ill whims! Himself, always. Here, he takes it into his head to dislike us, and he won't come to dine with us. What's the consequence? He don't lose much of a dinner.

WIFE: Indeed, I think he loses a very good dinner. *(The others agree with her, and must be allowed to be competent judges for they have just finished dinner, and are at dessert, clustered around the fire, by lamplight.)*

FRED: Well! I'm very glad to hear it, because I haven't great faith in these young housekeepers. What do *you* say, Topper?

TOPPER: Topper had clearly got his eyes upon one of Scrooge's niece's sisters, for he answered that a bachelor was a wretched outcast, who had no right to express an opinion on the subject.

PLUMP GIRL: Whereas Scrooge's niece's sister - the plump one with the lace tucker; not the one with the roses - blushed.

WIFE: Do go on, Fred. *(clapping her hands)* He never finishes what he begins to say! He is such a ridiculous fellow.

FRED: *(revels in a laugh, which everyone follows though the plump girl tries to stop it with aromatic vinegar)* I was going to say that the consequence of his not making merry with us is that he loses some pleasant moments, which could do him no harm. I am sure he loses pleasanter companions than he can find in his own thoughts.

WIFE: After tea they had some music.

FRIENDS: And knew what they were about when they sung a Glee or a Catch, I can assure you.

PLUMP GIRL: For they were a musical family,

TOPPER: especially Topper, who could growl away in the bass and never get red in the face.

WIFE: Scrooge's niece played well upon the harp *(plays)*;

FRIEND: and played among other tunes a simple little air,

WIFE: a mere nothing: you might learn to whistle it in two minutes.

SCROOGE: *(listening)* Scrooge softened more and more, and thought that if he could have listened to it often, years ago, he might have cultivated the kindnesses of life.

PRESENT: But they didn't devote the whole evening to music.

FRIEND: After a while they played at forfeits!

FRED: For it is good to be children sometimes,

PRESENT: and never better than at Christmas, when its mighty Founder was a child himself.

WIFE: Stop! There was first a game at blind-man's buff.

FRIEND: Of course there was. *(They start)*

SCROOGE: The way he went after that plump sister in the lace tucker, was an outrage on the credulity of human nature.

TOPPER: Knocking down the fireirons, tumbling over the chairs,

PLUMP GIRL: wherever she went there went he,

TOPPER: bumping against the piano, smothering himself among the curtains.

SCROOGE: He always knew where the plump sister was.

PRESENT: He wouldn't catch anybody else.

(Others fall against him, get in his way, he makes a feint of endeavoring to catch them, and sidles off toward the plump girl.)

PLUMP GIRL: She often cried out that it wasn't fair.

SCROOGE: And it really was not.

TOPPER: But when at last, he caught her;

PLUMP GIRL: when, in spite of all her silken rustling, and her rapid flutterings past him,

TOPPER: he got her into a corner whence there was no escape;

PLUMP GIRL: then his conduct was the most execrable.

TOPPER: For his pretending not to know her;

PLUMP GIRL: his pretending it was necessary to touch her headdress,

TOPPER: and a certain chain about her neck;

PLUMP GIRL: was vile, monstrous!

SCROOGE: No doubt she told him her opinion of it, when, another blind-man being in office,

PRESENT: they were so very confidential together, behind the curtains.

(The group start making music, playing, singing, whistling. Exeunt, pulling off curtains.)

SCROOGE: Scrooge noticed that the Ghost was older, clearly older; its hair was gray. Are Spirit's lives so short?

PRESENT: My life upon this globe, is very brief. It ends tonight.

SCROOGE: Tonight! *(Fog appears.)*

PRESENT: Tonight at midnight. *(chimes)* Hark! The time is drawing near.

SCROOGE: Forgive me, but I see something strange, and not belonging to yourself, protruding from your skirts. Is it a foot or a claw!

PRESENT: It might be a claw, for the flesh there is upon it. Look here. From the folds of its robe, it brought two children: wretched, abject, frightful, miserable. Oh, Man! look here. Look, look, down here! *(They are a boy and a girl, meager, scowling.)*

SCROOGE: Where angels might have sat enthroned, devils lurked and glared out menacing.

PRESENT: No change, no degradation, no perversion of humanity, in any grade, through all the mysteries of wonderful creation, has monsters half so horrible and dread.

SCROOGE: Spirit! Are they yours?

PRESENT: They are Man's. And they cling to me, appealing from their fathers. This boy is Ignorance. This girl is Want. Beware them both, but most of all beware this boy, for on his brow I see that written which is Doom, unless the writing be erased. *(bitterly)* Deny it! *(pointing towards the city)* Slander those who speak of it! Admit it for your factious purposes, and make it worse.

SCROOGE: Have they no refuge or resources?

PRESENT: Are there no prisons? Are there no workhouses? *(Exeunt)*

(The bell strikes twelve; the Ghost vanishes. Scrooge sees:)

SCROOGE: Remembering the prediction of old Jacob Marley, Scrooge saw a solemn phantom coming, like a mist along the ground. *(Fog.)*

STAVE FOUR: *Christmas Future*
The Last of the Three Spirits

(Stave IV sign is brought on. Scrooge bends down upon his knee before the gloom and mystery)

SCROOGE: *(in dread)* I am in the presence of the Ghost of Christmas Yet To Come?

(The Spirit answers not, but points onward with its hand.)

SCROOGE: You are about to show me shadows of the things that have not happened, but will happen in the time before us. Is that so, Spirit?

(The robe which conceals the Spirit shows it has inclined its head.)

SCROOGE: Lead on! Lead on! The night is waning fast, and it is precious time to me, I know. Lead on, Spirit! *(Traveller opens to SLIDE No. 10, MELANCHOLY LONDON)*

(The Spirit moves away. They are in the city. A funeral is in process; music. Four or five men enter, observing the coffin pass.)

  - Well! Old Scratch has got his own at last, hey?

  - So I see. Cold, isn't it?

  - What has he done with his money?

  - Left it to his Company, perhaps. He hasn't left it to *me*. That's all I know.

  - It's likely to be a very cheap funeral. I don't know of anybody to go to it.

  - Suppose we make up a party and follow the hearse.

  - Is there to be lunch? I must be fed if I go. *(a laugh)*

SCROOGE: *(shuddering)* Spirit! I see, I see. The case of this unhappy man might be my own. My life tends that way now. *(He recoils in terror, for suddenly a corpse is carried on by four to six figures, the body under a sheet.)* Merciful Heaven, what is this! *(Scrooge looks wildly about him. The Phantom points to the head. A motion of Scrooge's finger would disclose the face.)*

CHORUS: Oh cold, cold, rigid dreadful Death, set up thine altar here: for this is thy dominion.

SCROOGE: No voice spoke and yet Scrooge heard these words.

CHORUS: He lies in the dark, empty house, with not a man, a woman, or a child, to say that he was kind to me, in this or that, and for the memory of one kind word I will be kind to him.

SCROOGE: Spirit! This is a fearful place. In leaving it, I shall not leave its lesson, trust me. Let us go!

(Still the Ghost points with unmoved finger to the head.)

SCROOGE: I understand you, and I would do it, if I could. But I have not the power, Spirit. I have not the power. *(CRATCHIT HOUSE SCRIM enters on wire.*

The Spirit spreads its dark robe like a wing; and withdrawing it reveals a room by daylight in Cratchit's house. The little children are still as statues; Peter is reading; the mother and her daughters are sewing.)

PETER: 'And He took a child, and set him in the midst of them.' *(He does not go on. The mother lays down her work and puts her hand up to her face.)*

MRS. CRATCHIT: The color hurts my eyes.

SCROOGE: The color? Ah, poor Tiny Tim!

MRS. CRATCHIT: They're better now again. Candle-light makes them weak; and I wouldn't show weak eyes to your father when he comes home, for the world. It must be near his time.

PETER: *(shutting his book)* Past it rather. But I think he's walked a little slower than he used, these few last evenings, mother.

(They are very quiet again.)

MRS. CRATCHIT: *(in a steady, cheerful voice, that only falters once)* I have known him walk with - I have known him walk with Tiny Tim upon his shoulder, very fast indeed.

PETER: And so have I. Often.

BELINDA: And so have I.

GIRL: So had all.

MRS. CRATCHIT: But he was very light to carry, *(intent on her work)* and his father loved him so, that it was no trouble - no trouble. And there is your father at the door! *(She hurries out to meet him. Bob enters in his comforter.)*

BELINDA: His tea was ready for him on the bob,

MARTHA: and they all tried who should help him to it most.

(The two young Cratchits get on his knees and each child lays a little cheek against his face.)

SCROOGE: As if they said, Don't mind it, Father. Don't be grieved!

CRATCHIT: Bob was very cheerful with them. *(looks at the work)* He praised the industry and speed of Mrs. Cratchit and the girls. They would be done before Sunday, he said.

MRS. CRATCHIT: Sunday! You went today then, Robert?

CRATCHIT: Yes, my dear. I wish you could have gone. It would have done you good to see how green a place it tis. But you'll see it often. I promised him that I would walk there on a Sunday. *(weeps)* My little child! My little child! *(Light on Tiny Tim, laid out behind scrim. Cratchit goes upstage behind the scrim, where Tiny Tim is laid out amidst Christmas decorations, sits in a chir, leans over and kisses the little face. He is reconciled. Returns.)* I am sure we shall none of us forget poor Tiny Tim - shall we - or this first parting that there was among us.

ALL: Never, Father!

CRATCHIT: And I know, my dears, that when we recollect how patient and mild he was; although he was a little, little child; we shall not quarrel easily among ourselves, and forget poor Tiny Tim in doing it.

ALL: No, never, Father.

CRATCHIT: I am very happy. I am very happy!

(Mrs. Cratchit kisses him, his daughters kiss him, the two young Cratchits kiss him, and he and Peter shake hands.)

SCROOGE: Spirit of Tiny Tim, thy childish essence was from God! Spectre, something informs me that our parting moment is at hand. I know it, but I know not how. Tell me what man that was whom we saw lying dead.

(The Spirit spreads its robe again like a wing: SLIDE No. 11, GRAVE-YARD appears; traveller opens and they are in a graveyard; Spirit stands among the graves pointing down at one.)

SCROOGE: Before I draw nearer to that stone to which you point, answer me one question. Are these the shadows of the things that Will be, or are they shadows of things that May be, only? Men's courses will foreshadow certain ends, to which, if persevered in, they must lead. But if the courses be departed from, the ends will change. Say it is thus with what you show me!

(The finger points downward to the gravestone. Scrooge creeps towards it and reads his own name.)

SCROOGE: *Ebenezer Scrooge. (falls to his knees)* Am *I* that man who lay upon the bed? *(The finger points to him and back to the grave.)* No, Spirit! Oh, no, no! I am not the man I was. Why show me this, if I am past all hope? Good Spirit, your nature intercedes for me and pities me. Assure me that I may yet change these shadows you have shown me, by an altered life! *(The kind hand trembles.)* I will honor Christmas in my heart, and try to keep it all the year. I will live in the Past, Present, and the Future. I will not shut out the lessons that they teach. Oh, tell me I may sponge away the writing on this stone! *(In his agony he grasps the spectral hand, which tries to free itself and does. Scrooge holds up his hands in a last prayer, and sees the Phantom change.)* It shrunk, collapsed, and dwindled down into a bedpost. *(GRAVE-YARD SLIDE out as scene ends.)*

STAVE FIVE: The End of It

(Players bring Stave V sign onstage. SLIDE No. 12: CHRISTMAS MORN.)

SCROOGE: Yes! And the bedpost was his own, the room was his own. Best and happiest of all, the Time before him was his own, to make amends in! Oh Jacob Marley! Heaven, and the Christmas Time be praised for this. I say it on my knees, old Jacob, on my knees! *(trying to dress, laughing and crying at once)* I don't know what to do! I am as merry as a schoolboy. I am as giddy as a drunken man. A merry Christmas to everybody! A happy New Year to all the world! I don't know how long I've been among the Spirits. I don't know anything. I'm quite a baby. Never mind. I don't care. *(A lusty peal of bells is heard; goes to window and calls down to a boy.)* What's today?

BOY: Eh?

SCROOGE: What's today, my fine fellow?

BOY: Today! Why, CHRISTMAS DAY.

SCROOGE: It's Christmas Day. I haven't missed it. The Spirits have done it all in one night. Hallo, my fine fellow.

BOY: Hallo!

SCROOGE: Do you know the poulterer's, in the next street but one, at the corner?

BOY: I should hope I did.

SCROOGE: An intelligent boy! Do you know whether they've sold the prize turkey that was hanging up there? The big one.

BOY: What, the one as big as me?

SCROOGE: What a delightful boy. It's a pleasure to talk to him. Yes, my buck!

BOY: It's hanging there now.

SCROOGE: Is it? Go and buy it.

BOY: Walker-ER!

SCROOGE: No, no. I am in earnest. Go and buy it and tell 'em to bring it here that I may give them directions where to take it. Come back with the man and I'll give you a shilling. *(the boy is off like a shot)* I'll send it to Bob Cratchit's! *(rubbing his hands and laughing)* He shan't know who sends it. It's twice the size of Tiny Tim. *(writes address down and goes to door)* I shall love this knocker as long as I live. *(pats it)* What an honest expression on its face. Here's the turkey. Hallo! Whoop! *(to man)* Merry Christmas! How are you!

MAN: *(under the weight)* It *was* a turkey! He never could have stood on his legs, that bird.

BOY: He would have snapped 'em short off in a minute,

MAN: like sticks of sealing wax.

SCROOGE: Why, it's impossible to carry that to Cratchit's, you must have a cab. *(reaches into pocket to pay for everything)* Then he went to church, and walked about the streets, and patted children on the head, and questioned beggars, and found that everything could yield him pleasure. *(walks with hands behind his back, a delighted smile on his face. Passerby respond to him.)*

PASSERS: Good morning, sir! A merry Christmas to you!

SCROOGE: Scrooge said often afterwards, that of all the blithe sounds he had ever heard, those were the blithest in his ears. In the afternoon he turned his steps towards his nephew's house. He passed the door a dozen times before he had the courage to knock. *(to maid)* Is your master at home, my dear? Nice girl! Very.

MAID: Yes, sir.

SCROOGE: Where is he my love?

MAID: He's in the dining room, sir, along with the mistress. I'll show you upstairs, if you please.

SCROOGE: Thank'ee. He knows me, *(in the entrance)* I'll go in here, my dear. *(enters)* Fred! *(the wife is startled)*

FRED: Why bless my soul! Who's that?

SCROOGE: It's I. Your uncle Scrooge. I have come to dinner. Will you let me in, Fred?

FRED: Let him in! It is a mercy he didn't shake his arm off!

SCROOGE: He was at home in five minutes. Nothing could be heartier.

WIFE: His niece looked just the same.

TOPPER: So did Topper when *he* came.

PLUMP GIRL: So did the plump sister, when *she* came.

OTHERS: So did everyone when *they* came.

FRED: Wonderful party,

WIFE: wonderful games,

OTHERS: wonderful unanimity,

TOPPER & PLUMP GIRL: won-der-ful happiness! *(exeunt omnes)*

SCROOGE: But he was early at the office next morning. If he could only be there first, and catch Bob Cratchit coming late! The clock struck nine. No Bob. A quarter past. No Bob. He was a full eighteen minutes and a half behind his time. *(Scrooge has his door open.)*

CRATCHIT: His hat was off, before he opened the door; his comforter too. He was on his stool in a jiffy; driving away with his pen as of he were trying to overtake nine o'clock.

SCROOGE: Hallo! What do you mean by coming here at this time of day?

CRATCHIT: I am very sorry, sir, I *am* behind my time.

SCROOGE: You are? Yes, I think you are. Step this way, if you please.

CRATCHIT: It's only once a year, sir. It shall not be repeated. I was making rather merry yesterday, sir.

SCROOGE: Now, I'll tell you what, my friend. I am not going to stand this sort of thing any longer. And therefore, *(leaps from his stool and digs Cratchit in the waistcoat so he staggers back to the Tank)* and therefore I am about to raise your salary!

CRATCHIT. *(Thinks of getting the ruler and knocking Scrooge down with it, and sending for the strait jacket.)*

SCROOGE: A merry Christmas, Bob! *(clapping him on the back)* A merrier Christmas, Bob, my good fellow, than I have given you, for many a year! I'll raise your salary, and endeavor to assist your struggling family, and we will discuss your affairs this very afternoon, over a Christmas bowl of smoking bishop. Bob! Make up the fires, and buy another coal-scuttle before you dot another i, Bob Cratchit!

(Chorus sings 'Joy to the World,' one verse. All of Cratchit's family enters and sings.)

CRATCHIT: Scrooge was better than his word. He did it all and infinitely more;

MARTHA: and to Tiny Tim,

GIRL: who did NOT die,

MARTHA: he was a second father.

MRS. CRATCHIT: He became as good a friend, and as good a man, as the good old city knew,

PETER: or any other good old city, town, or borough,

BOY: in the good old world.

SCROOGE: Some people laughed to see the alteration in him, but he let them laugh, and little heeded them; for he was wise enough to know that nothing ever happened on this globe, for good, at which some people did not have their fill of laughter. His own heart laughed: and that was quite enough for him.

MRS. CRATCHIT: and it was always said of him, that he knew how to keep Christmas well,

CRATCHIT: if any man alive possessed the knowledge.

BELINDA: May that be truly said of us, and all of us!

PETER: And so, as Tiny Tim observed,

TINY TIM: God bless us, Every One!

CURTAIN

RAINER MARIA RILKE'S

STORIES OF GOD

Translated by M. D. Herter Norton

Adapted for the stage

by

Paul Sills

STORIES OF GOD
Copyright © Paul Sills, 2000

INTRODUCTION TO STORIES OF GOD

Twenty years after *Stories of God* was published, Rilke wrote: "...these youthful fantasies were almost entirely improvised out of an instinct which, if I were to specify it more particularly, I might describe as busied with transferring God from the sphere of rumor into the realm of direct and daily experiencing; the recommending by every means a naive and lively taking-in-use of God with which I seemed to have been charged since childhood."

The thirteen tales first appeared under the title *Of God and Other Matters/Told to Grownups for Children.* Rilke wanted children to know that a "taking-in-use of God" was possible for them. A relationship with God can be "direct, naive, 'lively'", not the kind adults have which usually takes place in "the sphere of rumor."

M.D. Herter Norton in her translator's note to *Stories of God* [1] comments that the thirteen stories were written in November, 1899, in a manner characteristic of his way of working, in the course of seven consecutive nights. Rilke refers to this in the foreword to his *Sonnets to Orpheus*, February, 1922, stating "...the whole first part (26 sonnets) was written down in a single breathless act of obedience, between the 2nd and 5th of February, without one word being doubtful or having to be changed. And this at a time when I had prepared myself for another big work and was already busy with that too." [2]

I adapted eight of the thirteen *Stories of God* in this story theater version. Several are Russian folk tales in origin, *bylini*, legendary stories. As Yeats wrote: "Folk-art is indeed the oldest of the aristocracies of thought...it is the soil where all great art is rooted." [3]

It is worth reminding ourselves that so many of the great poets were storytellers. Shakespeare had a theater for stories, but Yeats, Rilke, Brecht, Dante, Chaucer, Rumi, Ovid and Homer each could have, I like to think, his own story theater. It is "a mode of drama" as Yeats wrote about his own "unpopular" poetry theater, "'that Shelley and Keats could have used without ceasing to be themselves." [4]

[1.] Published by W.W. Norton & Company, Inc., 500 Fifth Ave., New York, N.Y. 10110

[2.] *Sonnet to Orpheus*, Foreword, W.W. Norton, Inc.

[3.] *Mythologies*, p. 139, The Macmillan Company, New York 10022

4. *Explorations*, p. 255, ibid.

Story theater can be regarded as choral work, all players being members of the chorus who step out to play roles and fall back into the choral group again. The Rilke stories are a clear example of this; the lines of prose are divided among the players for each to speak individually. Note the angels in *The Hands of God*, the beggars in *The Proud Young Lady* and the Ukrainians on the steppe in *The Song of Justice*. What is asked of the player is not character voices and mannerisms, but a focus on telling the story. When the players have lost this focus, acting takes over, and a story theater show begins to slip.

The first production of Rilke's *Stories of God* was at New Actors Workshop [5] in New York with the graduating class of 1994. [6]

---

5. New Actors Workshop, 259 W. 30th St, New York , NY 10001, a two-year gradu-ate-level program begun in 1988 with fellow teacher/directors Mike Nichols and George Morrison.

6. The cast included Jordan D. S. Ancel, Charlie Banks, Stephanie Bell, Susan Bob, Corrina B. Colldeweih, Christopher Cushman, Margaret Devine, Antoinette Feer, Stephanie Gillman, Trevor Hardwick, Leeanne Lisk, Christian Miller, Matthew Skollar Diez, Sharone Soker, David Stein, Kristin Tanzer and Alyssa Weiss. Movement, Beatrice Lees; music composed and performed by Greg Reeves; stage design, C.B. Sills.

Stories Of God

ACT I

I *The Hands of God*

God

Angels

St. Nicholas

Left Hand of God

Right Hand of God

St. Paul

Archangel

II *How Treason Came to Russia*

Poet

Lame Person

Tsar Ivan

Old Peasant

Princes (Three)

Wise Men

Counselors

Messenger

III *How the Thimble Came to be God*

Poet

Clouds (Three)

Children (Seven)

Persons (Two)

A Woman

IV *The Song of Jusice*

Poet

Lame Person

Chorus of 5 or 6 (people of the steppe)

Peter Akimovitch

Akulina

Daughter

Alyosha

Ostap

Woman

INTERMISSION BETWEEN ACTS

ACT II

V *The Beggar and The Proud Young Lady*

Poet

Schoolmaster

Palla

Tomaso

Young Man

Strozzi

Beatrice

Waiting Woman

Children (two or three)

Beggars (five speakers)

VI *How Old Timofei Died Singing*

Poet

Lame Person (Uta or Ewald)

Young Persons (three)

Timofei

Yegor

Ossip

Neighbors (three)

VII *A Scene From the Ghetto of Venice*

Poet

Herr Baum

Children (four)

Marcantonio

Esther

Melchizedek

Townspeople (six speakers)

VIII *A Story Told to the Dark*

Poet

Georg

Sophie (Georg's sister)

Second Sister

Councilor (Sophie's husband)

Klara

I THE HANDS OF GOD

CHORUS: These are the stories the poet Rainier Maria Rilke called the Stories of God.

CHORUS: Rilke wanted these stories told to children but he said he couldn't do it. He got embarrassed when he had to talk to children.

CHORUS: That wasn't so bad, but the children might think he was embarrassed because he felt himself telling lies.

CHORUS: And the truth of his stories was very important to him.

CHORUS: "You repeat them to the children," he said, "you will surely do it better."

CHORUS: We start with the first story in his book, *The Hands of God.*

CHORUS: The wind was already moving among the mountains, which were so like the clouds it had already known,

CHORUS: but it still shunned the trees with a certain mistrust.

GOD: *(Who could also be played by a male.)* And that was quite right with God. Things she had fashioned so to speak in her sleep, and only when she came to the animals did the work begin to interest her. *(The Chorus roar or cluck and take on physicality of animals.)* She bent over it and only seldom raised her broad brows to cast a glance down at the earth. Then she began to create man.

CHORUS: Suddenly there was a rush of wings about her. *(Chorus become angels.)*

ANGEL ONE: An angel hurried by, singing: 'Thou who seest all...'

ALL: *(singing)* Thou who seest all...

GOD: God started. In creating man she had forgotten to watch the earth. She thus caused that angel to speak falsely. She quickly peered down.

ANGEL: Look. A little bird is fluttering as though it were frightened,

GOD: and God was in no position to help it home,

ANGEL: for she had not seen out of *which* forest the poor creature had come.

GOD: *(vexed)* The birds are to sit still where I put them: But then she remembered at the request of the angels she had lent them wings so that on earth too there would be something like angels,

ANGEL: and this circumstance annoyed her even more. *(God stamps about.)*
Now in such a state of mind nothing is so salutary as work.

GOD: And busied with the construction of man, God quickly grew happy again.

ANGEL: She had the eyes of the angels before her as mirrors,

ANGEL: measured her own features in them, and was slowly and carefully modeling, on a ball in her lap,

ANGEL: the first face. She had succeeded with the forehead. Much more difficult for her was making the two nostrils symmetrical.

ANGEL: She bent lower and lower over the work, till a wind passed over her again.

ANGEL ONE: The same angel was circling around her;

ANGEL: no hymn was to be heard this time,

ANGEL: for with his lie the angel's voice had been extinguished,

GOD: but God could see by his mouth that he was still singing:

ANGEL ONE: *(mutely)* Thou who seest all…

ST. NICHOLAS: At that moment Saint Nicholas, who stands especially high in God's esteem came up to her: Your lions are sitting quite still, and very haughty beasts they are, I must say. But a little dog is running round on the very edge of the world, a terrier, see, he'll be falling off in a moment.

GOD: I see it,

ST. NICHOLAS: dancing about in the neighborhood of Scandinavia, where the earth is already so fearfully round.

GOD: She was exceedingly angry. If you don't like my lions, you should try and make some yourself. *(thunder)*

ST. NICHOLAS: Whereas Saint Nicholas walked out of heaven and slammed the door so hard,

ANGEL: that a star fell down,

ANGEL: right on the terrier's head. *(dog howls, yelps, off)*

ANGEL: Now the mischief was done,

GOD: and God had to admit to herself that it was all her own fault; and she determined not to take her eyes off the earth any more.

ANGEL: And so it was.

(The Hands are behind God or under her cloak; we see their arms and hands.)

RIGHT HAND: She left the work to her hands, which of course are wise themselves,

LEFT HAND: and although she was extremely curious to find out what man might look like,

GOD: she continued to gaze fixedly down at the earth, where now, as if out of spite, not a leaf would stir.

RIGHT HAND: To have at least some little pleasure after all this trouble,

LEFT HAND: she had bidden her hands to show her man first before they should deliver him over to life.

GOD: Repeatedly she asked, as children ask when they play hide-and-seek, Ready?

LEFT HAND: Not yet!

GOD: It seemed very long to her. Then *(whoosh)* suddenly she saw something falling through space. Filled with evil foreboding, she called to her hands.

RIGHT HAND: They appeared,

LEFT HAND: all blotched with clay,

RIGHT HAND: hot and trembling.

GOD: *(thundering)* Where is man?

RIGHT HAND: The right hand flew at the left: You dropped him!

LEFT HAND: Excuse me, you insisted on doing everything by yourself, you wouldn't even let me have anything to say.

RIGHT HAND: *(draws back as if to strike)* But you ought to have held him!

LEFT HAND: He was so impatient, man.

RIGHT HAND: He was in such a hurry to live. It is not our fault.

LEFT HAND: Really, we are both innocent.

GOD: *(pushing them away)* I've finished with you from now on; go and do as you like!

RIGHT HAND: And that is what her hands have been trying to do ever since.

LEFT HAND: But whatever they start they can only begin.

RIGHT HAND: Without God there is no perfection.

LEFT HAND: And so at last they tired of it.

RIGHT HAND: Now they are on their knees all day long doing penance.

(PAUSE.)

GOD: Dense clouds had lain between her and the earth for many days, so that she hardly knew any more whether she had not merely dreamed everything - the world and men and time - she called her right hand

RIGHT HAND: which had so long been banished from her sight. It came willingly, for it believed that God wanted at last to forgive it.

GOD: You are to go down to earth. You are to take on the form you will see there among men, and to stand, naked, upon a mountain, so that I can observe you closely. As soon as you arrive below, go to a young woman and say to her, but very gently: I want to live. At first there will be a little darkness about you and then a great darkness, which is called childhood, and then you will be a man, and climb the mountain as I have commanded you. All this will of course last but a moment. Farewell.

RIGHT HAND: The right hand then took leave of the left, called it many gracious names - indeed it has even been declared that it suddenly bowed down before it and said: Hail Holy Ghost.

ST. PAUL: But here Saint Paul stepped up and *(chop!)* smote off God's right hand;

ARCHANGEL: The archangels caught it up and bore it away under their wide mantle.

GOD: But God held the wound

LEFT HAND: with her left hand

GOD: so that her blood should not stream over the stars

LEFT HAND: and fall down in sorrowful drops upon the earth.

ST. PAUL: A short time after, God,

GOD: watching attentively all that went on below,

ST. PAUL: saw that certain men in iron garments were busying themselves about one mountain more than all others.

GOD: And she expected to see her hand climb up there.

ARCHANGEL: But there came only a man in, as it seemed, a red cloak,

ST. PAUL: who was dragging upwards some black swaying thing.

LEFT HAND: At the same instant, God's left hand, lying over her open wound, began to grow restless,

GOD: and suddenly, before God could prevent it,

LEFT HAND: it left its place and rushed madly among the stars, crying: O poor right hand, and I cannot help you!

GOD: Therewith it tugged hard at God's left arm

LEFT HAND: trying to tear itself free.

ARCHANGEL: And the whole earth was red with God's blood,

ST. PAUL: and it was impossible to see what was happening beneath it.

GOD: At that time God had very nearly died. With a last effort she called her right hand back;

RIGHT HAND. (*enters*) it came pale and trembling and lay down in its place like a sick animal.

LEFT HAND: And even the left hand, which already knew a good deal, could not learn from it what had further happened on that hill.

ARCHANGEL: It must have been something terrible.

RIGHT HAND: For God's right hand has not yet recovered from it and suffers under its memories no less than under the ancient wrath of God,

GOD: who has still not yet forgiven her hands.

II HOW TREASON CAME TO RUSSIA

POET: I have a friend here in the neighborhood.

LAME PERSON: This is a dark-haired lame woman (*or man; Uta or Ewald*) who has her chair, summer and winter, close by the window.

POET: She can look very young;

LAME PERSON: in her listening face there is often something girlish.

POET: But there are also days on which she ages, when the minutes pass over her like years and suddenly she is an old woman, whose dim eyes have already let go of life.

LAME PERSON: Good morning, I have not seen you for a long time.

POET: Good morning, Uta, I was away.

LAME PERSON: Where have you been?

POET: To Russia.

LAME PERSON: Oh, so far! What kind of a country is it, Russia? Very large isn't it?

POET: Yes, it is large, and besides -

LAME PERSON: *(blushing)* Was that a stupid question?

POET: No, Uta, on the contrary. Your asking, what kind of country is it? makes various things clear to me. For instance, how Russia is bounded.

LAME PERSON: On the East?

POET: *(reflecting)* No.

LAME PERSON: On the North?

POET: You see *(an inspiration)* - the reading of maps has spoiled people. There, everything is flat and level, and when they have noted the four points of the compass, they think that's all. But a country is no map. It has mountains and precipices. It must touch against something both above and below.

LAME PERSON: Hm - you are right. On what could Russia border in those two directions? *(Suddenly aware of something.)*

POET: You've got it!

LAME PERSON: Perhaps on God?

POET: Yes, on God.

LAME PERSON: So *(nodding, then doubtful)* But is God a country?

POET: I don't think so, but in primitive languages many things have the same name. There is probably a kingdom called God, and he who reigns over it is also called God. Simple peoples cannot always distinguish their country from their king; both are great and good, terrible and great.

LAME PERSON: *(slowly)* I understand. And does one notice this proximity in Russia?

POET: One notices it all the time.

LAME PERSON: Oh, so you don't say 'Your Majesty'?

POET: No, you call them both 'Little Father'

LAME PERSON: And you kneel to them both as well?

POET: You throw yourself down before both of them, touch the earth with your forehead, and weep and say: I am a sinner, forgive me,

Little Father. We, seeing that, call it slavery and most unworthy. I think differently about it. What does kneeling signify? It is meant to declare: I am full of reverence. That is why it is good, where there is still room and time to do so, to write the gesture out in full, the whole beautiful and weighty word: reverence.

LAME PERSON: Yes, if I could, I too would kneel down -

POET: But in Russia, many other things too come from God. One feels that everything new is introduced by him, every garment, every dish, every virtue and even every sin must first have his sanction before it comes into use. *(reassuring the other)* It's only a fairy-tale I refer to, a so-called *bylina*, something that has been, as we would say. I will briefly tell you the substance of it. The title is: How Treason Came to Russia.

TSAR IVAN: *(Enters.)* The terrible Tsar Ivan wanted to lay tribute upon the neighboring princes and threatened them with a great war if they would not send gold to Moscow, the white city.

PRINCE ONE: The princes, *(riding in on horseback)*

PRINCE TWO: after due deliberation, spoke as one person:

PRINCE THREE: We give you three riddles to solve. *(handing over a scroll)*

PRINCE ONE: Come on the day we appoint, to the East,

PRINCE TWO: to the white stone, where we shall be gathered,

PRINCE THREE: and tell us three answers. If they are correct, we will at once give you

PRINCE ONE: the twelve barrels of gold that you demand! *(Exeunt.)*

TSAR IVAN: At first Tsar Ivan Vassilievitch reflected, but the many bells of his white city of Moscow disturbed him.

WISE MAN: So he called his wise men and counselors before him,

TSAR IVAN: and each one who could not answer the riddles

COUNSELOR: he caused to be led out to the great red square,

WISE MAN: where the church of Vassily the Naked was just being built,

COUNSELOR: and simply beheaded.

TSAR IVAN: Thus occupied, time passed so quickly for him that he suddenly found himself on the way to the East, to the white stone by which the princes waited. To none of the three questions had he any answer, but the ride was long and there was still the possibility of meeting a wise man;

WISE MAN: *(A troop of Wise Men enter and exit hurriedly.)* for at that time many wise men were in flight,

WISE MAN: as all kings had the habit of ordering their heads cut off if they did not seem to them wise enough.

TSAR IVAN: One morning the Tsar saw an old bearded peasant who was building a church.

OLD PEASANT: *(climbing on and off a box)* He had already got as far as the frame-work of the roof and was laying on the small shingles.

TSAR IVAN: It seemed very odd that the old peasant should climb down from the church over and over again in order to fetch one by one the narrow shingles which were piled below,

OLD PEASANT: instead of taking a lot at a time in his long caftan.

TSAR IVAN: In this way he had to climb up and down continually,

OLD PEASANT: and there seemed no prospect of his ever getting all those hundreds of shingles into place.

TSAR IVAN: Idiot, you ought to load yourself up well with your wood and then crawl up on the roof; that would be much simpler.

OLD PEASANT: *(shielding his eyes with his hand)* That you must leave to me, Tsar Ivan Vassilievitch; every man knows his own craft best; Nevertheless, as you happen to be riding by I will tell you the answer to the three riddles, which you will have to know when you get to the white stone in the East. *(whispering in his ear)* And he urgently impressed the three answers in turn upon the Tsar's mind.

TSAR IVAN: The Tsar could hardly manage to thank him for astonishment. What shall I give you in reward?

OLD PEASANT: Nothing. *(fetching a shingle and starting up)*

TSAR IVAN: Stop, this will never do. You must wish for something.

OLD PEASANT: Well, Little Father, since you so command, give me one of the twelve barrels of gold you will get from the princes of the East.

TSAR IVAN: Good, I will give you a barrel of gold. *(mounts and rides off)*

OLD PEASANT: I'll take your word for it.

TSAR IVAN: Later, when the Tsar had returned from the East with the twelve barrels of gold, he shut himself up in the Kremlin and emptied one barrel after the other on the shining tiles of the hall, so that a mountain of gold cast a great black shadow on the floor. In his forgetfulness the Tsar had emptied the twelfth cask too. He wanted to fill it up again, but it grieved him to have to take away so much gold from the glorious pile. In the night he went down into the courtyard, scooped fine sand into the barrel until it was three quarters full, crept softly back into his palace, laid gold over the sand, and next morning

MESSENGER: *(messenger enters, mounts and rides)* sent the cask by messenger to that part of the broad land of Russia where the old peasant was building his church.

OLD PEASANT: *(still laying shingles on roof)* You need come no nearer, my friend. Go back, with your barrel which is three-quarters full of sand. I do not need it. Tell your master that up to now there has been no treason in Russia. And it is his own fault, should he notice that he cannot rely on any man, for he has now shown the way of betrayal, and from century to century his example will find throughout Russia many imitators. I do not need the gold, I can live without gold; I did not expect gold from him, but truth and righteousness. But he has deceived me. Say that to your master, the terrible Tsar Ivan Vassilievtch, who sits in his white city of Moscow with his evil conscience, in a golden dress.

MESSENGER: After riding a while, the messenger looked back once more: the peasant and his church had vanished. And the piled shingles no longer lay there; it was all empty, flat land. At that the man tore back in terror to Moscow, *(Tsar enters)* stood breathless before the Tsar and told him somewhat incoherently what had happened, and how the supposed peasant was no other than God himself. *(Exeunt.)*

POET: It was no other than God himself.

LAME PERSON: Could he have been right?

POET: Perhaps - though, you know, the people are - superstitious. But I must go now, Uta.

LAME PERSON: Too bad. Won't you tell me another story soon?

POET: Gladly, but under one condition.

LAME PERSON: Namely?

POET: You must, when you have a chance, repeat them all to the children in the neighborhood. I know that nothing is closer to their minds and hearts than God.

LAME PERSON: Oh, the children come to me so seldom now.

POET: *(consoling)* They'll come all right. Evidently you have not felt like telling them anything of late, and perhaps you had nothing to tell, or too much. But if someone knows a real story, do you believe that can remain a secret? Never fear, it gets told around, especially among the children! Goodbye.

LAME PERSON: And the children heard the story on the self-same day.

III HOW THE THIMBLE CAME TO BE GOD

POET: When I stepped away from the window, the evening clouds were still there. They seemed to be waiting. Should I tell them a story too? I proposed it. But they didn't even hear me. To make myself understood and to diminish the distance between us, I called out: I am an evening cloud too. They stopped still, evidently taking a good look at me. Then they stretched towards me their fine, transparent, rosy wings. That is how evening clouds greet each other. They had recognized me.

YOUNG CLOUD: (entering in slow motion) We are lying over the earth, more exactly, over Europe. And you?

POET: There's a country here -

CLOUD: What does it look like?

POET: Well, twilight, with things -

YOUNG CLOUD: (laughing) Europe's like that too.

POET: Possibly, but I have always heard that the things of Europe are dead.

CLOUD: (scornfully) Yes, of course! What nonsense would that be - living things! (all clouds laugh)

POET: All the same, mine are alive. So that's the difference. They can become various things, and one that comes into the world as a pencil or a stove, need not yet despair on that account of advancing in life. A pencil may someday turn into a staff, or, if all goes well, into a mast: and a stove at least into a city gate.

YOUNG CLOUD: You seem to me to be a very simpleminded evening cloud.

POET: I see it will not be easy for us to come to an understanding. Allow me, and I will simply tell you what I saw below me recently; that will probably be the best way.

WISE OLD CLOUD: Please do.

POET: People are in a room. I am fairly high up, you must know, and so it is that to me they look like children; *(children enter)* two, five, six, seven children. It would take too long to ask them their names. Besides, they seem to be having an earnest discussion, so there's a good chance that a name or two will be given away in the course of it. They must have been at it for some time already, for the eldest is speaking in a tone of finality: *(Clouds and Poet exeunt.)*

ELDEST CHILD: No, it certainly cannot remain like this. I have heard that parents used always to tell their children stories in the evening - or at least on evenings when they had been good - till they went to sleep. Does anything like that happen now? *(short pause)* It doesn't happen, anywhere.

CHILD TWO: I have an aunt, and she sometimes tells me stories.

CHILD THREE: Oh, go on, aunts don't count, *they* tell lies. Besides, we are above all concerned with our parents, for it is their duty, in a way, to instruct us in these matters; others do it more out of kindness, we can't expect it of them.

CHILD FOUR: But just listen now: what do our parents do? They go around with cross-annoyed faces, nothing suits them, they shout and scold, and yet they are really so indifferent that if the world came to an end they would hardly notice it.

CHILD FIVE: I think it's like this, children: that our parents neglect us is sad, certainly. But we would put up with that if it were not a sign that grown-ups generally are growing stupider, deteriorating, if one may say so.

CHILD SIX: They take off their hats to each other, but if a bald spot comes to light, they laugh.

ELDEST CHILD: Anyhow, they're always laughing. If we hadn't sense enough to cry now and then, even these matters would get entirely out of balance. And they're so arrogant. But apart from everything superfluous they've got, the grown-ups have something that most certainly cannot be indifferent to us - I mean, God.

CHILD SEVEN: I've not seen him with any one of them yet - but that's just what looks suspicious, they may have lost him somewhere. But he is something absolutely necessary.

CHILD FIVE: All sorts of things can't happen without him; the sun can't rise, babies can't come, and even bread would stop; even if it does come out of the baker's, God sits and turns the big mills.

ELDEST CHILD: *(rising)* It's easy to find lots of reasons why God is something we cannot do without. But this much is certain: the grown-ups aren't bothering about him, so we children must do it. Listen to a plan I've thought out. There are just seven of us children. Each of us must carry God about for one day, then he will be with us the whole week and we shall always know where he is at the moment.

CHILD FOUR: How was that to be done?

CHILD FIVE: Could one take God into one's hand or put him in one's pocket? - DUH!

CHILD SIX: Once I was all alone in the room. A little lamp burned beside me and I sat up in bed and said my evening prayer - very loud. Something moved inside my folded hands. *(shows hands)* It was soft and warm like a little bird. I couldn't open my hands, because the prayer wasn't over. But I wanted very badly to know and I prayed awfully fast. When I got to the Amen, I went like this *(stretching out hands and spreading out fingers)* but there was nothing there.

(All picture this to themselves)

ELDEST CHILD: How stupid! Anything can be God. One has only to tell it. An animal won't do. It runs away. But a thing, you see, stays where it is; you come into the room, by day, by night: it is always there, it can very well be God.

(Gradually others become convinced)

ELDEST CHILD: But we need a small object, something you can carry everywhere, otherwise it's no good. Empty all your pockets.

ALL CHILDREN: scraps of paper / penknife / an eraser / feathers / a bit of string / pebbles / screws / a whistle / wood chips / I don't know what this is but you can have it. *(children hold them in their hands)*

CHILD THREE: I have a thimble which my mother gave me.

CHILD SEVEN: It was bright,

CHILD TWO: as though made of silver.

ELDEST CHILD: For its beauty's sake, it will be God.

CHILD SEVEN: _____ put it in her pocket, for she had the first turn.

(All follow, as in follow the leader.)

CHILD TWO: The other children followed her about all day long and were proud of her.

CHILD FIVE: Only it was hard to agree on who should have it next day,

ELDEST CHILD: So _____ in her foresight drew up the program for the whole week, so that no quarrel should break out.

CHILD THREE: One could see at first glance who had God.

CHILD SIX: For that particular child walked more stiffly and solemnly

CHILD FOUR: and wore a Sunday face.

ELDEST CHILD: For the first three days, the children spoke of nothing else.

CHILD TWO: At every instant one of them was asking to see God,

CHILD THREE: and though the thimble hadn't changed a wit under the influence of its great dignity,

CHILD FOUR: the thimblyness of it now seemed but a modest dress about its real form.

CHILD FIVE: Everything proceeded as arranged. On Wednesday _____ had it,

CHILD FOUR: on Thursday _____.

ELDEST CHILD: Then came Saturday. The children were playing tag (*not it!*) and romping in breathless confusion. Wait! Who has God now?

CHILD THREE: They all stood still.

CHILD TWO: Each looked at the other.

ELDEST CHILD: _____ counted off whose turn it was;

CHILD SIX: the fact came out:

CHILD TWO: it was little Marie's.

ELDEST CHILD: Marie, where's God?

MARIE: What was she to do? (*scratches around in her pockets*) Then only did she remember that he had been given to her.

CHILD: She had probably lost him here while playing.

MARIE: And when all the other children went home, (*all others exit*) little Marie stayed behind on the green, searching. The grass was fairly high.

PERSON: (*entering*) Twice people passed and asked whether she had lost anything.

MARIE: A thimble. (*goes on looking*)

PERSON: The people helped her for a time, but soon tired of stooping.

PERSON: You had better go home now, you can always buy a new one.

MARIE: But still little Marie went on searching. The meadow grew more and more mysterious in the dusk, and the grass began to get wet.

WOMAN: Then another woman came along. What are you looking for?

MARIE: *(not far from tears, but brave and defiant)* I am looking for God.

WOMAN: *(smiles, takes her by the hand)*

MARIE: She let herself be led as though all were well now.

WOMAN: And just look, what a beautiful thimble I found today! *(Gives it to Marie. Exeunt.)*

POET: The evening clouds had been impatient to leave. One of them turned to me:

CLOUD: Pardon me, but may I ask what the country is called - over which you...?

POET: But the other clouds ran laughing into the sky and dragged that one along with them.

IV THE SONG OF JUSTICE

POET: The next time I passed Uta's window, she waved to me and smiled.

LAME PERSON: Do you know some more Russian stories?

POET: Yes.

LAME PERSON: I want so much to hear more about those singular men. I don't know how it happens, I always imagine if one of them were to come in here - but of course that would hardly be possible.

POET: Why should it not be possible, Uta? Many things might come to you that are not vouchsafed to people who can use their legs, because they pass so much by and run away from so many things. God has destined you to be a calm point amidst all the hurry. Don't you feel how everything moves around you? But you, my friend, simply sit at your window and wait; and to those who wait something always happens. You have a quite particular destiny.

LAME PERSON: Yes, I cannot even go to meet Death. Many people find him as they go their ways. He fights shy of entering their houses, and calls them away to foreign lands, to war, up onto a high tower, onto a swaying bridge, into some bewilderment or into madness. Most of them at least fetch him from somewhere outside and then carry him home on their shoulders all unwittingly. For Death is lazy: if people were not always disturbing him, who knows, he might even fall asleep. *(ponders)* But to me he will have to come when he wants me. Here into my sunny little room, where the flowers keep fresh so long *(hands Poet a flower)*, over this old carpet, past this cupboard, between the table and the foot of the bed. And he will have to do all this in the usual way, like any visitor, without noise, without knocking anything over, without doing anything out of the ordinary. It will all be acted out on this narrow stage, and that is why this episode will not differ so very much from all the other events that have taken place here and are yet to come. Among people one can't even remember the Lord's Prayer. One must go apart into some inaccessible stillness; and perhaps the dead are such as have withdrawn in order to reflect upon life. *(silence)* Is that a story too?

POET: No, it is a feeling, an emotion.

LAME PERSON: But couldn't one convey it to the children too - that emotion?

POET: Perhaps.

LAME PERSON: And how?

POET: By another story...It was at the time they were fighting for freedom in southern Russia.

LAME PERSON: Forgive me, how am I to understand that? Did the people want to get rid of the Tsar? That wouldn't correspond with my idea of Russia, and would be inconsistent with what you have told me before. If that is the case, I should prefer not to hear your story. For I love the picture I have made for myself of things there, and want to keep it unspoiled.

POET: The Polish Pans were masters in southern Russia and in those silent, solitary steppes that are known as Ukraine. They were hard masters. The city itself, Kiev, the holy, the place where Russia first gave account of herself with four hundred church domes, sank always more into itself and consumed itself in fires as if in sudden, lunatic thoughts, behind which the night only grows more and more immense.

(music and chorus)

CHORUS: The people of the steppe did not rightly know what was happening. But, seized with singular unrest, the old people would leave their huts at night and gaze silently into the high, eternally windless heavens,

CHORUS: and by day one could see figures appear on the ridges of the kurgans and stand waiting, silhouetted against the flat distance.

CHORUS: These kurgans are burial-mounds of bygone generations and spread across the entire plain like a frozen, sleeping succession of waves.

PETER AKIMOVITCH: And in this country, where graves are the mountains, men are the abysses.

CHORUS: Deep, dark, silent are these people and their words are but weak, swaying bridges over their real being.

CHORUS: Sometimes dark birds fly up from the kurgans. Sometimes wild songs drop down into these crepuscular people and vanish deep inside them, while the birds are lost in the sky.

CHORUS: In all directions, everything seems limitless.

ALYOSHA: Even the houses are no protection against this immeasurableness; their little windows are full of it.

PETER AKIMOVITCH: Only in the darkening corners of the rooms the old ikons stand, like milestones of God,

CHORUS: and the glint of a tiny light runs over their frames like a lost child through the starry night. *(exeunt chorus)*

PETER AKIMOVITCH: *(setting a box to sit on)* So it comes that Peter Akimovitch, properly a shoemaker by profession, also paints ikons. When he tires of the one labor, he changes, after he has crossed himself three times, to the other, and over his sewing and hammering, as well as his painting, the same piety holds sway.

AKULINA: *(setting table)* The greater part of his life he has spent all alone, never mingling in the excitement which came of his wife Akulina bearing him children and of these dying or getting married.

PETER AKIMOVITCH: Not till his seventieth year had Peter got in touch with those who had been dwelling in his house,

DAUGHTER: and whom he now for the first time looked upon as really present.

AKULINA: These were: Akulina, his wife, a quiet, humble person, who had spent herself almost wholly in her children;

DAUGHTER: an aging, bellicose daughter,

ALYOSHA: and Alyosha, a son, who was only seventeen.

PETER AKIMOVITCH: This son Peter wanted to train in painting; for he realized that he alone would not be able to cope much longer with all the orders. But he soon abandoned the lessons.

ALYOSHA: Alyosha had painted the most holy Virgin,

PETER AKIMOVITCH: but had so little achieved the austere and correct image he was copying,

DAUGHTER: that his handiwork looked like a portrait of Mariana, the daughter of Golokpytenko the Cossack -

PETER AKIMOVITCH: that is, like something thoroughly sinful - and old Peter hastened, after crossing himself many times, to paint over the offended panel *(does so)* with a Saint Dimitri,

DAUGHTER: whom for some unknown reason he set above all other saints.

ALYOSHA: Nor did Alyosha ever again try to begin a picture.

PETER AKIMOVITCH: When his father had not ordered him to gild a halo, he was usually out on the steppe,

DAUGHTER: no one knew where. Nobody kept him at home.

AKULINA: His mother wondered about him and was shy of speaking to him,

ALYOSHA: as though he were a stranger or an official.

DAUGHTER: His sister had always beaten him when he was a child, and now that Alyosha had grown up she began to despise him because *he* did not beat *her.*

ALYOSHA: Neither was there anybody in the village who bothered about the boy.

DAUGHTER: Mariana, the Cossack's daughter, had laughed at him when he told her he wanted to marry her,

ALYOSHA: and thereafter Alyosha had not asked the other girls if they would accept him as a bridegroom.

AKULINA: Once he had run away to the nearest monastery,

DAUGHTER: but the monks did not take him in -

ALYOSHA: and so only the plain remained to him, the broad billowing plain. A hunter had once given him an old gun, loaded with God knows what. Alyosha always dragged it about with him, but never fired it, first, because he wanted to save the bullet, and then, because he did not know what to shoot.

PETER AKIMOVITCH: One warm quiet evening at the beginning of summer

AKULINA: they all sat together at the rough-hewn table,

DAUGHTER: on which stood a dish of meal.

PETER AKIMOVITCH: Peter ate,

ALYOSHA: and the others watched him and waited for what he should leave.

PETER AKIMOVITCH: Suddenly the old man stopped with his spoon in mid-air.

AKULINA: They all listened.

DAUGHTER: Outside, along the walls of the hut, there was a sound as though some night-bird were gently brushing against the beams with its wings;

AKULINA: but the sun had scarcely set,

DAUGHTER: and anyway, nocturnal birds rarely ventured into the village.

ALYOSHA: And then again it seemed as though some other large animal were tapping its way round the house. *(Alyosha rises quietly)*

PETER AKIMOVITCH: At the same moment something pushed the whole evening aside -

ALL: Ostap!

DAUGHTER: And now they all recognized him.

ALYOSHA: It was one of the blind kobzars,

OSTAP: an old man who wandered through the village with a twelve string bandura and sang of the great fame of the Cossacks, of their braveness and loyalty, of their hetmans Kirdiaga, Kukubenko, Bulba,

AKULINA: and other heroes, so that everyone loved to listen.

OSTAP: In whose house might I be?

DAUGHTER: In ours, little father, in the house of Peter Akimovitch, the shoemaker.

PETER AKIMOVITCH: He was a lover of song, and glad of this unexpected visit.

OSTAP: Ah, Peter Akimovitch, the one who paints ikons. *(pause)*

PETER AKIMOVITCH: Then there was silence.

OSTAP: In the long six strings of the bandura a sound began. *(Music.)* The fine strong voice of the kobzar soon filled the house and called the people out of the neighboring huts too.

DAUGHTER: But not of heroes did the song tell this time.

ALYOSHA: The fame of Bulba

DAUGHTER: and Ostranitza

PETER AKIMOVITCH: and Nalivaiko

ALYOSHA: seemed already secure.

AKULINA: Nor of their deeds did the song tell that day.

PETER AKIMOVITCH: No one moved a leg or raised a hand.

DAUGHTER: Like Ostap's head, so were the other heads bowed,

AKULINA: growing heavy with the sorrowful song:

OSTAP: *(Speaks to music.)* There is no Justice more in the world.

Justice, who can find her? There is no Justice more in the world: for all Justice has become subject to the laws of Injustice.

Today Justice lies wretched in chains. And Wrong laughs at her, we have seen it, and sits with the Pans in their golden seats and sits in the golden hall with the Pans.

Justice lies on the threshold imploring! Wrong, which is evil, is the guest of the Pans, who beckon it laughing into their palace and they pour Wrong a cup full with mead.

Oh, Justice, little mother, little mother mine, with a wing that is like to the eagle's, there may yet come a man who wants to be just, to be just; then help him God, He alone can, and makes light the days of the just.

ALYOSHA: And only with effort were the heads lifted

AKULINA: and on all brows stood silence. *(others arrive in the doorway)*

OSTAP: Three times Ostap sang his Song of Justice.

DAUGHTER: And each time it was a different song.

PETER AKIMOVITCH: If the first time it was a lament, upon repetition it seemed a reproach,

OSTAP: and finally, when at the third time the kobzar with high-thrown head shouted it like a chain of curt commands,

ALYOSHA: a wild fury broke from the quivering words and took possession of the listeners

WOMAN: and carried them all away in a spreading yet anxious enthusiasm.

MAN: Where do the men meet?

OSTAP: The old man named a place nearby.

MAN: The men dispersed rapidly,

MAN: sharp calls were heard,

MAN: the stir of arms, and

WOMAN: women wept in the doorways. *(crowd leaves)*

PETER AKIMOVITCH: Peter offered the kobzar a glass of cider in the hope of learning more from him.

OSTAP: The old man sat and drank, but only gave brief replies to the shoemaker's many questions. Then he thanked his host and went.

ALYOSHA: Alyosha led the blind man over the threshold. And may everybody go to the war?

OSTAP: Everybody. *(exit)*

ALYOSHA: When all were asleep, Alyosha took his gun and went forth. Outside, he felt himself suddenly embraced and gently kissed on the hair. Mother?! A strange feeling came over him. *(hesitates; a door opens and closes, a dog howls: he slings the gun over his shoulder and strides away)*

PETER AKIMOVITCH: In the house they all acted as though they did not notice Alyosha's absence. *(rises, goes to icon)* He lit a candle before the Znamenskaya. *(Exeunt)*

OSTAP: *(crossing the stage)* Meanwhile, Ostap, the blind old man, was already on his way through the next village, beginning sadly and with gently lamenting voice the Song of Justice. *(Exit)*

LAME PERSON: Did you promise the children something definite?

POET: How so?

LAME PERSON: Well, they might complain that God did not come into the story.

POET: *(startled)* What, a story without God? But how is that possible?

LAME PERSON: You must not take it to heart. I imagine one can never tell whether God is in a story before one has finished it completely. For if only two words of the telling are still missing - indeed if nothing but the pause after the last word is still outstanding, he may yet come. It is the same as in the story about treason. That old man was God.

POET: *(tingling at the thought)* Oh, and I didn't know!

LIGHTS OUT

INTERMISSION

ACT II
V THE BEGGAR AND THE PROUD YOUNG LADY

POET: It happened that we -

SCHOOLMASTER: the schoolmaster

POET: and I - were witnesses to the following little incident. We have an old beggar who sometimes stands at the edge of the wood.

SCHOOLMASTER: Today too he was there again,

POET: poorer, more miserable than ever, almost indistinguishable, through a sort of sympathetic mimicry, from the boards of the rotted wooden fence against which he leaned.

SCHOOLMASTER: But then it happened that a very little girl came running up to give him a small coin. The way she did it was surprising.

POET: She made her very best curtsy, tendered her little gift to the old man hurriedly, as though no one should see, curtsied again and was gone. But those two curtsies were worthy of at least an emperor.

SCHOOLMASTER: This annoyed our schoolmaster quite particularly. He started towards the beggar,

POET: probably to drive him from his fence post; for as we know,

SCHOOLMASTER: he was director of the local charities and committed to the prevention of street-begging.

POET: I held him back.

SCHOOLMASTER: *(protesting)* But, we are helping these people, I may even go so far as to say we support them. And now if they beg on the streets, too, it's sheer - impertinence!

POET: Dear Mister Schoolmaster, I must tell you a story.

SCHOOLMASTER: *(venomously)* So urgently?

POET: Yes, right away. Before you forget what we chanced to observe just now. *(sees mistrust in the other)* Not about God, really not. God is not even mentioned in this story. It is something historical...With that I had won. Just say the word 'history' and every schoolmaster will prick up his ears; for history is something thoroughly respectable... *(Schoolmaster polishes his glasses)* He was polishing his glasses, a sign that his powers of vision had shifted to his ears. I began: It was in Florence. Lorenzo de Medici, young and not yet in power, had just composed his poem 'Trionfo di Baccho ed Arianna', and already it was echoing through all the gardens. Those were the days of living songs. Out of the darkness of the poet's soul they arose in men's voices and were wafted upon them, as on silver skiffs, fearless, into the unknown. The poet began a song, and all who sang it brought it to completion. The refrain: Quant e bella giovinezza

> che si fugge tuttavia.
> Chi vuol esser lieto, sia!
> Di doman non c'e certezza.

Literally,

> How beautiful is youth
> though it be ever fleeing.
> Who would be happy, let him be so today!
> For of tomorrow there is no certainty.

Is it to be wondered at that the men who sang such lines strove to pile up all festivity tower-like on this 'to-day', upon the only rock on which it is worth while to build? This spirit of impatience naturally found its clearest expression in the young men. *(They withdraw.)* *(Young men enter.)*

PALLA: In a loggia, a little apart from the rest stood Palla degli Albizzi

TOMASO: with his friend Tomaso, the painter.

PALLA: They were arguing with increasing excitement,

TOMASO: till Tomaso cried: That you will never do, I wager you never will!

YOUNG MAN: The others now took notice.

STROZZI: *(strolling up with friends)* What's the matter?

TOMASO: Palla says that at the festival he is going to kneel down before Beatrice Altichieri, that proud girl, and beg her to permit him to kiss the dusty hem of her robe. (All laugh)

STROZZI: Palla will think twice about that.   He well knows that the fairest women have a smile for him which at other times one never sees upon their faces.

YOUNG MAN: And Beatrice is still so young. Her lips are still too child-ishly firm to smile. That is why she seems so proud.

PALLA: No! She *is* proud, but that is not the fault of her youth. She is proud as marble is in the hands of Michelangelo, proud as a flower in a picture of the Madonna, proud as a ray of sunlight passing over diamonds.

TOMASO: And you, Palla, are not you proud also? To hear you, one would think you wanted to take your place among the beggars who wait about the hour of vespers in the courtyard of the Santissima Annunziata, till Beatrice Altichieri passes and, with averted face, gives each of them a soldo.

PALLA: I will do even that! *(pushing his friends aside and going)*

STROZZI: *(Tomaso is about to follow, Strozzi holds him back.)* Let him be. He must be left to himself now;   then he will come to his senses sooner.

YOUNG MAN: And the young men dispersed into the gardens. *(Exeunt)*

(Beggars enter.)

BEGGAR ONE: In the forecourt of Santissima Annunziata that evening, some twenty beggars, men and women, waited for vespers.

BEGGAR TWO: Beatrice, who knew them all by name and would some-times visit the children and the sick in their wretched homes at the Porta San Niccolo,

BEGGAR THREE: used to present each one of them, in passing, with a small silver piece.

BEGGAR TWO: Today she seemed to be a little late; the bells had already rung their call,

BEGGAR FOUR: and only threads of their sound still hung about the towers above the darkening air.

BEGGAR FIVE: An uneasiness spread among the mendicants, also because a new beggar,

PALLA: a stranger, had slunk into the shadow of the porch,

BEGGAR FIVE: and they were about to drive him off in their jealousy,

BEATRICE: *(entering)* when a young girl in a black, almost nunnish dress, appeared in the forecourt and, hampered in her progress by her pitying kindness, went from one to the other, *(they kneel before her)*

WAITING WOMAN: while one of her waiting women held open the purse from which she took her little gifts.

BEGGAR FOUR: The beggars fell on their knees, sobbed,

BEGGAR THREE: and sought to lay their shriveled fingers for one second on the train of their benefactress's simple gown,

BEGGAR ONE: or kissed its bottom hem with their wet, stammering lips.

BEATRICE: She had passed them all, and not one of the figures so well known to her was missing. But suddenly she became aware under the shadow of the porch, of another figure in rags, a stranger. She was startled. She became confused. She had known all her poor friends as a child, and to help them had become as natural to her, as, say, the dipping of one's fingers in the marble font of holy water that stands at the entrance of every church. It had never occurred to her that there might be beggars one did not know. How should one have the right to give these something too, since one had not earned the confidence of their poverty by somehow knowing of it? Would it not have been an unheard-of presumption to offer a stranger alms? And filled with the conflict of these dark emotions, the girl passed the new beggar by as though she had not noticed him and stepped quickly into the cool, high church. *(All transform into congregation entering, chanting)* But inside, as the service began, she could not remember a single prayer. A fear seized her that after vespers she might no longer find the poor man in the porch.

WAITING WOMAN: Signing to one among her waiting-women, she slipped out with her.

PALLA: The stranger still stood there, *(leaning against a pillar)* and seemed to listen to the singing that came from the church, strangely remote, as if from heavens.

WAITING WOMAN: His face was almost entirely hidden, as is sometimes the case with lepers.

BEATRICE: *(hesitating)* Beatrice was carrying the little purse herself and felt it contained only a few small coins. *(goes up to him)* I would not offend you, sir...I think if I recognize you aright, I am in your debt. Your father, I believe, made the fine balustrade in our house, of wrought-iron, you know, that adorns the staircase. Later - they found - in the room where he sometimes used to work - a purse- I think he must have lost it - surely - But the helpless lie upon her lips forced the girl to her knees before the stranger. *(presses purse into his hands)* Forgive me - For an instant Beatrice felt the beggar tremble. Then she fled back into the church

WAITING WOMAN: followed by her frightened waiting-woman. *(Exeunt)*

PALLA: Through the briefly opened door there burst a short jubilant peal of voices.

POET: *(entering with Schoolmaster)* That is the end of the story. Messer Palla degli Albizzi remained in his rags. He gave away all he had and went forth barefoot and destitute into the land.

SCHOOLMASTER: Oh, those times, those times! What's the good of it all? He was on his way to becoming a profligate and through this incident he turned into a vagabond, an eccentric. I am sure nobody remembers him today.

POET: Oh, but they do. His name is mentioned now and then in the great litanies of the Catholic Church, among those intercessors to whom they pray, for he became a saint. *(Enter, two children)*

CHILD: The children have heard this story too and they declare, to the annoyance of the schoolmaster

CHILD: that God does come into it. *(they chase him off repeating: God does come into it.)*

POET: I am rather surprised at that, myself, for I *had* promised the good schoolmaster to tell him a story without God in it. But, of course, the children must know!

LIGHTS OUT

VI How Old Timofei Died Singing

POET: What a pleasure it is to tell stories to a lame person! Healthy people are so changeable. And I was very glad when she called to me from her window:

BOTH: Good morning, good morning.

LAME PERSON: I must ask you something. Where did you get the Russian story you told me last time? Out of a book?

POET: *(sadly)* Yes, the historians have kept it buried there, since it died; that is not so very long ago. Only a hundred years since, it lived - quite carelessly, for sure - on many lips. But the words that people use now, those heavy words one cannot sing, were its enemies so that in the end it lived, most withdrawn and impoverished, on one pair of dry lips, as on a miserable widow's portion.

LAME PERSON: And it was very old when it died?

POET: Four to five hundred years; some of its relations attained an even greater age.

LAME PERSON: How, without ever coming to rest in a book?

POET: So far as I know, they were traveling from mouth to mouth all the time.

LAME PERSON: And did they never sleep?

POET: Oh yes, rising from the singer's lips, they might stay now and then in some heart, where it was warm and dark.

LAME PERSON: *(incredulous)* But were people so quiet that songs could sleep in their hearts?

POET: They must have been. It is said that they spoke less, and above all, they did not laugh loudly, as one hears them do today, despite our general high state of culture.

LAME PERSON: *(about to question)* I ask and ask - but perhaps you are about to tell me a story?

POET: A story? I don't know. I only wanted to say that these songs were the heritage of certain families. One had taken it over and one passed it on, like an old bible that is handed down from parent to child...Thus Yegor Timofeievitch, for example, against the will of his father, old Timofei, married a beautiful young wife *(The young couple cross the stage, turning as in a dance and exit.)* and had gone with her to Kiev, to the holy city, besides which the graves of the greatest martyrs of the Holy Orthodox Church are gathered. Father Timofei, who counted as the most adept singer within ten day's journey *(Exeunt Poet and Lame Person when Timofei says his first sentence.)*

TIMOFEI: *(enters)* cursed his son and told his neighbors he was often convinced that he had never had any such son at all. Nevertheless he grew dumb in rancor and sorrow. And he sent away all the young people who came crowding into his hut

YOUNG PERSON ONE: in order to become the inheritors of the many songs that were locked up in the old man

YOUNG PERSON TWO: as in a dust-covered violin.

YOUNG PERSON THREE: Father, our little father, give us just one song or another.

YOUNG PERSON TWO: See, we will carry it into the villages, and you shall hear it in every farmyard

YOUNG PERSON ONE: as soon as evening comes and the cattle in the stables have quieted down.

TIMOFEI: The old man, who sat continually on the stove, shook his head all the day long.

YOUNG PERSON THREE: He no longer heard well,

TIMOFEI: and as he never knew whether one of the young people had not just asked for a song again, he would sign with his white head: No, no, no, till he fell asleep and even then a while - in sleep. *(Young People exeunt)* He would gladly have done as the young people asked: he himself was sorry that his dumb, dead dust was to lie upon these songs, perhaps quite soon now. But what about his own Yegoruska? *(a sobbing behind every word)* Old Timofei had begun very early to teach his only son Yegor certain songs -

YEGOR: *(entering)* and as a boy of fifteen Yegor could already sing more, and more correctly, than all the grown-up youths in the village and the neighborhood.

TIMOFEI: Yegoruska, my little dove, I have already taught you to sing many songs, many bylini,

YEGOR: *(dancing in the Russian manner)* and also the legends of the Saints, one for every day almost.

TIMOFEI: But as you know, I am the most accomplished singer of the whole government, and my father knew, so to speak, all the songs of the whole of Russia,

YEGOR: and also Tartar stories as well.

TIMOFEI: You are still very young, and so I have not yet told you the most beautiful bylini, in which the words are like ikons and not at all to be compared with ordinary words, and you have not yet learned to sing those melodies that no man ever, were he Cossack or peasant, has been able to listen to without weeping.

YEGOR: This Timofei repeated to his son every Sunday and on all the many holidays of the Russian year - that is, quite often. Until Yegor, after a violent scene with the old man, disappeared,

Ustionka: simultaneously with the beautiful Ustionka, the daughter of a poor peasant. *(Exeunt)*

Timofei: In the third year after this event, Timofei fell ill, at the very time when one of those many pilgrimages to Kiev was about to start.

Ossip: *(enters)* His neighbor, Ossip, came to see the sick man. I am going with the pilgrims, Timofei Ivanitch, permit me to embrace you before I go. *(sobbing)* I have sometimes offended you, forgive me my little heart, it happened in drunkenness, and then one can't help it, as you know. Now I will pray for you and light a candle for you. Farewell, Timofei Ivanitch, my little father, perhaps you will get well again, if God wills it; then you will sing for us once more. Ah, yes, it is a long time since you have sung. What songs those were! The one about Diuk Stepanovitch, for instance, do you think I have forgotten it? How stupid you are! I still know it perfectly. Of course, not like you - God has given you *that*, to another he gives something *else*. To me, for instance...

Timofei: *(lying on stove, turns to say something, groans)*

Ossip: It sounded, very softly, like Yegor's name. Perhaps he wanted to send him a message. *(at door, leaving)* Did you say something, Timofei Ivanitch? *(Old man shakes his head gently, no. Ossip exits.)*

Poet: All the same, God knows how it happened, hardly a year after Ossip had gone away, Yegor quite unexpectedly returned. The aged man did not recognize him at once,

Timofei: for it was dark in the hut,

Yegor: and the old eyes were reluctant to take in a new, unfamiliar figure.

Timofei: But when Timofei heard the stranger's voice, he started and jumped down from the stove on his rickety old legs.

Yegor: Yegor caught him, and they clasped each other in their arms.

Timofei: Timofei wept.

Yegor: Have you been ill a long time, Father? *(repeatedly)*

Timofei: And your wife? *(severe tone)*

Yegor: *(pause, Yegor spits)* I have sent her away, you know, with the child. *(silence)* One day Ossip comes to see me. Ossip Nikiforovitch? say I. Yes, she *(he)* answers, it is I. Your father is sick, Yegor. He can no longer sing. It is all silent now in the village, as though it had no soul any more, our village. Nothing knocks, nothing stirs, no one weeps any more, and there's no real reason to laugh either. I think it over. What's to be done? So I call my wife, 'Ustionka - say I - I must go home, no one else is there now, *it is my turn.* Father is sick.' 'Good' says Ustionka. 'But I cannot take you with me, I explain, Father, you know, won't have you. And probably I shall not come back to you either, once I am there again and singing.' Ustionka understands me. 'Well, God be with you. There are many pilgrims here now, there'll be alms aplenty. God will help, Yegor.' And so I went away. And now, Father, tell me all your songs.

POET: The rumor spread that Yegor had come back and that old Timofei was singing again.

NEIGHBOR ONE: But that autumn the wind went so violently through the village that none of those who passed by could tell for sure whether there really was singing in Timofei's house or not.

NEIGHBOR TWO: And the door was not opened to any one who knocked.

NEIGHBOR ONE: The two wanted to be alone.

YEGOR: Yegor sat on the edge of the stove on which his father lay, *(box can make surface to lie on)* now and then bringing his ear close to the old man's lips, for he was indeed singing.

TIMOFEI: His aged voice bore, somewhat bent and trembling, all his most beautiful songs to Yegor,

YEGOR: and Yegor would sometimes sway his head or swing his hanging legs, quite as though he were already singing himself. This went on for many days.

TIMOFEI: Timofei kept finding some still more beautiful song in his memory; often at night he would wake his son *(gesturing uncertainly with twitching hands)* and sing one little song and then another and yet another -

YEGOR: till the lazy morning began to stir.

TIMOFEI: He had often bitterly complained in his last days that he still carried a vast quantity of songs within him and had no time left to impart them to his son. From time to time he would sit upright, sway his head to and fro for a while,

YEGOR: move his lips - and at length some faint little song would come forth;

TIMOFEI: but now for the most part, he kept singing the same verses about Diuk Stepanovitch, which he particularly loved,

YEGOR: and his son had to appear astonished and pretend he was hearing them for the first time, in order not to anger him.

TIMOFEI: Soon after singing the most beautiful, he died.

POET: After his death, the house, in which his son now lived alone, remained shut up for a time.

YEGOR: Then, in the following spring, Yegor Timofeievitch, who now had quite a long beard, stepped out of his door,

NEIGHBOR: and began to walk about the village and sing. *(music)*

YEGOR: Later he visited the neighboring villages too,

PEASANT ONE: and the peasants began to tell each other that Yegor had become at least as accomplished a singer as his father Timofei;

YEGOR: for he knew a great number of grave and heroic songs,

PEASANT TWO: and all those melodies to which no man, were he Cossack or peasant, could hear without weeping.

PEASANT ONE: Besides, his voice is supposed to have had such a soft and sorrowful tone as had never been heard from any other singer. *(Exeunt peasants)*

POET: And this quality always appeared, quite unexpectedly, in the refrain, which was therefore particularly moving in effect. So at least I have heard tell.

LAME PERSON: Then he did not learn that tone from his father?

POET: No, it is not known how he came by it. *(steps away)*

LAME PERSON: *(calling after)* Perhaps he was thinking of his wife and his child. Tell me, did he never send for them, his father being dead?

POET: No, I don't think so. At least he was alone later on when he died. *(music out)*

LIGHTS OUT

VII A SCENE FROM THE GHETTO OF VENICE

POET: Herr Baum,

HERR BAUM: householder, Chairman of the Borough Council, Honorary Chief of the Volunteer Fire Brigade, and various other things as well - or

POET: to put it briefly, Herr Baum, must have overheard one of my conversations with the lame person. Herr Baum and I have known each other by sight for a long time. But the other day, the chairman of the Borough Council stops, raises his hat a little,

HERR BAUM: so that a small bird could have flown out in the event one had been caught under it

POET: and opens our acquaintance:

HERR BAUM: You travel sometimes?

POET: (*vaguely*) Oh yes - I very well may.

HERR BAUM: (*confidentially*) I believe we are the only two here who have been in Italy.

POET: Indeed - well, then of course it is urgently necessary that we should talk together.

HERR BAUM: (*laughs*) Italy, to be sure - that really is something. I am always telling my children - . Take Venice, for example:

POET: You still remember Venice?

HERR BAUM: But I put it to you, how could I fail to? When once you've seen it - that Piazzetta - don't you agree?

POET: Yes, I remember with particular pleasure the ride through the Canal, that soft soundless gliding along the borders of things past.

HERR BAUM: The palazzo Franchetti!

POET: The Ca d'Oro -

HERR BAUM: The Fishmarket -

POET: The Palazzo Vendramin -

HERR BAUM: Where Richard Wagner -

POET: (*nodding*) The Ponte, you remember?

HERR BAUM: (*smiling*) Of course, and the Museum, not to forget the Academy, where a Titian...

POET: When you pass along under the Ponte di Rialto, skirting the Fondaco de Turchi and the Fishmarket, and tell your gondolier 'to the right!' he will look surprised and even ask 'Dove?' But you insist on going to the right, you leave the gondola in one of the dirty little canals, bargain with the gondolier, tell him what you think of him, and walk away through narrow alleys and black, smoke-darkened archways, out onto an empty, open square. All this for the simple reason that my story takes place there.

HERR BAUM: *(diffidently touching his arm)* Pardon me, what story?

POET: Oh, just a little story, my dear sir, nothing remarkable at all. I cannot even tell you when it happened. Perhaps under Doge Alvise Mocenigo IV, but it may also have been somewhat earlier or somewhat later. Only the real Venice is concerned, the city of palaces, of adventures, of masques and pale nights on the lagoon, which carry like no other nights the sound of clandestine romances. In the bit of Venice of which I shall tell, there are only poor ordinary sounds, the days pass monotonously over it, as though they were but a single day, *(music of lamentation, Jewish)* and the songs one hears there are swelling plaints that do not mount upward but settle like curling smoke over the alleys. *(Entering, children.)*

CHILD: As soon as twilight comes much furtive humanity mills about the streets,

CHILD: countless children have their homes upon the squares and in the narrow cold doorways

CHILD: and play with chips and leavings of varicolored glassy flux,

CHILD: the same from which the masters pieced together the stern mosaics of San Marco.

MARCANTONIO: A noble seldom finds his way into the Ghetto.

CHILD: Only when the Jewish maidens gather at the well,

MARCANTONIO: one may sometimes notice a figure, black, in cloak and mask.

PERSON: Certain people by experience know that this figure carries a dagger hidden in those folds.

CHILD: Somebody is supposed to have seen the young man's face once in the moonlight,

CHILD: and since then they declare this dark slim visitor to be Marcantonio Priuli,

PERSON: son of the Proveditore Niccolo Priuli and the beautiful Caterina Minelli.

CHILD: He waits under the porch of Issac Rosso's house;

MARCANTONIO: then, when the people are gone, walks straight across the square and enters the house of old Melchizedek, the wealthy goldsmith,

PERSON: who has many sons and seven daughters, and by his sons and daughters many grandchildren.

ESTHER: Esther, the youngest granddaughter, awaits him, *(leaning against her grandfather's shoulder)*

MARCANTONIO: in a low dark chamber in which many objects glitter and glow,

ESTHER: and silk and velvet hangs soft over the costly vessels,

MELCHIZEDEK: as though to quench their full, golden flames.

MARCANTONIO: Here Marcantonio sits on a silver-embroidered cushion at the feet of the venerable Jew and tells of Venice,

ESTHER: as he would tell a fairy-tale that never anywhere happened quite like that.

MARCANTONIO: He tells of the theatre, of battles fought by the Venetian army, of foreign visitors, of pictures and statues of the 'Sensa' on Ascension Day, of the carnival,

ESTHER: and of the beauty of his mother Caterina Minelli.

MARCANTONIO: All these have for him much the same meaning, being different expressions of power and love and life.

ESTHER: To his two listeners it is all strange; for the Jews are strictly excluded from all society but their own,

MELCHIZEDEK: and even the wealthy old Melchizedek never sets foot within the domain of the Great Council,

ESTHER: although as a goldsmith and because of the general respect in which he is held, he might have dared to do so.

MELCHIZEDEK: In the course of his long life, the old man had obtained from the Great Council many privileges for his co-religionists,

ESTHER: who looked upon him as a father;

MELCHIZEDEK: but again and again he had had to endure the rebound. Every time a calamity befell the state, vengeance was taken on the Jews.

MARCANTONIO: The Venetians themselves were much too kin with them in spirit to use them, as other nations did, for commercial purposes;

MELCHIZEDEK: they plagued them with taxes, robbed them of their possessions, and restricted the boundary of the Ghetto more and more,

ESTHER: so that the Jewish families, which in the midst of all their hardships increased fruitfully, were forced to build their houses up into the air,

MELCHIZEDEK: one upon the roof of the other. And their city, which did not lie by the sea, thus slowly grew up into the sky as into another sea,

ESTHER: and all around the square with the well the steep buildings rose on all sides like the walls of some giant tower.

MELCHIZEDEK: The wealthy Melchizedek, in the eccentricity of old age, had made an odd proposal to his fellow-citizens, sons and grandsons.

ESTHER: He wished always to inhabit whichever was the highest of these tiny houses pushing upward, one above the other, in countless stories.

MELCHIZEDEK: So the old man would move two or three times a year, and

ESTHER: Esther, who refused to leave him, was always with him. In the end they were so high that when they stepped from the confinement of their room out upon the flat roof,

MELCHIZEDEK: there began at the level of their eyes another country, of the customs of which the old man would speak in dark words, half psalmodizing. *(Exeunt)*

MARCANTONIO: It was a long way up to them now;

PERSON: *(entering)* through the lives of many strangers, over steep and slippery steps,

WOMAN: past scolding women,

CHILD: and the onslaught of hungry children that way led,

PERSON: and its many obstacles kept all visitors away. *(Exeunt)*

MARCANTONIO: Even Marcantonio no longer came to visit,

ESTHER: Esther hardly missed him. In the hours when she had been alone with him, she had looked at him so large-eyed and so long that it seemed to her that he had plunged deep into her dark eyes and died, and that now there was beginning, in herself, his new, everlasting life, in which he as a Christian had of course believed. With this new feeling in her young body, she would stand all day on the roof, seeking the sea. But high though her house might be, there were only to be seen the gable of the Palazzo Foscari, some tower or other, the cupola of a church, a more distant cupola that seemed to shiver in the light, and then a lattice of masts, beams, poles against the rim of the humid, quivering sky.

MELCHIZEDEK: Towards the end of that summer the old man, though the climbing was already hard for him,

ESTHER: despite all protest

MELCHIZEDEK: moved once more;

PERSON ONE: for a new hut, high above all, had been built.

MELCHIZEDEK: As he crossed the square again after so long a time, *(leaning on Esther's arm)* people gathered round him,

PERSON TWO: and bent low over his fumbling hands and begged for his advice in many matters;

PERSON THREE: for he was to them like one dead who rises from his grave because a certain time is fulfilled.

PERSON ONE: And so indeed it seemed.

PERSON TWO: The men told him that there was a revolt in Venice, the nobles were in danger, and soon the boundaries of the Ghetto would fall and all would enjoy the same freedom.

MELCHIZEDEK: The old man answered nothing, and only nodded as though all this had long been known to him and much more besides. He entered the house of Issac Rosso, on the very top of which his new abode was perched, and spent half a day climbing the stairs. *(Exeunt)*

ESTHER: *(enters)* Up there Esther bore a delicate, blond child. When she recovered, she took it in her arms out upon the roof and for the first time let its open eyes be filled with the whole golden sky. It was an autumn morning of indescribable clearness. One caught sight from this highest spot of that which no one had ever seen from the Ghetto before - a still and silvery light: the sea. And only now, when Esther's eyes had grown accustomed to the glory, did she notice, at the roof's very edge,

MELCHIZEDEK: Melchizedek. He rose with outspread arms, forcing his dim eyes to gaze into the slowly unfolding day. His arms remained uplifted, a radiant thought upon his brow;

ESTHER: it was as though he were offering a sacrifice.

MELCHIZEDEK: Then he leaned forward again and again and pressed his venerable head upon the rough, jagged stones.

ESTHER: Had he seen the sea or God, the eternal, in his glory? *(Exit)*

POET: *(Entering, with Herr Baum.)* Had he seen the sea or God, the eternal, in his glory?

HERR BAUM: The sea probably, it really is impressive.

POET: Goodbye, goodbye, don't forget to tell your children this incident.

HERR BAUM: The children? But you know, that young nobleman, that Antonio or whatever his name is, he is not at all a nice character, and then the baby - that baby! That seems rather - for children -

POET: Oh, you have forgotten, my dear sir, that all babies come from God. Why should the children wonder that Esther had one, since she lived so near the sky! *(Exeunt. Two or three children enter.)*

CHILD ONE: This story too the children have heard,

CHILD TWO: and when you ask them what *they* think it may have been that the old Jew Melchizedek saw in his ecstasy,

CHILD ONE: they say without stopping to think:

CHILD TWO: Oh, the sea too.

CHILD ONE: Oh, the sea too.

LIGHTS OUT

VIII A STORY TOLD TO THE DARK

POET: I wanted to put on my coat and go to my friend Uta *(or Ewald)*. But I had lingered over a book, an *old* book at that, and evening had come, as in Russia spring comes...The lame person would surely no longer be at her *(his)* window. So I stayed at home. What was it I had wanted to tell her? I no longer knew. But after a while I felt that someone was entreating me for this lost story - some lonely soul, perhaps, standing far away at the window of her dusky room, or perhaps this very darkness itself that surrounded me and her and all things. So it happened that I told my story to the dark. And it leaned ever closer to me so that I could speak more and more softly, quite as befits my story. It takes place in the present, by the way, and begins: After a long absence Doctor Georg Lassman was returning to the simple home of his birth. He had never possessed much there, and now he had only two sisters still living in his native city, both married, apparently well married; to see them again after twelve years was the purpose of his visit.

GEORG: So he himself believed. But in the night, unable to sleep in the overcrowded train, it became clear to him that he was really going for the sake of his childhood, hoping to rediscover something in those old streets: a doorway, a tower, a fountain, anything to induce some joy or some sorrow by which he might recognize himself again. One loses oneself so in life. And then he remembered many things: the little apartment in the Heinrichgasse with the shiny doorknobs and the dark-colored tiles, the well-cared for furniture and his parents, those two threadbare beings standing almost reverently beside it; the hurrying and harassed week-days and the Sundays that were like cleared-out rooms, the rare visitors whom one received laughing and embarrassed, the out-of-tune piano, the old canary, the heirloom armchair in which one might not sit, a name-day, an uncle who came from Hamburg, a puppet-show, a barrel-organ, a children's party and someone calling:

FEMALE VOICE: Klara!

GEORG: The doctor has almost dropped off. They are in a station, lights run by and the listening hammer goes ringing along the wheels. And that is like Klara. Klara, who was Klara anyway? And next instant he becomes aware of a face, a child's face with blond, straight hair. Until the day he went to boarding-school, at the age of about ten, he shared with her everything that happened to him. But since then he had never asked anyone about her. How was that possible? She had been a pious child. What can have become of her?

SOPHIE: *(enters)* The reunion with his two married sisters passed off not without embarrassment.

SECOND SISTER: The three had forgotten how far apart they had always remained,

GEORG: and endeavored for a while to act like brothers and sisters.

SECOND SISTER: However they soon silently agreed to take refuge behind that polite mediate tone which social intercourse has invented for all occasions. *(exits)*

SOPHIE: It was at the house of his younger sister, whose husband was in particularly comfortable circumstances, *(setting object on table)*

COUNCILOR: *(enters)* a manufacturer with the title of Imperial Councilor,

GEORG: and it was after the fourth course at dinner that the doctor asked: Tell me, Sophie, what ever became of Klara?

SOPHIE: Klara who?

GEORG: I don't remember her name. The little one, you know, a neighbor's daughter, with whom I played as a child.

SOPHIE: Oh, you mean Klara Sollner?

GEORG: Sollner, that's it, Sollner. Now I remember, old Sollner was that awful old man - but what of Klara?

SOPHIE: *(hesitating)* She married - and now she lives altogether in retirement.

COUNCILOR: Yes *(sliding his knife across his plate)*, quite retired.

GEORG: You know her too?

COUNCILOR: Y-ye-es - just slightly; she's pretty well known here, of course. *(husband and wife exchange look of understanding; she gets up and leaves the men to their coffee.)*

COUNCILOR: This Klara, *(sly smile, watching ash fall from cigar)* wasn't she supposed to be a quiet child, and homely too? *(The doctor says nothing. The Councilor moves confidentially closer.)* That was a story! Did you never hear of it?

GEORG: But I haven't seen anybody to talk to.

COUNCILOR: Talk to? *(laughs cunningly)* You could have read it in the papers.

GEORG: *(nervously)* What?

COUNCILOR: Why, she ran off and left him - *(waits for the effect; takes a business-like, injured tone)* Well, they had married her to Lehr, of the building council. You wouldn't have known him. Not an old man - my age. Rich, thoroughly respectable. She hadn't a penny and in addition she had no looks, no bringing-up etc. Still, Lehr didn't want a great lady, just a modest housekeeping wife. But Klara - she was taken into society all over, everybody was kindly disposed towards her - really, they acted - well, you know, she could easily have made a position for herself - but Klara, one day - hardly two years after the wedding, off she goes. Can you imagine: gone. Where? To Italy. A little pleasure-trip, not alone, naturally. All that last year we hadn't invited them - as though we had suspected! Lehr, a good friend of mine, a man of honor, a man -

GEORG: And then? *(rising)*

COUNCILOR: Oh, yes - well, the chastisement of heaven fell upon her. You see, the man in question - an artist, they say, you know - a casual sort of bird, naturally, just- Well, when they got back from Italy, to Munich: good-bye, and she saw him no more. Now she's sitting there with her child!

GEORG: *(striding excitedly up and down)* In Munich?

COUNCILOR: Yes, in Munich. *(rising)* They say she's having a pretty miserable time -

GEORG: How, miserable?

COUNCILOR: Well, pecuniarily, and then anyhow - God, what an existence - *(laying hand on the other's shoulder)* You know *(clucking with pleasure)* You know they also used to say that she lived on - *(The doctor turns short and walks out the door. The Councilor needs time to recover; goes to wife)* Sophie! *(angrily)* I've always said so, your brother is decidedly queer.

SOPHIE: *(yawning)* Oh, Lord yes. He's always been that way. *(Exeunt)*

GEORG: A short time later the doctor departed. He knew all at once that he must seek his childhood elsewhere. In the Munich directory he found: Klara Sollner, the name of the suburb, Schwabing, the street and number. He announced his coming and drove out.

KLARA: A slender woman greeted him in a light-filled room. Georg, and you still remember me?

GEORG: *(in amazement)* So this is *you*, Klara. You were writing?

KLARA: Yes, I'm translating.

GEORG: For publication?

KLARA: Yes, for a publishing house.

GEORG: There were some Italian photographs on the walls. Among them Giorgione's 'Concert'. Are you fond of this? *(steps up nearer to it)*

KLARA: And you?

GEORG: I have never seen the original; it's in Florence, isn't it?

KLARA: In the Pitti. You must go there.

GEORG: For the purpose?

KLARA: For the purpose. What's the matter, Georg? Won't you sit down?

GEORG: I've been sorry *(faltering)* I thought - but - but you aren't in the least miserable!

KLARA: *(smiling)* You have heard my story?

GEORG: Yes, that is -

KLARA: Oh, *(interrupting quickly)* it's not people's fault if they speak differently of it. The things we experience often cannot be expressed, and any one who insists on telling them nevertheless, is bound to make mistakes. *(A pause.)*

GEORG: What has made you so kind?

KLARA: *(softly and warmly)* Everything. But why do you say: kind?

GEORG: Because - because you really ought to have grown hard. You were such a weak, helpless child; children of that sort later either grow hard or -

KLARA: Or they die, you mean. Well, I died too. Oh, I died for many years. From the time I last saw you at home, until - *(reaches for something from the table)* See, this is his picture. It flatters him a little. His face is not so clear-cut, but - nicer, simpler. I'll show you our child in a moment, it's asleep in the next room. It's a boy. Called Angelo, like him. He is away now, traveling, far away.

GEORG: And you are all alone?

KLARA: Yes, I and the child. Isn't that enough? I will tell you how it is. Angelo is a painter. His name is little known; you would never have heard of it. Until lately he had been struggling with the world, with his plans, with himself and with me. Yes, with me too; because for a year I've been begging him to travel. I felt how much he needed it. Once he asked jokingly: Me or a child? A child, said I, and then he went.

GEORG: And when will he be back?

KLARA: When the child can say his name, that's how we arranged it. *(laughs)* And as it's a difficult name, it will take a while yet. Angelino won't be two till summer.

GEORG: Extraordinary.

KLARA: What, Georg?

GEORG: How well you understand life. How big you have grown, how young! What have you done with your childhood? We were both such - such helpless children. But that can't be altered or made never to have happened.

KLARA: You mean, we ought to have *suffered* from our childhood, by right?

GEORG: Yes, I mean just that. From that heavy darkness behind us with which we preserve such feeble, vague relations. There comes a time when we have deposited in it all our firstlings, all beginning, all confidence, the seeds of all that which might perhaps some day come to be. And suddenly we realize: All that has sunk in a deep sea, and we don't even know just when. We never noticed it. As though someone were to collect all his money, and buy a feather with it and stick the feather in his hat: whish! the first breeze will carry it away. Naturally he arrives home without his feather, and nothing remains for him but to look back and think when it could have flown off.

KLARA: You are thinking of that, Georg?

GEORG: Not any more. I've given it up. I begin somewhere behind my tenth year, at the point where I stopped praying. The rest doesn't belong to me.

KLARA: And how is it, then, that you have remembered *me*?

GEORG: That is just why I have come to you. You are the only witness to that time. I believed I could find again in you - what I can *not* find in myself. Some gesture, some word, some name, that would carry a suggestion - some *enlightenment* - *(his head sinks into his hands)*

KLARA: *(ponders)* I remember so little of my childhood, as though there were a thousand lives between. But now that you remind me of it so, something comes back to me. One evening. You came to us, unexpectedly; your parents had gone out, to the theatre or something of the sort. Our house was all lit up. My father was expecting a guest, a relative, a distant wealthy relative, if I remember rightly. He was coming from, from - I don't know where, but in any case from some distance. We had already been awaiting him for two hours. The doors were open, the lamps were burning, my mother went over from time to time and smoothed an antimacassar on the sofa, my father stood at the window. Nobody dared to sit down for fear of displacing a chair. As you happened to come, you waited with us. We children listened at the door. And the later it grew, the more marvelous a guest did we expect. Yes, we even trembled lest he came before he should have attained that last degree of gloriousness to which with every minute of his not-coming he drew nearer. We were not afraid that he might not appear at all; we knew for certain he would come, but we wanted to leave him time to grow great and mighty.

GEORG: *(raising his head)* So we both know that - that he *didn't* come. I had not forgotten it either.

KLARA: No, he didn't come - *(pause)* But it was lovely all the same!

GEORG: What?

KLARA: Oh, well, - the waiting, the many lamps - the stillness - the festive spirit.

GEORG: Something stirred in the room.

KLARA: Excuse me. *(leaves, comes brightly and serenely back)* We can go in now. He's awake and smiling. - But what was it you wanted to say just now?

GEORG: I was just wondering what could have helped you to - to yourself, to this calm possession of yourself. Life certainly hasn't made it easy for you. Evidently something helped you that I haven't got.

KLARA: What should that be, Georg? *(sits near him)*

GEORG: It is strange; when I first remembered you again, one night three weeks ago, on the train, I thought: She was a pious child. And now, since I have seen you, although you are so entirely different from what I had expected - in spite of that, and yet, I would almost say, only the more surely, I feel that what led you through all dangers was your - your piety.

KLARA: What do you call piety?

GEORG: Well, your relation to God, your love of God, your belief.

KLARA: *(closes her eyes)* Love of God? Let me think. *(speaks slowly as her thoughts come to her)* As a child - did I love God? I don't believe so. Why, I never even - it would have seemed to me insane presumption - that isn't the right word - like the worst sin, to think: He is. As though I had thereby compelled him to be *in me*, in that weak child with the absurdly long arms, in our poor apartment where everything was imitation and false, from the bronze wall-plaques of papier mache' to the wine in bottles that bore such expensive labels. And later - *(parrying gestures, eyes closed as though afraid to see something dreadful)* - why, I would have had to drive him out of me if he had been living in me then. I had forgotten *everything*. - Not until I came to Florence, when for the first time in my life I saw, heard, felt, realized and simultaneously learned to be thankful for all those things, did I think of him again. There were traces of him everywhere. In all the pictures I found bits of his smile, the bells were still alive with his voice, and on the statues I recognized the imprints of his hands.

GEORG: And you found him there?

KLARA: I felt that he *was* - at some time once *was*...why should I have felt *more*? That was already more than enough.

GEORG: *(The doctor gets up and goes to window)* One could see a stretch of field and the little old village church of Schwabing, and above it sky, no longer quite untouched by evening. *(without turning around)* And now? *(comes back)*

KLARA: *(faltering, then raising her eyes to his face)* Now - now I sometimes think: He will be. *(He takes her hand for a moment.)* What are you thinking of, Georg?

GEORG: I'm thinking that it's like that evening once more: *you* are again waiting for the wonderful guest, for God, and know that he will come - And I have joined you by chance -

KLARA: *(rises, calm and happy)* Well, this time we'll really wait until it happens. Come see my child. *(Exeunt)*

POET: In this story there is nothing that children may not know. Still, the children have *not* heard it. I have told it only to the dark, to no one else. And the children are afraid of the dark, and run away from it, and if some time they have to stay in it, they press their eyes shut and put their fingers in their ears. But for them also the time will come when they love the dark. From it they will learn my story, and then they will understand it better, too.

FADE OUT

CURTAIN

R U M I

SIXTEEN STORIES OF JALALUDDIN RUMI,
IN STORY THEATER FORM, TRANSLATED BY
COLEMAN BARKS
AND ADAPTED FOR THE STAGE BY PAUL SILLS
WITH THREE ADDITIONAL STORIES

RUMI
Copyright © Paul Sills and Coleman Barks, 2000

INTRODUCTION

This production, titled *RUMI*, has been adapted by Coleman Barks[1] from literal translations by John Moyne[2] and the translations of A.J. Arberry and Reynold Nicholson, the Cambridge Islamicists, of the writings of the celebrated Islamic poet Jalalludin Rumi, (1207-1273).

His father was a theologian, jurist and mystic, who led his family out of Afghanistan (then a part of the Persian Empire), fleeing invading Mongol armies, arriving finally at Konya, Turkey. At his father's death, Rumi took over the position of sheikh (pronounced shake) in the dervish (Sufi) learning community. For the last twelve years of his life he dictated the six volumes of *Mathnawi*. These stories are from that work.

To quote Coleman Barks, "The *Mathnawi* runs over fifty-one thousand verses, complete in twelve-beat lines, in which the hemistichs, or half-lines, also rhyme. I have set these versions of the *Mathnawi* in the free verse of American poetry, one of the strongest and most spiritually open and questing traditions in Western writing. To use Rumi's own metaphor, the *Mathnawi* is an ocean of ecstatic poetry, folklore, the *Qur'an*, stories of saints and teachers, myth, the sayings of Muhammed, jokes from the street, and whispered asides to Husan, Rumi's scribe. It is a sacred text that invites one to drown in it."

In the Spring of '98 when it was time to do my annual show with the graduating students[3] at *New Actors Workshop* in New York, my friend, W. A. Mathieu[4] contacted his friend Coleman Barks, who gave me permission to use his sublime translation of Rumi's teaching stories [5] as a story theater show, and to publish them in this volume.

I divided my cast into two groups, one for each act, and rehearsed the groups separately. Both acts ended with a scene using all the

---

1. *The Essential Rumi*, translated by Coleman Barks, with John Moyne, Harper San Francisco, Harper Collins Publishers, 10 E. 53rd St. New York, N.Y. 10022

2. Emeritus Head of Linguistics at the City University of New York.

3. Scott Becker, Kevin Biacsi, Chandelle Binns, Jose Luis Bouchon, Jeanne Boyle, Darren Cappozi, Laurie Devino, Kelly Eads, Quinten Gordon, Mary Haley, Simone Kowitz, Bronwyn Knox, Mark Lieber, Nicole Mack, Jacqueline Maloney, Nicole Marshall, Troy Metcalf, Naomi Nissen, Karen Oughtred, Suzanne Petkus, Ajna Pisani, Shea Ryan, John Slaninka, Ryan Soteres and Amy Zimmerman.

4. W. A. Mathieu was the first musician/composer at *The Second City* as he was at the *Compass* before that, and the San Francisco *Committee* after that.

5. MAYPOP, 196 Westview Drive, Athens, GA 30306. (404)543-2148.

players of that group. There are very few female roles as such in these stories and fifteen of my cast of twenty-five were women. They easily fit into the text, playing the Voice of God, The Mouse and the Frog, The Dream That Must Be Interpreted, Spiritual Seniority, Birds, Sufis, The Halvah Seller and Creditors in The Debtor Sheikh, The Three Fish, The Shroud Maker, and other parts as well as specifically female roles. Costume "friends" were asked to volunteer and they helped fellow cast members find the appropriate dress for their stories. Shadow screens were used and projections made that were both abstract and Arabic in their design quality.

In Winter of 1999 I mounted a workshop production of thirteen of these Rumi stories in Los Angeles with professional actors, all of whom had been with me at Second City or Story Theater: Hamilton Camp, Paul Dooley, Mina Kolb, Paul Sand, Avery Schreiber, Christopher Allport and Rachel MacKinnon, with music composed and played by Fred Kaz. Both productions began with *The Dream That Must Be Interpreted* and ended with *Breadmaking*. The order of stories was dependent on casting.

The stories in RUMI are folktales, some known worldwide, others stories of saints and teachers of Islam which the poet retold to point to the spiritual journey all of us are on, and this he did merrily, with wit, and in a theater the audience laughs freely at the contradictions.

Like so many of the greatest poets, Rumi knew the way of the storyteller. At the beginning of the Mathnawi, Rumi tells of being asked to speak of his dearest friend. He refuses with these words. [6]

> It's better that the friend remain in veils!
>
> Come, listen to the content of the tales:
>
> It's better that his mysteries be told
>
> In other people's stories, tales of old!

> Mathnawi, Volume I, Line 141

[6.] Translated by Annemarie Schimmel in her book *I Am Wind You Are Fire, The Life and Work of Rumi*, Shambala Publications Inc., 300 Massachusetts Ave. Boston, MA 02115

RUMI

The Dream That Must be Interpreted
Narrator
Shadows (two)

Baghdad, Dreaming of Cairo
Man
Wife
Dream Voice
Night Patrol (two)

Sexual Urgency
Caliph
Man
Captain
King
Soldiers
Girl
Lion (Shadow)

Spiritual Seniority
Camel
Ox
Ram

The Mouse and the Frog
Mouse
Frog
Raven

Muhammed and the Huge Eater
Muhammed
The Huge Eater
Maids (two)
Friends/Unbelievers (Ensemble)

Moses and the Shepherd
Moses
Shepherd
Voice of God

A Song About a Donkey
Wanderer
Servant
Sufis (Ensemble)
Donkey (Shadow)

The Trick of Hiding in a Box
Juhi
Juhi's Wife
Judge
Porters
Deputy

Nasuh
Nasuh
Flute Player
Bathers (Women)
Gnostic Saint (Shadow)
Princess
Lady Chamberlain

The Law Student and the Shroud Maker
Jahan
Beggar Woman
Law Student
Other Law Students
Widows (Ensemble)

The Debtor Sheikh
Sheikh Ahmad
Sufis
Creditors
Halvah Seller
Flute Player
Hatim's Servant

The Indian Parrot
Merchant
Servants (three)
The Indian Parrot
Parrots
Voice

The Three Fish
Fish One
Fish Two
Fish Three
Fisherman One
Fisherman Two

*The Woman Who Wanted to
Learn the Language of Animals*
Woman (or Man)
Moses
Voice of God
Dog
Rooster

Breadmaking
King
Harem
Musicians
Cupbearer
Scholar
Scholar's Lover
Dancers

*THREE ADDITIONAL
STORIES OF RUMI:*

Snow and the Voice
Bu'l
Bestami

Spilling the Rose Oil
Grocer
Parrot
Customers
Dervish
Second Dervish

The Camel Driver's Song
Sufi
Slave
Merchant

Hamilton Camp, Paul Sand, Christopher Alport, Avery Schreiber, Mina Kolb and Paul Dooley, February, 1999, in a scene from The Debtor Sheikh, *RUMI*

Sophie Olmsted

THE DREAM THAT MUST BE INTERPRETED

SPEAKER: This place is a dream.
 Only a sleeper considers it real.
 But there's a difference with this dream.
 Everything cruel and unconscious
 done in the illusion of the present world,
 all the mean laughing,
 all the quick, sexual wanting,
 all that does not fade away at the death-waking.

It stays, and it must be interpreted.

And this groggy time we live,
this is what it's like:

A man goes to sleep in the town
where he has always lived, and dreams he's living
in another town.
 (shadow of man awakening, rising)
In the dream he doesn't remember
the town he's sleeping in his bed in. He believes
the reality of the dream town.
 (shadow of man pulling woman up)
The world is that kind of sleep.
The dust of many crumbled cities
 (shadows move in expression of the poetry)
settles over us like a forgetful doze,
but we are older than those cities.
 (shadows sink down like dusty rocks.)
We began
as a mineral. We emerged into plant life
 (fingers arise as sprouts)
and into the animal state,
 (figures rise up transforming to animal, then human)
and then into being human,
and always we have forgotten our former states,
except in early spring when we slightly recall
being green again.
 (shadows move joyfully)
That's how a young person turns

toward a teacher.
    (they bow to each other)
That's how a baby leans
toward the breast,
    (she holds the baby)
without knowing the secret   *(he is a father)*
of its desire, yet turning instinctively.

Humankind is being led along an evolving course,
through this migration of intelligences,
    (they settle back to sleep)
and though we seem to be sleeping,
there is an inner wakefulness
that directs the dream,
and that will eventually startle us back to the truth of who we are.

    (on the word "startle", they awaken)

IN BAGHDAD, DREAMING OF CAIRO

MAN: There was once a man
    who inherited a lot of money and land.

WOMAN: *(His wife)* But he squandered it all too quickly. Those who in-
    herit wealth don't know what work it took to get it.

MAN: In the same way, we don't know the value of our souls,
    which were given to us for nothing!

WOMAN: So the man was left alone without provisions, an owl in the
    desert. *(They prepare to go to sleep.)*

MAN: The Prophet has said
    that a true seeker must be completely empty like a lute
    to make the sweet music of Lord, Lord.

WOMAN: This man was empty, and the tears came.
    His habitual stubbornness dissolved.
    This is the way with many seekers.
    They moan in prayer, and the angels say, 'Answer
    this prayer. This worshiper has only you and
    nothing else to depend on. Why do you go first
    to the prayers of those less devoted?'

God says,
'By deferring my generosity I am helping him. *(man moans)*
His need dragged him by the hair into My Presence.
If I satisfy that, he'll go back to being absorbed
in some idle amusement. Listen how passionate he is.
    (the man moans and cries out)
That torn-open cry is the way he should live.'

MAN: So this man with nothing, who had inherited everything
and squandered it, kept weeping, Lord, Lord!
    (they go to sleep)
Finally in a dream he heard a Voice.

VOICE: Your wealth is in Cairo. Go there to such and such
a spot, and dig, and you'll find what you need.

MAN: So he left on the long journey, *(embraces wife and leaves)*
and when he saw the towers of Cairo,
he felt his back grow warm with new courage.
He had no money, of course, so he begged
among the townspeople, but he felt ashamed doing that.
He decided, I will go out at night
and call like the night-mendicants that people
throw coins into the street for.
Shame and dignity and hunger
were pushing him forward and backward and sideways!

PATROL ONE: *(entering)* Suddenly he was seized by the night-patrol.

PATROL TWO: *(entering)* It so happened that many had been robbed
recently in Cairo at night,
PATROL ONE: and the Caliph had told the police
to assume that anyone out roaming after dark was a thief.

PATROL TWO: They gave him a sound drubbing,

PATROL ONE: and blows without number.

MAN: Have mercy! Don't strike! Let me tell the truth about it all.
Wait! I can explain!

PATROL TWO: Tell me.

MAN: I am not a criminal. I am new to Cairo.
    I live in Baghdad. And then he told
    the story of his dream and the buried treasure,

PATROL TWO: and he was so believable in the telling that
    the night patrolmen began to cry.

PATROL ONE: Always the fragrance of truth has that effect.

PATROL TWO: Passion can restore healing power,
    and prune the weary boughs to new life.

PATROL ONE: The energy of passion is everything!

PATROL TWO: I know you're not a thief.
    You're a good man, but you're kind of a fool.
    I've had that dream before. I was told in my dream
    that there was a treasure for me
    in Baghdad, buried in a certain quarter of the city
    on such-and-such a street.

MAN: The name of the street that he said
    was where this man lived!

PATROL TWO: And the dream-voice told me, 'It's in
    So-and-so's house, under the iron stove.
    Go there and get it!'

MAN: Without knowing either,
    he had described the exact house,
    and mentioned this man's name!

PATROL TWO: But I didn't do what the dream said to do,
    and look at you, wandering the world,
    fatigued and begging in the streets!

MAN: So it came quietly to the seeker,

though he didn't say it out loud,
What I'm looking for lives in my poor house in Baghdad!

He was filled with joy. He breathed continuous praise.
My good fortune depended on my suffering these blows:
   (*he is home again, his wife greets him, they dance, he feels under the
stove to find a box*)
the Water of Life has been under my stove all the time.

WIFE: What a long way he had to go to find out.

SEXUAL URGENCY

MAN: Someone offhand to the Caliph of Egypt:
   The King of Mosul has a concubine like no other,
   more beautiful than I can describe.
   She looks like this.
   He draws her likeness on paper.

CALIPH: The Caliph drops his cup.
   Immediately he sends his Captain to Mosul
   with an army of thousands.

CAPTAIN: The siege goes on for a week,
   (*battle in shadow*) with many casualties, the walls
   and towers unsteady, as soft as wax.

KING: The King of Mosul comes as his own envoy:
   Why this killing? If you want the city,
   I will leave and you can have it!

   If you want more wealth, that's even easier.
   What do you want?

CAPTAIN: The Captain takes out the piece of paper
   with the girl's picture on it. This.

KING: The strong King of Mosul is quick to reply.
   Lead her out. The idol belongs with the idolater.

      (*girl enters, circles the captain, exits*)

CAPTAIN: When the Captain sees her, he falls in love
     like the Caliph. Don't laugh at this.
     This loving is also part of infinite Love,
     without which the world does not evolve.
     This Captain thinks the soil looks fertile,
     so he sows his seed. Sleeping, he sees the girl
     in a dream. (*shadow of girl*) He makes love to her image
     and his semen spurts out.

     After a while he begins to wake.
     Slowly he senses the girl is not there.
     I have given my seed into nothing.
     I shall put this tricky woman to a test.

     A leader who is not captain of his body is not one
     to be honored, with his semen spilled so in the sand.
     Now he loses all control. He doesn't care
     about the Caliph, or about dying.
     I am in love!

     The Captain does not return straight to the Caliph,
     but instead camps in a secluded meadow.
     Blazing, he can't tell ground from sky.
     His reason is lost in a drumming sound,
     worthless radish and son of a radish.
     The Caliph himself a gnat, nothing.
          (*Goes behind shadow screen, as into her tent.*)

     But just as this cultivator tears off the woman's pants
     and lays down between her legs, his penis
     moving straight to the mark, there's a great tumult,

          (*howls off*)

SOLDIER: a rising cry of soldiers outside the tent.

CAPTAIN: He leaps up with his bare bottom shining
     and runs out, scimitar in hand. (*runs onstage*)

SOLDIER: A black lion from a nearby swamp
     has gotten in among the horses. Chaos.

The lion jumping twenty feet in the air, (*shadow of lion*)
tents billowing like an ocean.

CAPTAIN: The Captain quickly approaches the lion, (*shadow with sword*)
splits his head with one blow, (*comes onstage*)
and now he's running back to the woman's tent.
When he stretches out her beauty again,   (*they are seen in shadow*)
his penis goes even more erect.

WOMAN: The beautiful one is amazed at his virility.
Immediately, with great energy she joins with his energy,

CAPTAIN: and their two spirits go out from them as one.

(*they enter together*)
WOMAN: A man and a woman together always
have a spiritual result. Be aware of this.

CAPTAIN: The Captain was not so aware. He fell,
and stuck like a gnat in a pot of buttermilk
totally absorbed in his love affair. Then,
just as suddenly, he's uninterested.
Don't say a word of this to the Caliph.

He takes her there,

CALIPH: and the Caliph is smitten.
She's a hundred times more beautiful than he's imagined.
So the Caliph is mightily in love with this girl.
His kingdom vanishes like lightning.
He has the idea of entering the beautiful woman,
and he comes to her to do his wanting.

But as he actually lays down with the woman,
there comes to him a decree from God
to stop these voluptuous doings.

VOICE: Stop these voluptuous doings!

CALIPH: A very tiny sound,
like a mouse must make. The penis droops,

and the desire slips away.

WOMAN: The girl sees his drooping
and sails into fits of laughing at the marvelous thing.
She remembers the Captain killing the lion
with his penis standing straight up.

CALIPH: Long and loud her laughter.

WOMAN: Anything she thinks of only increases it,
like the laughter of those who eat hashish.
Everything is funny.

CALIPH: The Caliph is furious. He draws his sword.
What's so amusing? Tell me everything you're thinking.
Don't hold anything back. At this moment
I'm clairvoyant. If you lie, I'll behead you.
If you tell the truth, I'll give you your freedom.

He stacks seven Qur'ans on top of each other
and swears to do as he says.

WOMAN: When she finally gets hold of herself
the girl tells all, in great detail. Of the camp
in the meadow, the killing of the lion,
and the Captain's return to the tent with his
penis still hard as the horn of a rhino.
And the contrast with the Caliph's own member
sinking down because of one mouse-whisper.

CALIPH: Hidden things always come to light.
Do not sow bad seed. Be sure, they'll come up.
Rain and the sun's heat make them rise into the air.
Spring comes after the fall of the leaves,
which is proof enough of the fact of resurrection.

The Caliph comes back to his clarity. In the pride
of my power I took this woman from another,
so of course, someone came to knock on my door.

Whoever commits adultery is a pimp
for his own wife.

If you cause injury to someone, you draw
that same injury toward yourself. My treachery
made my friend a traitor to me. This repetition
must stop somewhere. Here, in an act of mercy.

I'll send you back to the Captain,
saying another of my wives is jealous,
and since the Captain was brave enough
to bring you back from Mosul, he shall have you in marriage.

CAPTAIN: *(enters)* This is the virility of a prophet.

WOMAN: The Caliph was sexually impotent,
but his manliness was most powerful.

CALIPH: The kernel of true manhood is the ability
to abandon sensual indulgences.

CAPTAIN: The intensity of the Captain's libido
is less than a husk

WOMAN: compared to the Caliph's nobility in ending
the cycle of sowing lust

CAPTAIN: and reaping secrecy

CALIPH: and vengefulness.

SPIRITUAL SENIORITY

CAMEL: *(enters)* A camel,

OX: *(enters)* an ox

RAM: *(enters)* and a ram

CAMEL: were ambling along a road,

(If women play these roles, call the animals a camel, a cow and a sheep.)

OX: when they saw a fresh tuft of barley grass

RAM: that they all wanted. *(jostling each other to get it)*

CAMEL: They stopped,

RAM: and the ram said, If we divide this,
none of us will be satisfied. Let us do
as Muhammed advised and give it to the eldest,
honoring his superior experience.

CAMEL: No one honors their elders these days
without some ulterior motive. The young
invite them to taste the food first
only when they suspect it's too hot.

OX: They invite them to cross the bridge ahead of them
only when they see dangerous cracks in the arches,
and no one bows to the Teacher in these times
without some scam in mind. So let us each declare his
age and settle this matter.

RAM: As for me, I don't know my exact years,
but I was once pastured with that ram
that Abraham sacrificed instead of Isaac.

OX: Well I can beat that! I was yoked
in the team that Adam plowed with when he left Eden.

CAMEL: The camel listened silently to their amazing lies,
reached his long neck down, plucked the luscious tuft,
and held it over their heads.
I don't know much about
this chronology, sweethearts, but I know
I'm taller than you two,
and that has obvious spiritual significance.

    (Exeunt as camel finds more tufts)

THE MOUSE AND THE FROG

MOUSE: A mouse *(enters with short bench)*

FROG: and a frog *(enters with short bench)*

MOUSE: meet every morning on the riverbank.

FROG: They sit in a nook of the ground and talk.

MOUSE: Each morning, the second they see each other,
they open easily, telling stories and dreams

FROG: and secrets, empty of any fear or suspicious holding back.

MOUSE: Friend sits by Friend and the tablets appear.

FROG: They read the mysteries off each other's foreheads.

MOUSE: But one day the mouse complains, There are times
what I want sohbet (spiritual conversation), and you're
out in the water, jumping around where you can't hear me.
Physically, we meet only at breakfast.
Your absence during the rest of the day
enters all my cravings! I drink
five hundred times too much. I eat
like a bulimic trying to die. Help me!
I know I'm not worth it,
but your generosity is so vast!
My friend, I know I'm ugly to you. I'm ugly to me!
I'm perfectly ugly! But look, you'll be sad
when I die won't you? You'll sit by my grave
and weep a little? All I'm asking is,
be with me that little bit of time
while I'm still alive!
Now, I want you NOW!
I'm always standing on the bank calling to you.
Have mercy. I can't follow you into the water.
Isn't there some way we can be in touch?

FROG: The two friends decided that the answer was a long string

MOUSE: A *longing* string

FROG: with the end tied to the mouse's foot
and the other to the frog's, (*they tie the space string connection*)
so that by pulling on it their secret
might be remembered (*they each pull the string and get response*)

MOUSE: and the two could meet

FROG: as the soul does

MOUSE: with the body. (*they embrace*)

FROG: The frog-like soul often escapes from the body
and soars in the happy water. (*dives in water*)

MOUSE: Then the mouse body pulls on the string,

FROG: and the soul thinks, Damn,
I have to go back on the riverbank and talk
with that scatterbrained mouse!

MOUSE: So the string was tied

FROG: even though the frog had a hunch some
tangling was to come.
Never ignore those intuitions.
When you feel some slight repugnance about doing something,
listen to it. These premonitions come from Allah.

MOUSE: So the love-string stretched into the water

FROG: with the frog diving to the bottom,

MOUSE: and the mouse on the riverbank.
(*a shriek and the shadow of a raven spreading wings to take off: enters on stage*)
Suddenly a raven grips the mouse and flies off.

FROG: The frog too, follows,

suspended in the air.
(frog is dragged around the stage)

PASSERBY:Whoever saw a raven
go underwater and catch a frog?

FROG: This is the force of friendship! *(the frog is dragged offstage)*
(the stage is empty, then frog and mouse return)

MOUSE: What draws friends together
does not conform to laws of nature.
(picks up his bench)

FROG: Gabriel was always there with Jesus, lifting him
above the dark-blue vault,   *(picks up his bench)*

MOUSE: the night-fortress world,

FROG: just as the raven of longing carried the flying frog.

(they exit carrying the benches)

MUHAMMED AND THE HUGE EATER

(a group is seen in shadow)

MUHAMMED: *(entering)* A large group of unbelievers
once came to see Muhammed, knowing
he would feed them.
 Muhammed told his friends,
Divide the guests among you and tend to them.
Since you are all filled with me,
it will be as though I am the host.

FRIEND: Each friend of Muhammed chose a guest,

MUHAMMED: But there was one huge person left behind.
(the man is seen in shadow)

MAID: He sits in the entrance to the mosque
like thick dregs in a cup.

MUHAMMED: So Muhammed invited the man to his own
    household, *(a servant leads the man in; a seat is given him)*

MAID ONE: where the enormous son of a Ghuzz Turk ate everything.

MAID TWO: *(serving him)* The milk of seven goats and enough food for
    eighteen!
        (could be maidservant and manservant)
MAID ONE: The others in the house were furious.
        (glancing at Muhammed, who gestures: 'give him more.')

MAID TWO: When the man went to bed, *(leading him there)*
    the maid slammed the door behind him
    and chained it shut, out of meanness

MAID ONE: and resentment.

EATER: Around midnight, the man
    felt several strong urges at once.
    But the door! He works it,
    puts a blade through the crack. Nothing.
    The urgency increases. The room contracts.
    He falls back into a confused sleep and dreams
    of a desolate place, since he himself
    is such a desolate place.
        (Muhammed, in shadow, is praying)
    So, dreaming he's by himself,
    he squeezes out a huge amount,
    and another huge amount.
    But he soon became conscious enough
    to know that the covers he gathers around him
    are full of shit. He shakes with spasms of the shame
    that usually keeps men from doing such things.
    My sleep is worse than my being awake.
    The waking is just full of food.
    My sleep is all this.

    Now he's crying, bitterly embarrassed,
    waiting for dawn and the noise of the door opening,
    hoping that somehow he can get out
    without anyone seeing him as he is.

MUHAMMED: I'll shorten it. (*he is at the door*)
The door opens. (*a gesture*)

EATER: He's saved!

MUHAMMED: Muhammed becomes invisible so the man
won't feel ashamed, so he can escape and wash himself
and not have to face the door-opener.

MAID ONE: (*appears*) Someone completely absorbed in Allah
like Muhammed can do this. (*exits*)

MUHAMMED: Muhammed had seen all that went on in the night,
but he held back from letting the man out,
until all happened as it needed to happen.

> (*both maids appear*)

MAID TWO: Many actions which seem cruel
are from a deep Friendship.
Many demolitions are actually renovations.

> (*the maids pick up the soiled sheet and bring it to Muhammed*)

MAID ONE: Look what your guest has done.

MUHAMMED: Muhammed smiles, himself a mercy given to all beings,
Bring me a bucket of water.

MAIDS No! Let us do this./ We live to serve you, and this
is the kind of hand-work we can do./ Yours is the
inner heart-work.

MUHAMMED: I know that, but this is an extraordinary occasion.
A Voice inside him is saying, 'There is great wisdom
in washing these bedclothes. Wash them.'

EATER: Meanwhile, the man who soiled the covers and fled
is returning to Muhammed's house. He has left behind
an amulet that he always carried.

He enters and sees the Hands of God
washing his incredibly dirty linen.

He forgets the amulet. A great love suddenly enters him.
He tears his shirt open. He strikes his head
against the wall and the door. Blood pours from his nose.

OTHERS: (*enter*) People come from other parts of the house.

EATER: He's shrieking, Stay away! (*Muhammed gestures them away*)
I have no understanding!
He prostrates himself before Muhammed.
You are the Whole. I am a despicable, tiny
meaningless piece. I can't look at you.
He's quiet and quivering with remorse.

MUHAMMED: Muhammed holds him and caresses him
and opens his inner knowing.

MAID ONE: The cloud weeps, and then the garden sprouts.

MAID TWO: The baby cries, and the mother's milk flows.

MUHAMMED: The Nurse of Creation has said, Let them cry a lot!

MOSES AND THE SHEPHERD

MOSES: Moses heard a shepherd on the road praying.
(*the part could be played by a man or a woman*)

SHEPARD: God, where are You? I want to help you,
to fix your shoes and comb Your hair.
I want to wash Your clothes and pick the lice off.
I want to bring You milk, to kiss Your
little hands and feet when it's time for You
to go to bed. I want to sweep Your room
and keep it neat. God, my sheep and goats are Yours.
(*animal sounds*)
All I can say, remembering You, is ayyyyy and ahhhhhh.

MOSES: Moses could stand it no longer. Who are you talking to?

SHEPARD: The One who made us,
and made the earth and made the sky.

MOSES: Don't talk about shoes and socks with God!
And what's this with 'Your little hands and feet'?
Such blasphemous familiarity sounds like
you're chatting with your uncles.
Only something that grows needs milk.
Only something with feet needs shoes. Not God!
Even if you meant God's human representatives,
as when God said, 'My servant and I are one,'
even then this tone would be foolish and irreverent.
Body-and-birth language are right for us
on this side of the river, but not
for addressing the Origin. Not for Allah.

SHEPARD: The shepherd repented and tore his clothes
and sighed and wandered out into the desert.

MOSES: A sudden revelation came then to Moses. God's voice:

VOICE OF GOD: You have separated Me from one of My own.
Did you come as a Prophet to unite, or to sever?
I have given each being a separate and unique way
of seeing and knowing and saying that knowledge.
What seems wrong to you is right for him. Ways
of worshiping are not to be ranked as better
or worse than another.
It doesn't matter which direction you point your prayer rug.
Don't scold the lover!

MOSES: (*speaking along with the Voice*) I am apart from all that.
It's not me that's glorified in acts of worship.
It's the worshipers!

VOICE OF GOD: I don't hear the words they say.
I look inside at the humility. Forget phraseology.

MOSES: I want burning, burning!
   (shepherd seen in shadow, dancing with tambourine)
   Moses ran after the shepherd.
   He followed the bewildered footprints,
   in one place moving straight like a castle
   across a chessboard. In another, sideways
   like a bishop. *(Moses becomes shadow crossing screen.)*

   (The shepherd enters joyfully playing a tambourine and dancing.)

MOSES: *(entering)* Moses finally caught up with him.
   I was wrong. God has revealed to me
   that there are no rules for worship.
   Your sweet blasphemy is the truest devotion.
   Through you a whole world is freed.
   Loosen your tongue and don't worry what comes out.
   It's all the light of the spirit.

SHEPARD: Moses, Moses, I've gone beyond even that.
   You applied the whip and my horse shied and jumped
   out of itself. The Divine Nature and my human nature
   came together. *(One hand represents the Divine and the other
   the human nature. They come together.)*
   Bless your scolding hand and your arm.
   I can't say what has happened. Now my state is
   beyond telling. What I'm saying now
   is not my real condition. It can't be said.

SHEPARD: The shepherd grew quiet. *(a flute plays)*

MOSES: The flute player puts breath into a flute,
   so who makes the music?

SHEPARD: Not the flute. The flute player!

   (Moses and shepherd dance off to flute and tambourine.)

A SONG ABOUT A DONKEY

TWO SUFIS: The following is about the dangers
of imitating others in your spiritual life./
Meet the Friend on your own. (*Exeunt.*)

WANDERER: (*Enters, followed by servant.*) A wandering Sufi came with his
donkey

SERVANT: to a community of Sufis who were very poor.

SUFIS: They greeted him warmly/ took his donkey and
led it to the stable/ (*shadow of donkey*) where they
fed it and gave it water (*in shadow*).

SERVANT: The wandering Sufi and his servant went inside.

SUFIS: Immediately, a group of the resident Sufis
sold the donkey. (*in shadow, the donkey is led off*)
They bought food and candles for a feast./
(*music, others enter*)/ There was jubilation in the monastery!/
No more patience and three-day fasting! /
(*to audience*) If you are rich and full-fed,
don't laugh at the impulsiveness of the poor./ They were not acting
from their souls, but/ they were acting out of some necessity.

WANDERER: The traveler joined in the festivities.

SUFIS: They paid constant attention to him,/ caressing him,/
honoring him./
The sema began./ (*All dance in a circle, right hand up, left down.*)
There was smoke from the kitchen,/ dust from the
feet hitting the floor,/ and ecstasy from the longing
of the dancers./ Their hands were waving./ Their
foreheads swept low across the dais./
It had been a long wait for such an occasion./
Sufis always have to wait a long time for their desire./
That's why they're such great eaters!/
The Sufi who feeds on light, though, is different/
but there's only one of those in a thousand./
The rest live under that one's protection./

The sema ran its course and ended.

POET: The poet began to sing a deep grief-song;
The donkey is gone, my son. Your donkey is gone.

SUFIS: Everyone joined in,/ clapping their hands
and singing over and over,/
The donkey is gone,
my son, your donkey is gone

(The Wanderer's servant comes to tell him what happened. He refuses to listen.)

WANDERER: And the visiting Sufi sang more passionately
than all the rest, *(sings)* Your donkey is gone,
(dances) my son, your donkey is gone! *(repeat)*

SUFIS: *(Cock crow)* Finally it was dawn,/ and they parted with many
goodbyes. *(exeunt)*

WANDERER: The banquet room was empty. The man brought
out his baggage and called to his servant,

Where's my donkey?

SERVANT: Look at you!

WANDERER: What do you mean?

SERVANT: Your donkey is gone! They sold your donkey. That's how we
had such a celebration!

WANDERER: Why didn't you come and tell me?

SERVANT: Several times I came near, but you
were always singing so loudly, 'The donkey's gone,
the donkey's gone', that I thought you had a secret
insight.

WANDERER: Yes. It was my imitation of their joy

that caused this. (*exeunt*)

SUFIS: (two *enter*) The imitation here came
from the man's desire to be honored./
It deafened him to what was being
so constantly said./ Remember, there's only
one reason to do anything:/ a meeting with the Friend
is the only real payment.

INTERMISSION

THE TRICK OF HIDING IN A BOX

JUHI'S WIFE: This world is a small piece of brocade,
a preposterous frontispiece at the beginning
of a wonderful book.

JUHI: Anyone who believes this place
is all there is, let him or her be called,
'King of the World!

WIFE: Or 'Queen of the World!'

JUHI: O Body! You have enslaved so many free men
and women for so long! Quit plotting for a moment.
Be free from yourself for a little while
before you die.

WIFE: Find some other companion.
I'm finished playing your games. Beguile somebody else.
Say goodbye to me. You've taken almost my entire life.
Find some other victim.

JUHI: Which reminds me of the story of Juhi and his Wife
Every year when they got poor,
Juhi would turn to his wife and say, Sweetheart,
you still have your traps and lures intact. Go out,
and catch us some game. Lay snares for a big bird!
Show the bait, but withhold it. Let him know
what he wishes for, but disappoint him. Let him

look at what he wanted from inside the trap! (*exits*)

WIFE: So his wife went to the local judge.
    (*the judge enters*)
Sir, my husband will not support me as he should.
He doesn't give me what I need.

JUDGE: That's the way she began, and to cut the story short,
the judge was hooked by her flirtatious ways.
(*he leans to her*) There's too much commotion
in this courtroom. If you could meet me at my house,
then we could discuss in detail how your husband
has mistreated you.

WIFE: But I'm sure that there, as here, there'll be a constant
coming and going of people who want to talk with you.

JUDGE: What shall we do, sweet one?

WIFE: We could go to my house. No one is there.
My husband has gone to the country.
It'll be very private. Come at night.
No one will see you. Come when everyone's asleep
as though they'd drunk too much wine, dead-asleep
as though they'd been beheaded by the huge
black executioner, Night.

JUDGE: The judge watched her lips
move as she said all this. Such excitement
she wove around him!

WIFE: Woman can do this
very easily. Satan often talked cunningly
with Adam, but only when Eve told him to eat,
did he eat.

JUDGE: So the wise judge came at night
to make love with Juhi's wife.

WIFE: She had set the table
with two candles, a sweet desert, and wine.

JUDGE: I can do without these. I am already drunk
with wanting you.

JUHI: At this moment Juhi knocked on the door, his own door.
(three loud knocks)

JUDGE: The judge looked for a place to hide.

WIFE: There was only an old chest.

JUDGE: He climbed in, trembling. *(she slams lid down and locks chest)*

JUHI: *(enters)* O Wife, why are you always complaining?
I have sacrificed everything for you,
I own nothing now but this chest, which has, indeed,
become a source of suspicion in the community.
People think it's full of gold,

and so no one will give me any charity.

It's an attractive piece, isn't it?
But it's quite empty, believe me.
(knocks or kicks chest; sound shakes up judge)   In fact
it's a perfect metaphor for hypocrisy.
Handsome and dignified outside,
but a snake within. (Knocks again)
Tomorrow, I'll carry it out into
the middle of the bazaar and publicly burn it,
so that everyone can see that nothing was in it,
nothing. *(Knocks)*

WIFE: No! There is no need for that!

JUHI: But Juhi was determined. He repeated his plan several times.
Early the next morning he hired two porters
to carry the chest.

(enter porters who carry box and judge or carry box by space handles as judge scuttles along on his knees)

PORTER ONE: And as the porter was going along,

JUDGE: the judge decided it was time to act. Porter! O Porter!

PORTER ONE: The man looked right and left. (*they dump the space chest*)

PORTER TWO: Is this the voice of God, or is it a genii calling us?

JUDGE: This is not a revelation. This is coming from
    (*hits chest from inside three times*)
  inside the chest.

WIFE: A lover of world things has put himself
    in just such a box. Though he appears to be free,
    he can see nothing but the inside of his chosen chest.

JUHI: He moves from tomb to tomb.
    There's no end to this subject.

JUDGE: (*to porters who are crouched near to listen*)
    Go tell the court deputy to come and buy this chest,
    and take it, unopened, to the judge's house. (*porters exit*)

WIFE: Lord, appoint such powerful helpers
    to get us out of our body-boxes!

JUHI: Among thousands, there are only a few who even know
    that they are trapped inside a chest.

WIFE: Such a one gets a glimpse of the spiritual world.

DEPUTY: (*entering followed by porters*) The deputy came to the market
    where the chest had been brought.
    How much do you want for it?

JUHI: They're offering nine hundred gold dinars,
    but I can't go lower than a thousand.
    Do you have that much?

DEPUTY: Have you no shame in your short felt tunic?
The chest is obviously not worth that much!

JUHI: Well, maybe you're right, and it's certainly wrong
to be buying something in the dark.
I'll open the chest, and if it's not worth
what I'm asking, don't buy it.

DEPUTY: The deputy quickly insisted,
Keep the lid on. I want to buy it as it is.

JUHI: The haggling continued for a while longer.

DEPUTY: Finally the chest was sold to the court deputy
for a hundred dinars,

PORTER: and the judge was lugged home.
(porters carry judge in chest, as before)

WIFE: Everyone has a stable
and a trainer appointed to him or her.

JUHI: If you break away, the trainer comes and gets you.

WIFE: You think you're making choices, but the trainer
is actually leading you around.

JUHI: You like to deny that you have a keeper.
You say, It's my powerful animal urges.

NASUH

NASUH: Some time ago there was a man named Nasuh.
He made his living shampooing women in a bathhouse.
He had a face like a woman, but he was not effeminate,
though he disguised his virility, so as to keep his job.

(Shadow screen shows naked women washing and showering.)

He loved touching the women as he washed their hair.
He stayed sexually alert, at full strength,
all the time, massaging the beautiful women,

(Musician enters followed by the princess and her lady chamberlain.)

especially the Princess and her ladies-in-waiting.

(Princess and entourage exit. Shadow screen fades.)

Sometimes he thought of changing jobs,
of doing something
where he wouldn't be so constantly lustful,
but he couldn't quit.
He went to a gnostic saint.

(Shadow screen shows seated figure, perhaps with six arms waving.)

Please remember me in prayer.

GNOSTIC SAINT: That holy woman was spiritually free, and totally opened to God. She knew Nasuh's secret,

NASUH: but with God's gentleness she didn't speak it.

GNOSTIC SAINT: May God cause you to change your life
in the way you know you should.
That prayer traversed the Seven Heavens.
The means were found to change Nasuh. *(Shadow fades.)*

NASUH: While he was pouring water over the Princess,

PRINCESS: she felt and discovered that a pearl
was missing from her earring.

LADY CHAMBERLAIN: Quickly they locked the doors.

WOMEN: *(Entering)* They searched the cushions/ the towels/ the rugs/ and the discarded clothes./ Nothing.

LADY CHAMBERLAIN: Now they search ears and mouths

and every cleft and orifice.
Everyone is made to strip (*All go behind the shadow screen.*)
and the Queen's lady chamberlain
probes one by one
the naked women.

(*this shadowing continues behind Nasuh's following speech*)

NASUH: Nasuh, meanwhile
has gone to his private closet, trembling.
I didn't steal the pearl,
but if they undress and search me,
they'll see how excited I get
with these nude ladies.
God, please,
help me!
I have been cold and lecherous,
but cover my sin this time, please!

Let me not be exposed for how I've been.
I'll repent!
He weeps and moans and weeps,
for the moment is upon him.

LADY CHAMBERLAIN: (*in shadow*) Nasuh!
We have searched everyone but you. Come out!

NASUH: A long pause.
A long waiting silence.

WOMAN: Then a shout from one of the women. Here it is! (*She runs on
with it. All clap and enter excitedly.*)

NASUH: Nasuh sees his new life sparkling out before him.

PRINCESS: The women come to apologize. We're so sorry we didn't
trust you.

WOMAN: We just knew that you'd taken that pearl.

ANOTHER: They kept talking about how they'd suspected him,

ANOTHER: and begging his forgiveness.

NASUH: I am much more guilty than anyone has thought or said.
Don't ask my pardon!
You don't know me. No one knows me.
God has hidden my sneakiness. God saw what I did,
but chose not to publicly reveal my sin
     (The women fall into a dance and bring him into it, holding hands.)
And now, I am sewn back into Wholeness!   *(Exit, women)*

 I said
Oh No!
Help me!
And that Oh No! became a rope
let down into my well. I've climbed out to stand here
in the sun. One moment I was at the bottom
of a dank, fearful narrowness, and the next,
I am not contained by this Universe.
I wish everyone could know what I know.

LADY CHAMBERLAIN: Some time later the chamberlain came to Nasuh
The young Princess would like for you to wash her hair.
She will let no one touch her but you.

NASUH: Nasuh and the Princess had been very close,
but he replied,
Nasuh is very sick. I've lost my touch.
Look for someone else to tend the women's hair.
I'm out of that business.

     (Lady Chamberlain exits)

NASUH: The cold way I was still frightens me. In it, I tasted
a kind of bitter living-death.
But this new life is real. I will stay in its grace,
until my soul leaves my body.

     (Return of the gnostic saint shadow image.)

SAINT: One delight can only be replaced by a greater delight.
Nasuh found a Friend lovelier than the Princess.

THE LAW STUDENT AND THE SHROUD MAKER

JAHAN: Consider the story of Sadri Jahan of Bukhara,
who was very generous with beggars.
He wrapped pieces of gold in bits of paper
and gave them away as the sun and the moon
gamble their light.

(Beggars enter.)

BEGGER ONE: Every morning Jahan chose a different set of people.
One day it might be the sick.   *(becomes sick.)*

BEGGER TWO: Another, the widows, *(wails and mourns.)*

BEGGER THREE: or the law students,

BEGGER FOUR: or those in debt,

BEGGER FIVE: or the ordinary country people.
(all do a country step or two, to music.)

BEGGER WOMAN: Everybody had a turn to receive Jahan's gold.

JAHAN: *(entering)* He only had one rule:
You mustn't ask out loud.

BEGGER WOMAN: When he walked out, the mendicants stood
like silent walls on either side of his path.

JAHAN: If anyone made a begging sound to get his attention,
the punishment was no alms, ever again.
His motto was,
'blessed are the silent'.

BEGGER WOMAN: One day a wandering Begger woman blurted
out suddenly, Please sir, I'm hungry.

JAHAN: Have you no shame, old woman?

BEGGER WOMAN: Ah, but you're more shameless than I, Jahan.

JAHAN: How?

BEGGER WOMAN: You enjoy this world, and in your greed for giving you try to bring the other world here to enjoy that one too.

JAHAN: Sadri Jahan laughed and gave her money, (*Beggars gasp*) but except for that one instance, he never gave to those who spoke when he went by. (*exits*)

BEGGER: Another day it was the poor law students.

LAW STUDENT: One of them began a little involuntary whining noise as Jahan approached. (*whimpers*)

JAHAN: Jahan heard and noted the impatience, and the punishment began. (*gives to all students but him. exits*)

LAW STUDENT: Next day the law student put splints on his legs and wrapped them in rags and stood among the crippled with his head down.

JAHAN: (*enters*) But Jahan recognized him. (*exits*)

LAW STUDENT: The next day he put on a woman's robe and tried to mix with the widows, totally veiled.

JAHAN: (*enters*) But Jahan somehow knew which outstretched hand not to put alms in. (*pushes student aside*)

LAW STUDENT: In desperation the student went to a shroud-maker.
(*Fearfully. Enters at a creaking door. The shroud maker is frightening to him.*)
Wrap me in black felt and set me out on the road.
When Jahan comes by, say nothing.
Just sit beside me, and anything he gives,
I'll split with you.

SHROUD MAKER: So there they were,
the student lying wrapped in his shroud,
and the other beside him.

JAHAN: (*enters*) Jahan paused and dropped some gold pieces
on the shroud.

LAW STUDENT: The dead man's hand shot out to grab it,

SHROUD MAKER: so the shroud-maker wouldn't run off with the take.

LAW STUDENT: (*unwrapping himself and getting up*) See, Jahan,
I found a way back into your generosity.

JAHAN: Yes, but you had to die to do it.

BEGGERWOMAN: (*entering*) Here is the mystery
of 'die before you die.' Favors come
only after you develop the skill of dying.
Be silent and wait.

THE DEBTOR SHEIKH

SHEIKH: (*Entering, supported by two Sufis.*) Sheikh Ahmed was continually in debt.

SUFI ONE: He borrowed great sums from the wealthy
and gave them out to the poor dervishes of the world.

SHEIKH: He built a Sufi monastery by borrowing,

SUFI TWO: and God was always paying his debts, turning sand
into flour for this Generous Friend.

(*The Sufis gently help the Sheikh sit and support him.*)

SUFI ONE: For years, until his death, he scattered seed
profusely.

SHEIKH: Even very near his death,

SUFI TWO: with the signs of death clear,

SHEIKH: he sat surrounded by creditors,
   (Creditors enter and sit at the Sheikh's feet.)

SUFI ONE: the creditors in a circle. and the Great
  Sheikh in the center gently melting
  into himself like a candle.

CREDITORS: The creditors were so sour-faced with worry/
  that they could hardly breathe.

SHEIKH: Look at these despairing men. Do they think
  God does not have four hundred gold dinars.

BOY: *(in shadow, calling out. The tray is seen in shadow.)*
  Halvah, a sixth of a direm
  for a piece! Fresh Halvah!

SHEIKH: Sheikh Ahmed, with a nod of his head

SERVANT: directed the famulus to go and buy
  the whole tray of halvah. *(exits)*

SHEIKH: Maybe if these creditors eat a little sweetness,
  they won't look so bitterly on me.

SERVANT: *(in shadow with the boy)* How much for the whole lump of halvah?

BOY: Half a dinar, and some change.

SERVANT: Don't ask too much from Sufis my son.
  Half a dinar is enough.

  (Servant and the boy enter.)

BOY: The boy handed over the tray *(a space tray onstage)*

SERVANT: and the servant brought it to the Sheikh,

SHEIKH: who passed it among his creditor guests.
   Please eat and be happy.

CREDITORS: The tray was quickly emptied,

BOY: and the boy asked the Sheikh for his half a gold dinar.

SHEIKH: Where would I find such money? These men can tell
   you how in debt I am, and besides,
   I am fast on my way into non-existence.

BOY: The boy threw the tray on the floor
   and started weeping loud and yelling. I wish
   I had broken my legs before I came in here! I wish
   I had stayed in the bathhouse today. You
   gluttonous, plate-licking Sufis, washing
   your faces like cats! O Sheikh,
   my master will beat me if I come back without anything.

CREDITORS: The creditors joined in./How could you do this?/
   You've devoured our properties, and now you add this
   one last debt before you die./ Why?

SHEIKH: The sheikh closes his eyes and does not answer.

BOY: The boy weeps until afternoon prayers.

SHEIKH: The Sheikh withdraws underneath his coverlet,
   pleased with everything, pleased with Eternity,
   pleased with death, and totally unconcerned
   with all the reviling talk around him.

SUFI ONE: On a bright-moon night, do you think the moon
   cruising through the tenth house,
   can hear the dogs barking down here?

SUFI TWO: Water does not lose its purity because
   of a bit of weed floating in it.

SUFI ONE: The king drinks wine on the riverbank until dawn, listening to the water music, not hearing the frog-talk.

CREDITOR: The money due the boy would have been just a few pennies from each of his creditors,

SHEIKH: but the Sheikh's spiritual power prevents that from happening.

CREDITOR: No one gives the boy anything.

(the boy howls and howls)

HATIM'S SERVANT: *(enters)* After afternoon prayers a servant comes with a tray from Hatim, a friend of Ahmad's, and a man of great property. A covered tray.

SHEIKH: The Sheikh uncovers the face of the tray,

SUFI ONE: and on it there are four hundred gold dinars,

SUFI TWO: and in one corner, another half a dinar wrapped in a piece of paper.
(it is thrown to the boy)

CREDITORS: Immediately the cries of abasement/ O King of Sheikhs/ Lord of the Lords of Mystery/   forgive us!/ We were bumbling and crazed./ We were knocking lamps over/ We...

SHEIKH: It's all right. You will not be held responsible for what you've said or done. The secret here is that I asked God and the way was shown that until the boy's weeping, God's merciful generosity was not loosened. *(He rises with help and making his exit, followed by all, speaks to audience.)*
Let the boy be like the pupil of your eye.
If you want to wear a robe of spiritual sovereignty, let your eyes weep with the wanting.

THE INDIAN PARROT

MERCHANT: There was a merchant setting out for India.
   (Claps hands; servants enter.)
   He asked each male and female servant
   what they wanted to be brought as a gift.

SERVANTS: Each told him a different exotic object:/
   a piece of silk/ a brass figurine/
   a pearl necklace. *(exeunt)*

MERCHANT: Then he asked his beautiful caged parrot,
   the one with such a lovely voice.

PARROT: *(She appears singing without words)* When you see the Indian
   parrots, describe my cage. Say that I need guidance
   here in my separation from them. Ask how
   our friendship can continue with me so confined
   and them flying about freely in the meadow mist.

   Tell them that I remember well our mornings
   moving together from tree to tree.

   Tell them that the sound of their quarreling
   high in the trees would be sweeter
   to hear than any music.

   Tell them to drink one cup of ecstatic wine
   in honor of me here in the dregs of my life.

CHORUS: *(enters)* This parrot is the spirit-bird in all of us,
   that part that wants to return to freedom,
   and is the freedom. What she wants from
   India is herself.

MERCHANT: So this parrot gave her message to the merchant
   and when he reached India, he saw a field
   full of parrots. *(Parrots, flying in space.)* He stopped
   and called out what she had said,

Tell them to drink one cup of ecstatic wine
in honor of me here in the dregs of my life.

A PARROT: One of the nearest parrots shivered
and stiffened and fell down dead.

> *(a parrot falls)*

MERCHANT: This one is surely kin
to my parrot. I shouldn't have spoken.

> *(The other birds scoop up the fallen parrot and take it off.)*

He finished his trading and returned home
with the presents for his workers.

PARROT: *(enters)* when he got to the parrot, she demanded her gift.
What happened when you told my story
to the Indian Parrots?

MERCHANT: I'm afraid to say.

PARROT: Master, you must!

MERCHANT: When I spoke your complaints to the field
of chattering parrots, it broke
one of their hearts.

She (he) must have been a close companion,
or a relative, for when she heard about you
she grew quiet and trembled, and died.

PARROT: As the caged parrot heard this, she herself
quivered and sank to the cage floor.

MERCHANT: This merchant was a good man. *(Enters cage area.)*
He grieved deeply for his parrot, murmuring
distracted phrases, self-contradictory-
cold, then loving-clear, then
murky with symbolism.

CHORUS: *(enters)* A drowning man reaches for anything!
　　The Friend loves this flailing about
　　better than any lying still,
　　and whatever you do, that king
　　watches through the window.

MERCHANT: When the merchant threw the 'dead' parrot
　　out of the cage,

PARROT: it spread its wings
　　and glided to a nearby tree!

MERCHANT: The merchant suddenly understood the mystery.
　　Sweet singer, what was the message
　　that taught you this trick?

PARROT: She told me that it was the charm
　　of my voice that kept me caged.
　　Give it up, and be released!
　　She told him one or two more spiritual truths,
　　and then a tender goodbye. *(Flies off and is seen on the shadow
　　screen, wings soaring)*

MERCHANT: God protect you, as you go on your new way.
　　I hope to follow you.

THE THREE FISH

FISH ONE: This is the story of the lake and the three big fish
　　that were in it, one of them intelligent,

FISH TWO: *(enters)* another half-intelligent,

FISH THREE: *(enters)* and the third, stupid.

FISHERMAN ONE: *(in shadow)* Some fishermen came to the edge of the
　　lake

FISHERMAN TWO:　　with their nets. *(net thrown, in shadow)*

FISH THREE: The three fish saw them. (*they pull back together, quickly*)

FISH ONE: The intelligent fish decided at once to leave,
to make the long difficult trip to the ocean.
She thought, I won't consult these two on this.
They will only weaken my resolve, because they love
this place so. They call it home. Their ignorance
will keep them here. It's right to love your home place,
but first ask, Where is that, really? I'm leaving.
(*the other two are seen moving their lips, making fish faces*)
Sometimes there's no one to talk to.
You must just set out on your own.
So the intelligent fish made its whole length
a moving footprint and, like a deer the dogs chase,
suffered greatly on its way, but finally made it
to the edgeless safety of the sea. (*exits*)

FISH TWO: The half-intelligent fish thought, My guide
has gone. I ought to have gone with her, but I didn't
and now I've lost my chance to escape.
I wish I'd gone with her. Don't regret what's happened.
If it's in the past, let it go. Don't even remember it.
I'll belly up on the surface and float like weeds float,
just giving myself totally to the water. To die before I die,
as Muhammed said to. So he did that.
He bobbed up and down, helpless,
within arm's reach of the fishermen.

FISHERMAN ONE: (*in shadow*) Look at this! The best and biggest fish is
dead!

FISHERMAN TWO: One of the men lifted him by the tail,
spat on him, and threw him up on the ground. (*seen in shadow*)

FISH TWO: He rolled over and over and slid secretly near
the water, and then, back in. (*exits*)

FISH THREE: Meanwhile, the third fish, the dumb one,
was jumping about, trying to escape
with his agility and cleverness.

The net, of course,
finally closed around him, and
    (to show skillet, add large opaque paper circle to the projection)
as he lay in the terrible frying-pan bed,
(sound of fish frying in a pan)   he thought,
If I get out of this,
I'll never live again in the limits of a lake.
Next time, the ocean! I'll make the infinite my home!
    (a great cry!)
The infinite!

THE WOMAN (OR MAN) WHO WANTED TO LEARN THE LANGUAGE OF ANIMALS

WOMAN: A woman asked Moses,
    Teach me the language of animals.
    Hopefully, listening to them will increase my Faith.
    Human language seems to be mostly about getting food and fame. It
    may be the animals have different concerns,
    like what the moment of death means.

MOSES: This is a dangerous ability for you to want.
    Wake yourself up in some other way. Try to learn
    about God directly, not from other people's words,
    not from books, not even from animal sounds.

WOMAN: Of course, that just makes the woman want to learn
    animal-language all the more. Moses,
    don't disappoint me in this. It's my last hope.

MOSES: Moses asks God, What shall I do? She's set on this
    one thing.

GOD'S VOICE: Teach her what she wants.

MOSES: But this special power is not suitable for her.

GOD'S VOICE: Give her what she's asking for.
    She's free to choose.

MOSES: *(to woman)* What you want will terrify you.

I don't think you really want it.

WOMAN: Yes I do. Teach me the language
of the dog and the chicken.

MOSES: (*squeezes her head*) It's done.
(*a cock's crow is heard*)

WOMAN: At daybreak, to test this out,
the woman stands in the doorway
(*a maid appears, shaking out a cloth*)
and watches a maid
shake out a tablecloth.

(*Woman sits at side of stage and watches the following:*)

ROOSTER: A piece of bread from the night before
falls to the ground, and a rooster quickly pecks it up.

DOG: A dog standing nearby says, This is not fair.
You eat grains of corn, which I can't. You enjoy barley
and all the rest. But that crust of bread!
You know how I
love the greasy leftover scraps. You should have
let me have it. That was such a mean thing for you to do,
to scarf it up before I could get to it.

ROOSTER: Do not complain. Be quiet. God will give you something
much better in place of this. The master's horse is
going to die tomorrow. Tomorrow will be a feast day for dogs!

WOMAN: As soon as the woman, who owned the horse, hears this,
she leads the horse to market and sells it.

ROOSTER: The next day the Rooster and Dog have a similar discussion.

DOG: You said the horse would die, but look,
the horse is gone. You lied.

ROOSTER: That horse did die,

but not here. The woman sold the horse
so the loss would be someone else's. Tomorrow though,
her mule will die.

WOMAN: Immediately the mule is sold,
and on the third day the dogs says,

DOG: Liar, Prince of Liars,
Where is my surprise banquet! Liar!

ROOSTER: I didn't lie. The mule is dead,
but, again, sold before it happened.
Tomorrow, I predict, and I'm always right, her slave will die,
and the next of kin will scatter out lots of bread
for beggars and dogs.

WOMAN: The woman, of course, hears and happily
sells her dying slave for a fine profit.
She laughs,   three times since I learned the language of dogs and
chickens, I have been saved from big losses.   *(Sits to watch)*

DOG: Rooster, what's your sniveling excuse this time?
Where are the bits and pieces you prophesied? Nothing
but lies roost in your nest, and nothing but lies
walk the dooryard.

ROOSTER: Not so, not so. Roosters are truthful.
We watch the sun inside us. You could turn a big basin
over the top of me, and I would still crow at dawn.
Such inner-sun-knowers are God's gift to mankind.
We wake people up and remind them of their prayers.

DOG: The dog said nothing.

ROOSTER: I have another prediction for you.
Tomorrow the owner herself will die,
and her heir, in mourning, will slaughter a cow.
Some of the leavings will reach you,
pieces of roast meat and thin, hardcrusted bread,
just what you like. *(Exeunt, Rooster and Dog)*

WOMAN: So the woman hears the rooster's prediction
and runs to Moses, save me, please save me.

MOSES: *(who has entered)* Why don't you sell yourself!
You've become so expert at avoiding loss.
Putting the suffering off on someone else!
I saw this coming on the side of a brick.
But you couldn't see it if were it in your mirror.

WOMAN: Moses, don't rub my nose in it. At least
bless my Soul before I die.
With that she began to feel
very sick.

MOSES: Yes, try to vomit up your profiteering!

WOMAN: The woman can't answer. *(Exits. Enters shadow area, showing sickness)*

MOSES: At dawn Moses gets up and prays, Lord, forgive her
her impudence. No one who can't keep her mouth shut
is fit to learn the secrets of the Unseen. Only seabirds
live on the ocean. This one is definitely a land-bird.
She's sinking. Help her.

GOD'S VOICE: *(Shadow of woman listening hopefully)*
Would you like me to raise her from the dead?
For you, Moses, I would raise everyone from the dead!

MOSES: No. Dying is proper for this world. *(Shadow of woman dismayed at this)*
Give her,
and everyone, the mercy of Faith in the next world.

GOD'S VOICE: And it was done.

BREADMAKING

COURTIER: There was a feast. *(company enter drinking)*

KING: The King was heartily in his cups.
   He saw a learned scholar walking by. (*in shadow, a man is
   reading a scroll*))
   Bring him in, and give him some of this fine wine.

SERVANTS: Servants rushed out and brought the man
   to the king's table. (*he is offered wine*)

SCHOLAR: But he was not receptive. I had rather drink poison!
   I have never tasted wine and never will!
   Take it away from me!

SERVANTS/DANCERS: He kept on with these loud refusals/
   disturbing the atmosphere of the feast./
   This is how it sometimes is at God's table./
   Someone who has heard about ecstatic love,
   but never tasted it, disrupts the banquet.

KING: The king gave orders. Cupbearer, do what you must.

CUPBEARER: This is how your invisible guide acts,
   the chess champion across from you that always wins.
      (*two of the men hold the scholar*)
   He cuffed the scholar's head. Taste! Again!

MUSICIAN: The cup was drained, (*a long pause as the scholar waits to see
   if he'll be affected; the cupbearer beats on a tambourine, the scholar's eye-
   twitches, etc.*)

SCHOLAR: and the intellectual started singing (*he dances, arms out,
   towards the women*)
   and telling ridiculous jokes. Did you hear the one about...
   Soon, of course, he had to pee.

   He went out, and there, near the latrine (*in shadow*)
   was a beautiful woman,

WOMAN: (*in shadow*) one of the king's harem.

SCHOLAR: His mouth hung open. He wanted her!

WOMAN: And she was not unwilling.

(They embrace and slowly fall to the ground, in shadow.)

(The following verses on breadmaking divided among the company:)

You've seen a baker rolling dough.
He kneads it gently at first,
then more roughly.

He pounds it on the board.
It softly groans under his palms.
Now he spreads it out
and rolls it flat.

Then he bunches it,
and rolls it all the way out again,
thin. Now he adds water,
and mixes it well.

Now salt,

and a little more salt.

Now he shapes it delicately
to its final shape,
then slides it into the oven,
which is already hot.

You remember breadmaking!
This is how your desire
tangles with a desired one.

And it's not just a metaphor
for a man and a woman making love.

Warriors in battle do like this too.
A great mutual embrace is always happening
between the eternal and what dies,
between essence and accident.

The sport has different rules
in every case, but it's basically the same,

KING: the way you make love is the way
God will be with you.

WOMAN: (*in shadow*) So these two were lost in their sexual trance.

SCHOLAR: (*in shadow*) They did not care anymore about feasting or wine.

WOMAN: Their eyes were closed like
perfectly matching calligraphy lines

KING: The king came looking for the scholar.
What he beheld was like the commotion
on the day of Resurrection.

    (shadow figures leap apart)

SCHOLAR: The scholar sprang up in terror,
(enters) and fleeing to the banquet-hall, seized a wine cup.
    (the girl enters)

KING: *(entering)* The king, full of fire and fury,
called out for the blood of the guilty pair.

SCHOLAR: O cup-bearer, why do you sit there dumbfounded!
Give him some wine and put him in good humor.

    (All look at king, who laughs. All laugh.)

KING: O sir, I am restored to my good humor; the girl is yours.
As Muhammed said, A good king must serve his subjects
from his own table.

    (All dance as lights go down. Lights come up on the curtain call.)

Three Additional Stories of Rumi:

SNOW AND THE VOICE

BU'L: After Bestami died, it happened
as he said it would, that Bu'l-Hasan
became the sheikh for the community,
and everyday he would go to Bestami's tomb
to receive instruction.

BESTAMI: *(in shadow)* Bu'l-Hasan had been told to do this
in a dream, by Bestami himself.

BU'L: Every dawn he went and stood facing the grave
until mid-morning.

BESTAMI: Either the spirit of Bestami
would come to talk to him,

BU'L: or in silence
the questions he had would be answered.
    (snow falls in shadow)
But one night a deep snow fell.
The graves were
indistinguishable.

Bu'l-Hasan felt lost.
Then he heard the sheikh's voice.

BESTAMI: *(walking, in shadow, through snow fall)*
    The world is made of snow. It falls and melts
and falls again. Don't be concerned
with that. Come toward the sound
of my Voice. Always move
in this direction. *(shadow light out.)*

BU'L: And from that day Bu'l-Hasan began to experience the enlightened
state
which he had only heard about before.

SPILLING THE ROSE OIL

GROCER: There was a grocer with a fine parrot,
which could talk intelligently to customers
in several languages, and to the merchants
bringing fruits and vegetables.

(parrot speaks foreign language gibberish to merchants and customers)

PARROT: He could also sing sweet songs in his
parrot language. *(sings in gibberish)*

GROCER: Once the grocer had to leave for a moment,

PARROT: And the parrot accidentally knocked over
some rose oil from off a shelf.

GROCER: The grocer
came back and sat down with great confidence
and high good-humor as a merchant always does
in front of his shop.
Then he realized that his clothes
were soaked with greasy rose oil. He bopped the parrot
on the head so that the top feathers came out

PARROT: and the parrot looked bald. *(looks in mirror, bemoans his looks)*

GROCER: For several days afterward
the parrot was quiet. It said nothing

PARROT: in any language, not even its own.

GROCER: The grocer felt
terrible. Three days and three nights he grieved
and repented that he had silenced his Friend.
He felt his well-being and his prosperity leaving him.

(a dervish enters crossing the stage)

DERVISH: He gave gifts to every dervish that he saw,

hoping to restore the speech of the parrot.

(second dervish enters)

SECOND DERVISH: Finally a bareheaded dervish came by
with a head as bald as a begging bowl.

PARROT: Hey-hey, screeched the parrot,
Here's another klutz who spilt the rose oil!

(exeunt second dervish and parrot, still cackling)

GROCER: A true human being is never what he or she
appears to be. Rub your eyes,
and look again.

THE CAMEL DRIVER'S SONG

SUFI: A sufi was on the path of clarity.
Every day he walked the desert, and every night
he slept in the emptiness of God's custody.
One night he came upon a merchant's
tent and felt the need for conversation.
He lifted the tent flap and saw a black slave

SLAVE: in chains unable to move,

SUFI: but shining
with intelligence like the moon.

SLAVE: *(whispering)* Help me.
My master will not refuse a guest.
Ask him to set me free.

MERCHANT: *(enters)* The merchant
welcomed the sufi to his tent and brought food.

SUFI: I cannot accept your generosity until you release
this poor man.

MERCHANT: I will. But first listen
   to what I have suffered because of him!
   I used to have many pure-bred camels, beautiful animals,
   with humps like mountains, swift as the wind over
   steeps and flat, powerful as rhinosceri,
   tall and dignified like elephants.
   Their crossing
   and recrossing this desolation were the source
   of my joy, their bells my most
   wished for sound.
   As they traveled this camel driver
   sang songs. They heard and carried their loads
   with courage and discipline. This time,
   though, when we unloaded them, they fled in every
   direction, vanished in the desert, all but
   the one still tied outside my tent.

SUFI: The sufi said,
   Let me hear the camel driver's song.

MERCHANT: The master gestured,

SLAVE: and the slave began.

   (sings)

SUFI: The visitor
   sat politely watching the tethered animal, but
   as the longing for freedom deepened in the song,
   the night-walker tore his clothes
   and fell on the ground,

MERCHANT: While the camel
   snapped its rope and escaped into the darkness.

   (The song ends.)

Frank Farrell in *The Golden Key*, seen in the light of an overhead projection, Learning Theater, Chicago, 1980

Norris McNamara

Overhead projection helps create the setting for *A Robber Bridegroom*. Kathy Kirk works in stage space at the Learning Theater

Norris McNamara

DESIGNING FOR STORY THEATER

In all stories the space transforms from cottage to castle, ground to sky, through the forest to under the sea and this must be shown by players with the help of lighting and changes in stage color, height and shape. Spolin's space walks will help the company relax bodily holds, flow through space and shape it as if it were a substance so they can play onstage, without scenery or props.

SHADOW SCREENS and SHADOW PLAY:

A genuine visual effect is possible with the use of shadows and projection of colored gels onto a playing area and shadow screen, changing with the story's transformations.

For instance, screens 4' or 5' wide x 8' tall surround a center screen 10' wide by 8' tall and are each backlit by 150 watt lamps on dimmers controlled by the lighting person. The stage muslin is stretched onto frames made of two by fours. The screens must be screwed into the stage floor and anchored from behind the top to the walls. Masking is used as necessary. The players move closely behind the screens; their shadows appearing when the screens are backlit. When onstage, players work with space substance objects, but when in shadow use real props to show objects. Thus, Simpleton may carry a cut-out cardboard goose shape when in shadow but emerge onstage carrying a space goose. The audience is delighted by this. Any offstage event can be shown this way. Clever Gretel preparing the chicken, feathers flying, cleaver swinging, followed by her entrance with a space chicken on a space spit. Another player or players on a mike provide sound effects.

By playing with the shadows, experimenting with the height of the light sources for the screens, we have filled the screens with the lower half of giants, and amplified their voices. Players become adept at finding shadow images for their parts. Long entrances or exits on two or three screens can be effective. A platform behind the screens to raise the action a few inches helps to show the full figure.

OVERHEAD PROJECTIONS

Overhead projectors are part of every school's equipment and can be borrowed or rented for productions. Stage lighting gelatins in a wide variety of colors can be cut into patterns with scissors and the pieces over-laid to create new color combinations upon a clear acetate ground, made to size,[1] in order to cover your shadow screen fully.

You can also paint on the acetate with colored inks or transparent theater projection dyes. [2] Opaques, either painted or cut-out, will read black on the shadow screen. The forms and colors are projected from the front so that the players' faces and bodies take the colored light, which can be very effective, or a leico or fresnel can wash it off the player while allowing the color to reach the back screens, as long as this lamp does not also spill onto the screens. A projector from each side of the playing area with two operators has been used, projecting onto large shadow screens stage left and stage right (with a pass-through between the two screens, stage center). In the case of a single projector covering a large screen, stage center, the operator works from the center of the front row of the audience and the projected beam can cover a width of twelve feet or more. Shadows can and do appear while projections are on. The projection must be not be too pale when the shadow light comes up or the shadow will not appear strongly. This may necessitate adding an abstract shape in a deeper

---

[1] The artwork, no larger than 8"x11" rests on the flat surface of the overhead projector. Pieces of colored gel are laid on clear acetate, inside an acetate folder. The gel can be attached on the outer edge with double sided tape, but not in the area of the art work that is projected, or it would be seen on the screen. The artist creating this design work must spend some time with the projector, once the shadow screen is up, working out the dimensions of the required art work in terms of the distance from the screen the projector will sit (say, 17 feet) and the area of the stage needing to be covered. The flat surface of the projector is masked, leaving an opening the size of the projections, which are placed on it manually by the operator at the beginning of each story, the stage having gone to black at the end of each story. At the end of a story, the projectionist covers the artwork with an opaque cover, removes the previous artwork with one hand and places the new artwork onto the surface. The opaque cover is removed at the beginning of the next story. Change can occur during a scene by lifting or adding layers of pattern or color. Much variation is possible. Keep each story's acetate folders in a separate manilla folder. The projector stays on the whole time; otherwise the operator can have a handheld switch to cue the projector to the music and/or action that initiates each scene or story. Before each performance, check the artwork and dust the gelatins.

[2] Roscoe lacquer dyes; brilliant transparent projection colors. Rosco Laboratories, Port Chester, NY 10573

hue at the moment it is needed, in its own sleeve of clear acetate. Generally, a new projection is made for each story, sometimes with two or more variations for scene changes within a story. Without a lighting expert and expensive equipment, really with only minimal general lighting, the effect can be gratifying. The richness of light and sound and color brought about by the play of all this provides a multitude of cues for the actors, and makes fellow players of the musicians, lighting and sound effects people and the projectionist.

SLIDE PROJECTIONS

Another approach to visual transformations of stage space are slides, which allow the projection of paintings[3] or photographs, usually from the back of the house, over the heads of the audience. As with overhead projections, everything depends upon the quality of the transparencies. The director must involve the artist(s) early in production, so that there is time for the work to be undertaken, and viewed during rehearsals. The slides must be completed before previews begin, which will give all (on-stage and off-stage) players the needed time to learn the cues. This is true for the overhead projection art work as well; even though trips to a darkroom won't be needed, changes will certainly be called for.

STAGE FURNITURE

For thrones, beds, carriage seats, chairs, all that is needed are two or three benches and/or wooden cubes with a cut-out in the top for picking up and moving them, which the players do. They must be painted to go with the production.

Carol Bleackley, 1999

---

[3] We did this effectively for our production of *A Christmas Carol*, and include cues for the slide changes in this edition.

MUSIC NOTES FOR STORY THEATER

Each story can be underscored whenever it is appropriate with traditional music such as folk songs, blues, country and western, talking blues, ballad, reggae and gospel. For instance, I am currently rehearsing *All Three of Us*, one of the stories in *The Blue Light and Other Stories*, to a rhythmic baseline found in reggae and setting *Our Lady's Child* to gospel such as the classic *Pale Horse* or the hymn Mahalia Jackson sang, *Trouble of the World*. Incidental music can be added where it is desired; piano, a folk rock group, wind instruments, drum; any orchestration. Each story and scene does have a musical quality that can be found. Music will underscore the emotional tone desired in a scene.

For Rilke's *Stories of God*, a couple of albums of Russian folk music will give your musicians the rhythm and tone for the three *bylini*, folk tales that he retold.

For all these stories, it is not a song itself we are after, but contact with the traditional sound and rhythm on which we can improvise.

For *RUMI*, Spring, '98 in New York, we used contemporary Arabic dance hall music, influenced by western rock bands, called *Rai*, "the young music of dissent."[1] To hear the music from a classic Mevlevi ceremony, order the CD *Wherever You Turn is the Face of God.*[2] The music for the workshop production, Winter '99, was composed and played on electric piano by Fred Kaz with flute and guitar music played by Christopher Allport.

---

[1]·The Music of North Africa, World Music Network, 6 Abbeville Mews, 88 Calpham Park Road, London SW4 7BX.

[2] Water Lily Acoustics, P.O. Box 91418, Santa Barbara CA 93190.

HORSEBACK RIDING

The trick of simulating riding on the stage is to use the legs as if they were the front legs of a horse, stamping the earth with the ball of the foot, lifting the knees to trot or gallop. In moving, the upper body should ride on the lower body, and one hand can seem to hold the reins while the other can carry a flag or lance or reach behind the rider as if slapping the horse's flank.

It is also possible to give a sense of the horse rearing on its hind legs, by imitating the way these legs would stamp the ground, and using the rider's arms and hands as if they were the front legs of the horse pawing the air to steady itself, as the rider leans back. In this way the audience can see the invisible body of the horse as if it were there.

For the sound of hoof beats, the two dry shells of a halved coconut can be held and tapped together in a right-sounding rhythm.

THEATER GAMES

FOR

STORY THEATER

Viola Spolin

Theater Games for Story Theater by Viola Spolin

Copyright © 2000 by Paul Sills

THEATER GAMES FOR
STORY THEATER

Introduction by Viola Spolin   p. 217

First Section of Theater Games for Story Theater   p. 219

A. Introductory Exercises   p. 220
B. Playground Series   p. 231
C. Part of a Whole Series   p. 236
D. Traditional Games   p. 243

Second Section of Theater Games For Story Theater   p. 245

A. Verbal Agility Series   p. 246
B. Vocal/Technical Series   p. 254
C. Integration of On & Offstage Activity Series   p. 259
D. Character/Technical   p. 262

Third Section: Preparing the Story for Performance   p. 270

A. Finding the Story
B. Story Becomes Group Support
C. Casting
D. Editing the Written Story for Performance
E. Run-Throughs for Performance

Alphabetical List of Theater Games for Story Theater   p. 271

Viola Spolin

INTRODUCTION

Story Theater is a way to tell myths, legends, folk and fairy tales as well as history and literature with theatrical integrity. Players, who both tell the story and play the character, work in open space which they shape to show the natural world, helping the audience see the invisible. Shadow screens, projections, curtains and music assist the transformation, as well as vocal sound effects and minimal lighting, with only the occasional need for blocks or ramps to give height or a touch of abstraction to a set.

This handbook was organized to give players the theatrical techniques necessary for story theater performance. The selection of theater games is an exerpt from the greater body of games in *Improvisation for the Theater*.[1] Lesson plans have been avoided as the time allowed for workshops or rehearsals will vary. It is suggested that you progress in sequence from section to section, drawing at least one game from each series in a section.

The First Section of Theater Games introduces players to space and space objects and will generate trust and a spirit of play within your group. The traditional games included here may be played as warmups to sessions or whenever energy levels begin to fall within a rehearsal.

The games presented in the Second Section will help to develop theatrical experience. Played during the rehearsal period,[2] these exercises[3] will introduce the sidecoaching vocabulary that brings rehearsals to life and help to give players specific theatrical techniques.

The Third Section: Preparing the Story for Performance is an outline for a group to begin work on a story and to engage in the process of arriving at a script.

Include time for storytelling. You tell stories and let the players tell stories.[4] For a story theater performance, whatever acting problems

---

[1] Northwestern University Press, 625 Colfax St, Evanston, IL , 60201

[2] See Paul Sills' introduction to *A Christmas Carol*, p. 59, for a short discussion of these exercises.

[3] SpolinTheater Games that Paul Sills has added to her original manuscript for this anthology, include Feeling Self with Self, two Slow Motion games, Gibberish Demonstration and Gibberish/English, Give and Take Warmup, No Motion, Extended Sound, Stage Picture and several traditional games from Neva Boyd's Handbook of Traditional Games (Dover Press): New York, Pussy Wants a Corner and Who Started the Motion?

[4] *Building a Story*, p. 247

need to be solved in rehearsal, the players' focus must be on telling the story. It is the spiritual passion of telling a story that unites player to player and players to audience.

The trap for most beginners, child or adult, is "in the head" acting. To escape the trap there must be focus. The games will give players experience of focus that can free them from their ideas of acting and make real what it means to tell a story on stage.

Viola Spolin, 1970

F<small>IRST</small> S<small>ECTION OF</small> T<small>HEATRE</small> G<small>AMES FOR</small> S<small>TORY</small> T<small>HEATRE</small>:

A. INTRODUCTORY EXERCISES

FEELING SELF WITH SELF:

Focus: on feeling self with self.

This exercise, which gives players a full body perception of self, can follow a traditional game to start workshops and may be used frequently, alone or leading into a **Space Walk**.

Description: Entire group sits quietly. Players physically feel what is against their bodies with their bodies as side coached. Side coach continuously. If necessary, coach players to keep their eyes open.

Side Coaching: **Feel your self with your self! Feel your feet with your feet! Feel your feet in your stockings and your stockings on your feet! Feel your slacks or skirt on your legs and your legs in your slacks or skirt! Feel your underclothing next to your body and your body next to your underclothing! Feel your shirt against your chest and your chest inside your shirt! Feel your ring on your finger and your finger in your ring! Feel the hair on your head! Your eyebrows on your forehead! Feel your nose against your cheeks! Your ears! Your tongue inside your mouth! Try to feel the inside of your head with your head! Feel all the space around you! Now let the space feel you!**

Evaluation: Was there a difference between feeling your ring on your finger and feeling your finger in the ring?

Space Walks and Space Shaping:

Introduction

Space Walks and **Space Shaping** exercises are ways of perceiving/sensing/experiencing the environment (space) around us as an actual dimension in which all can enter, communicate, live and be free. Each player becomes a receiving/sending instrument capable of reaching out beyond the physical self and the immediate environment. As water supports and surrounds marine life, space substance surrounds and supports us. Objects made of space substance may be looked upon as thrusts/projections of the (invisible) inner self into the visible world, intuitively perceived/sensed as a manifest phenomenon, *real!* When the invisible (not yet emerged, inside, unknown) becomes visible - seen and perceived - theater magic! This is the fertile ground of the poet, the artist, the seeker.

SPACE WALK #1 (EXPLORATION):

Focus: on feeling space with the whole body.

Description: Players move around and physically investigate space as an unknown substance. Leader walks with players during side coaching.

Side Coaching: **Move through the substance and make contact with it! Use your whole body to make contact! Feel it against your cheeks! Your nose! Your knees! Your hips! Let it (space) feel you! Feel your body shape as you move through it!** (If players tend to use hands only, coach: **Let your hands be as one with the rest of your body! Move as a single mass!**) **Explore the substance! You never felt it before! Make a tunnel! Move back into the space your body has shaped! Shake it up! Make it fly! Make it ripple! Eyes open!**

SPACE WALK #2 (SUPPORT AND EFFORT)

Focus: on letting space support you or holding yourself together as side coached.

Description: Players walk around, moving through the space substance, open to the side coaching. After the players are responding to the support of space, coach them to support themselves. Then, coach players to go back to letting space support them. Calling out parts of the body helps to release muscle holds. Change back and forth until the difference between space support and holding self together is realized by players.

Side Coaching: A: **As you walk, let the space substance support you! Rest on it! Lean into it! Let it support your head! Your chin! Your eyeballs! Your upper lip, etc.!** *B:* **Now, you are your sole support! As you walk, you are holding yourself together! Your face!**

Your arms! Your whole skeleton! If you quit holding yourself together, you would fly into a thousand pieces! You are hanging onto
your arms! Your mouth! Your forehead (calling out that which is held
rigid)! **Note what you feel when you are your sole support!** *C:* **Now
change! Walk through the space and let the space support you!
Don't worry about what that means! Your body will understand!
Let the space take over where you were holding! Note your body
feeling! Let the space support you! Let space support your eyes!
Your face! Your shoulders! Your upper lip! You go through the
space and let the space go through you!** (Continue to change back
and forth between support and effort until players experience the difference.)

Evaluation: To players: How did you feel when space was supporting you? When you were your own support? To audience: Did you perceive a difference between support and no support in the way players
walked and looked?

Point of Observation:

When players hold themselves together, are their own gravity
line, so to speak, some shrink up, some seem to be afraid of falling,
while others appear anxious, lonely and still others look aggressive. In
fact, many 'character qualities' appear. When, on the other hand, players lean on space, an expansiveness and fullness can be noted as they
move through the environment. It is as if they knew the environment
will support them if they allow it to.

SPACE WALK #3 (SKELETON)
(Warm Up: **Space Walk #1, #2**)

Focus: on physical movement of one's skeleton in space.

Description: Full group. Players walk through space focusing on
skeletal movement of bones and joints.

Side Coaching: **You go through the space and let the space go
through you! Feel your skeleton moving in space! Avoid seeing a
picture of your skeleton! Feel your skeleton with your skeleton!
Feel the movement of every joint! Allow your joints to move
freely! Observe where you are interfering! But don't do anything
about it! And don't not do anything about it! Feel the movement
of your spine! Your pelvic bones! Your leg bones! Let your head**

rest on its own pedestal! Feel your skull with your skull! Now put space where your brains are! Where your cheeks are! Around your arm bones! Between each disc in your spinal column! Put space where your stomach is! But hang on to your skeleton! Feel your skeleton moving in the space! Heighten the movement of your joints! Feel your own form once more! The outer outline of your whole body in space! Feel where the space ends and you begin! You walk through the space and let space through you! Take note of your skeleton moving in space! Everybody close your eyes! When I call "Open your eyes!", you will be in a new place! Now, open your eyes! See the new place you are in! (Repeat this 2 or 3 times.) Your next step is into an unknown place! You are now stepping into an unknown place!

Evaluation: Did you begin to get the feeling of your own skeleton in space?

Points of Observation:

1. Younger children who may be put off by the word 'skeleton' should be made aware of the fact that the skeleton is the basic frame of every person's body. This exercise will help.

2. When body space is connected to outer space in this exercise, some players can experience anxiety. Should anxiety appear at this point, bring players back to their own body form quickly.

SPACE SHAPING/SINGLE

Focus: on allowing space substance to take shape as an object.

PART ONE:

Description: Single players find any object they wish, emerging out of the space substance.

Side Coaching: **Play with the space substance! If an object begins to take shape, go with it! Feel the object! Stay with it!**

PART TWO:

Description: Single players pull space substance around as though it cannot be separated from itself.

Side Coaching: **Experiment! Move it about! Pull it! Let it pull you!**

Point of Observation:
          Most players can gather and handle the space substance as they would any other pliable mass, finding objects with confidence that show exactness and reality. Perhaps this is so because the player does not construct (invent) the object from the imagination but discovers (intuits) it as it comes up out of space.

SPACE SHAPING/ENSEMBLE

Focus: on allowing objects to take shape in the space substance between players

PART ONE:
     Description: Two or more players allow an object animate or inanimate to appear out of the space substance and then keep it between them through play.
     Side Coaching: **Play with the space substance! Use full body energy! Go with it! Let it emerge! Keep it between you!**

PART TWO:
     Description: Coach players to pull the space substance about, keeping it attached in space, to swing on it, let it pull them, to wind it around each other, etc.
     Side Coaching: **Head to toe involvement! Follow the follower! Keep the space substance between you!**

MIRROR

Focus: on exact mirror reflection of initiator's movements.

Description: Divide groups into teams of two by counting off. One player on each team is A; one is B. All teams play simultaneously. A faces B. B will initiate all movement. A will reflect B. Movements are to be full body movement and reflection is to be complete. After a time, leader will call "Change!" and A becomes the initiator of movement and B becomes the mirror without any stop in the flow of movement. Leader should call "Change!" frequently.

Side Coaching: **A, reflect B's movements! Keep the mirror between you! Reflect fully from head to toe! Change the mirror! B is the mirror! Keep the mirror between you! A, know when you initiate! Change the mirror! A, know when you reflect! B, know when you initiate! Change the mirror! B, know when you reflect! Reflect only what you see - - not what you think you see!** (Repeat as needed.)

Evaluation: After playing for awhile, ask players: Did you know for sure when you were initiating and when you were reflecting? What is the difference between imitation and reflection?

Points of Observation:

1. In the same session, go on to **Who is the Mirror**? which increases tension between players and brings in audience participation.

2. For the teacher, imitation is cerebral, i.e., player sees right hand and uses right hand, etc. Reflection requires a present time environment. Reflection takes players out of old frames of references (conditioned response) and has players work on what is at hand.

WHO IS THE MIRROR?

Focus: to conceal which player is the Mirror.

Description: Teams of two. Before going on stage, the two players secretly decide between themselves which one will be the Reflector and which the Initiator. The game is played exactly as in **Mirror** - with one player initiating all movement and the other reflecting fully all movement. During the game, leader will call out the name of one of the players. Members of the audience are to raise hands if they feel that player is the Mirror. The Mirror and Initiator are to continue playing until audience is unanimous on one or the other player or cannot decide for either player unanimously.

Side Coaching: (leader will not coach players; just ask for hands on which player is the Mirror by calling player's names.)

Evaluation: To players: which one of you was the mirror?

Point of Observation:

The effort to confound the audience demands a heightened concentration and produces a more intense involvement with the problem and each other. This game is an early step in breaking down the walls between player and player and between player and audience.

Gibberish:

INTRODUCTION

Developing fluency in "no symbol" speech brings with it a release from word patterns that may not come easily. You may even have to practice your own fluency before presenting Gibberish to the group. An illustration might consist of initiating a simple communication by asking a player, in Gibberish, to stand up: *Gallorusheo!* accompanying the sound with gesture. If the player is slow to respond, strengthen the gesture and repeat the sound, or utter a new phrase in Gibberish. You might ask other players to sit down *(Moolasay!)* move about *Rallavo!)* or sing *(Plagee?)* for example. The following exercise may now be played by the entire group.

GIBBERISH/INTRODUCTION

Focus: on speaking in Gibberish.

Description: Ask the whole group to turn to neighbors and carry on conversations in Gibberish as if speaking an unknown language, and converse as if making perfect sense.

Sidecoaching: **Use as many different sounds as possible! Exagerrate mouth movements! Vary the tone! Try gum-chewing movements! Keep your usual speech rhythm! Let the Gibberish flow!**

Evaluation: Was there variety in the Gibberish? Did the Gibberish flow?

Points of Observation:

1. Keep the conversation going until everyone participates.

2. Have those who are more fluent in Gibberish converse with those who stick with a monotonous *dadeeda* sound.

3. While most of the group will be delighted at their ability to converse in Gibberish, there may be one or two who are so tied to speech for communication that they will be almost paralysed physically as well as vocally. Treat this casually, and in subsequent Gibberish, flow of sound and expression should become one.

GIBBERISH/ENGLISH

Focus: on communication.

Description: Choose two players to select a topic and conduct a conversation. Explain to group that you will coach players to switch from English to Gibberish and back again, even if caught mid-word. Proceed to side coach. Conversation is to flow normally and advance in meaning. When playing is understood, divide workshop into teams of three. Many teams, each with its own side coach, play simultaneously. After a time, call **Change!** for the side coaches so that all have a chance to side coach and to converse in Gibberish/English with both team-mates.

Side Coaching: **Gibberish! English! Gibberish! English!** and so on.

Evaluation: Did the conversation flow and have continuity? Was communication maintained throughout? Players, do you agree?

Points of Observation:

l. This game develops side coaching skills within all age ranges.

2. If Gibberish becomes painful for any player, immediately change to English for a time. In all side coaching help the player who withdraws energy from the problem.

3. The moment of change should be when the speaker is off-guard, in mid-word or sentence. In the off-balance moment the source of new insights is tapped.

4. A group of four can play, one as interpreter, the others speaking Gibberish, if the class size is uneven.

NO MOTION

Focus: on the 'no motion' within movement.

PART ONE:

Description: Ask players to raise their arms in space, breaking up the flow of movement into a series of stills or frames as on a filmstrip. Arms are to move up and down in regular speed and players are to focus on feeling the periods of 'no motion' within the total flow of movement.

Side Coaching: **Raise your arms as in a series of stills and focus on the feeling of 'no motion' as you raise your arms! You do nothing and focus on doing nothing! Lower your arms in 'no motion'! You stay out of it! Raise your arms in regular speed, focusing on 'no motion'! Triple your speed, focusing on 'no motion'! Up and down! Normal speed, in 'no motion'!**

Evaluation: To players: How many of you got the feeling of 'no motion', the feeling that the arms were moving by themselves?

Point of Observation:

If properly executed, this exercise gives a physical understanding and feeling of keeping out of the way. By focusing on 'no motion', limbs move without the effort of conscious volition. You are at rest in 'no motion' - without attitude about the action.

PART TWO:

Description: Full group walks around the room focusing on 'no motion'.

Side Coaching: **As you walk, focus on the periods of 'no motion'! You do nothing! Let your body walk around the room! You stay in 'no motion'! As you walk, let your sight go out into the whole room and see all the objects and people around you! Walk and move in 'no motion'! See your fellow players in 'no motion'! Take a ride on your own body and view the scenery around you!**

Evaluation: To players: Are you beginning to get the feeling of yourself doing nothing? Of the body moving itself?

Point of Observation:

"No motion!" used as a side coach keeps the player quiet and off the subject. This loss of concern releases fear and anxiety holds, leaving a clear, blank mind through which something new might come forth. You can use **No Motion!** as a side coach with other theater games or during rehearsal.

SLOW MOTION/FREEZE TAG

Focus: on moving in complete slow motion.

Description: Establish a relatively small area for play, no larger than 20' x 20'. After a short warmup of Tag played in normal speed, stop and tell players they will play a game of freeze tag in very slow motion within restricted boundaries. Appoint the first 'it'. Immediately upon tagging another player, 'it' must freeze in the exact tagging position. If the group is overlarge, two taggers are recommended. Coach players to run, breathe, duck, look, laugh, etc., in very slow motion. The new 'it' proceeds in slow motion, attempting to touch untagged players who must stay within bounds and move in very slow motion around frozen players as around trees in a forest. Game continues until all are frozen.

Side Coaching: (Side coach in slow motion.) **Run in slow motion! Breathe in slow motion! Slooooow moootiiiooon! Tag in slooow moootion! Freeze in slooow moootion! Duck away from 'it' in slooooow motion! Stay within bounds in very slooooow motion!**

Evaluation: To players: Is there a difference between moving slowly (start, stop, start, stop) and moving in slow motion (even fluidity of movement)?

Points of Observation:

1. If the space is not restricted the game becomes time-consuming. If two taggers are used, at the end coach "Taggers, tag each other!"

2. If the game bogs down, coach "Normal speed!" for a while and then coach "Slooooow moooootioooon!" We are after present-time energy and fluidity of movement. The game is a warmup for the Theater Game **Slow/Fast/Normal.**

SLOW/FAST/NORMAL

Focus: on exploring the **Who, What** and **Where** in different time frames.

This 4-part exercise allows players to be in a state of play. In Part Two they go back and replay in slow motion the normal speed action of Part One. In Part Three they do so in fast time, and in Part Four they replay the same action in normal speed

PART ONE: Normal Speed
Description: Two or more players agree on **Who, What** and **Where** and play their agreed **Who, What** and **Where** in normal speed. Keep the playing time fairly short, just long enough for players to be in relation to one another and the **Where**

Side Coaching: **Use your Where Play with each other!**

PART TWO: Slow Motion

Focus: on replaying Part One in slow motion.

Description: Players go through the **Who, What** and **Where** again, this time in slow motion.

Side Coaching: **Slowww motiooonnnn! The Space is in slow motion! See each other in slow motion! Very slooow motion!**

PART THREE: Fast Time

Focus: on repeating in fast time.

Description: Players re-do the action as fast as they can.

Side Coaching: **Fast!! Double time!! As fast as can be! Faster! Faster! Keep going!**

PART FOUR: Normal Speed

Focus: on playing the scene in normal speed.

Description: Players repeat scene in normal time with no side coaching.

Evaluation: To audience: Was there a difference between the first and last playing? Was there more depth or defined relationships between the players? To players: Do you agree?

Points of Observation:

1. It is not necessary that players repeat the action and dialogue exactly each time. They will intuitively edit elements that are not essential to the playing. This is an exercise in self-editing.

2. Watch for players who are acting out slow motion, rather than being in a state of slow motion.

GIVE AND TAKE WARM-UP

Focus: on trying to move within the rules of the game.

Description: Players stand in a circle. One (any) player may 'take', start a movement, and when any player 'takes', all other players must 'give'; hold their own movement, waiting to move. Any player can 'take' (move) at any time, into the space of the circle, but must hold if another player starts a motion. Sounds may be considered 'taking'.

Side Coaching: **Hold when another player takes! Give! Take! Even the slightest movement takes it! Hold your movement - ready to continue the flow of your movement when the chance arises! Take! Give!**

Evaluation: None.

Points of Observation:

    1. Even a beginning group can play this game successfully.

    2. Players sensing another player 'taking' are said to be 'giving'.

    3. The word 'hold' is used instead of 'freeze'. 'Freeze' is total stoppage; 'hold' is waiting to move as soon as one can do so.

B. Playground Series:

PLAY BALL

Focus: on keeping the ball in the space between players - - and out of individual player's heads. (No pretending.)

Description: Teams of many players (half the group is suggested.) Team members agree on the type and size of ball they will play catch with, i.e., baseball, basketball, etc.. The game is to be played as regular catch, with members tossing the ball back and forth between themselves. However, the ball is not visible. There is no real ball. The chosen ball is to be made of air or 'space'. Once the game is in motion, the teacher/director is to call out changes in the weight of the ball.

Side Coaching: **Keep the ball in space - - not in your heads! Use your full body to throw the ball! Get your shoulders into the action! Keep your eye on the ball! The ball is one hundred times lighter! Play with your whole body! The ball is one hundred times heavier! Use your whole body to catch the ball! The ball is normal again! Keep it going!**

Evaluation: (after each team plays) To audience players: Did they show you the weights of the ball? Were they all playing with the same ball? Did they keep the ball in space? Or were they pretending? To team players: Was the ball in the space or in your heads?

Points of Observation:

    1. After evaluation have the next team play. Be sure to ask the players whether or not they benefited from the first team's evaluation.

2. Side coach with energy and enthusiasm during the game. Keep the pace up and emphasize the necessity of using the full body to keep the ball in motion. Players should leave this game with all the physical effects of having actually played an active game of catch, i.e. warm, out of breath, pink cheeks, etc. If this has not occurred even partially, then you may be sure your players were pretending.

3. Words used in the first presentation of this problem must be carefully chosen. Players are not asked: a) to pretend the ball is there; b) to imagine the ball is there; or c) to make the ball real. Players are simply instructed to keep the ball in space - - not in their heads.

4. Remember, when the ball does 'appear', it can be regarded as a physical connection that is as real as if a ball/ball had been used. Everyone will know when and if it does happen.

KEEP AWAY
(Prerequisite: **Play Ball**)

Focus: on keeping the ball in space - - out of the head.

Description: Full group or teams of many players. Players form a circle with one player in the center. After agreeing on the type of space ball to be used, circle players throw ball back and forth trying to keep the center player from catching it. If the center player catches the ball, the player who threw it takes his place.

Side Coaching: **Keep the ball going! Play with your whole bodies! Keep your eye on the ball! Get your legs working! Your back muscles! Your arms!** (if ball is caught) **Change places! Keep the ball in space - - out of your heads! Use your full bodies!**

Evaluation: To audience players: Were they all playing with the same ball? Was the ball in space - - or in their heads? To team players: Was the ball in space - - or in your heads?

Point of Observation:

Be sure to ask both the audience and the players whether the ball was in the space or in their heads. The whole premise of rote-teaching and dependency on authoritarianism (right/wrong) is shaken by the simple question, "Was it in your head or in the space?"

DODGE BALL
(Prerequisite: **Play Ball**)

Focus: on keeping the ball in space - - out of the head.

Description: Full group or teams of many players. Each team agrees on the type of space ball to be used. Players form a circle with one player in the center. Circle players try to hit the center player with their space basketball, baseball, or whatever. If the center player is hit, he/she changes places with the one who hit him/her. No hitting above the waist.

Side Coaching: **Play with your whole bodies! Keep your eye on the ball! Keep the ball in space - - out of the head! No hitting above the waist! Use your full body to throw and catch! Keep the ball in space - - not in your head!** (If player is hit: **Change places with the one who threw it!)**

Evaluation: To players: Was the ball in space? Or was the ball in your head? To audience players: Was the ball in space or in their heads?

TUG OF WAR

Focus: on keeping the rope in space - - and out of the head; full attention on the rope between them.

Description: Divide group into teams of two by counting off. Playing one team at a time, each player tries to pull the other player over a center line, exactly as in playground Tug of War. Here, the rope is not visible, but a space rope.

Side Coaching: **Keep the rope in space! And out of the head! Keep the rope between you! Use your full bodies to pull! Pull with your leg muscles! Your back! Your feet! Keep the rope between you! Keep the rope in space and out of the head! Stay on the same rope!**

Evaluation: To audience: Were the two players on the same rope? Did the rope connect the players? Was the rope in space or in the players' heads? Ask the players: Was the rope in space or in your head? Do players agree with audience? Does audience agree with players?

Points of Observation:

1. Play the space rope and space ball games with your group until the phenomena of objects in space, not in the head, has been experienced and understood by your group.

2. As your group becomes facile with this game played in pairs, add more and more players to both ends of the rope.

JUMP ROPE

Focus: on keeping the rope in space, not in the head.

Description: Three or more players per team. As in regular jump rope, two players turn the rope and others jump in. The jumper who misses must exchange places with a player turning the rope. The rope is not a real rope, but a 'space' rope.

Side Coaching: **Keep the rope in space! Out of the head! Turners, stay on the same rope! Use your whole body to play the game! Keep the rope in space! Out of the head!**

Evaluation: To audience: Was the rope in space or in the players' heads? To players: Was the rope in space or in your head?

Points of Observation:

1. Variations: If space allows, have the whole group play **Jump Rope** simultaneously. The group will enter this play with all the pleasure, excitement, relaxation of playground games. The invisible will indeed become visible. Some teams can play single rope jumper; Double Dutch; Higher and Higher; Lindy Loop, or any jump rope game they wish.

2. The author likes to join in each game around the playing area by jumping on or into each team's rope.

IT'S HEAVIER WHEN IT'S FULL

Focus: on showing the variations in weight between empty and filled receptacles.

Description: Two large teams line up on opposite sides of the room or stage facing each other. Type of receptacles and objects to be placed in receptacles are agreed upon. First team carries empty space receptacles to players on team Two who fill the receptacles with space objects. First team returns to its original place carrying filled receptacles. (Examples: baskets and apples; chests and treasure; pails and water, etc.)

Side Coaching: **Feel the weight in your legs! Your back! Not only your arms! Feel weight with the whole body!**

Evaluation: To audience: Did you see the difference in weight between full and empty receptacles? To players: Was the difference in weight in your heads or in the space?

Point of Observation:

If your players are preparing for a theater performance, this game is valuable for giving reality to objects. Discussion can include simple facts such as there being no actual water in the well on stage, no weight to the space substance objects used in a scene.

PLAYGROUND #1

Focus: on keeping space objects in the Space and out of the head.

Description: Full group. Players can select their own fellow players or can be counted off into teams of three, four and five. Teams of players play any game they wish. Teams will play many different playground games simultaneously around the playing area. Suggest Marbles, Jacks, Four Squares, Knives, or a repeat of Tug of War, Play Ball, Jump Rope, etc. All games are to be played with space objects.

Side Coaching: **Keep it (the ball, rope, bat, marble, etc.) in the space - - out of the head! Play with your whole body! More energy! Faster! Keep it in space and out of the head! Full bodies!**

Evaluation: (as in other space object games) Was it (the playing object) in your head or in the space?

Point of Observation:

If your players are beginning to grasp the idea of playing with space objects, the whole area should be full of excitement, energy, and fun.

PLAYGROUND #2

Focus: on keeping the space objects in the space and out of the head.

Description: Space permitting, have the full group play any of the following games with space objects: Baseball, Badminton, Volleyball, Basketball, Ping Pong. The author has seen as many as five innings of baseball played this way. As in all space object games, players are to: **Keep the ball in space, not in the head!**. (Side Coaching, Evaluation, etc., will follow the same format as in previous games in this series.)

C. Part of a Whole Series

PART OF A WHOLE ACTIVITY (**What**)
(Warm-Up: **New York**)

Focus: on showing (and seeing) a project, through an activity.

Description: Teams of six to ten players agree on a first player who secretly chooses a group project and begins an activity related to it. When the nature of the project becomes apparent, other players freely join in, one at a time, and take a part in the project. For Example, setting up camp, spring cleaning, building a house. (This game should be fun. Don't be dismayed if the stage becomes chaotic or if you end up with ten players raking ten piles of leaves.)

Side Coaching: **Show us! Don't tell! Avoid dialogue! Other players, give yourselves time to see the whole project before joining! Show! Don't tell! Other players, take a risk! Join the project!**

Evaluation: To audience: What was the whole project? Did players show or tell us? To on-stage players: Were you sharing the different activities within the project, or were you all doing the same thing? Did you give yourselves enough time to *see* what the project was before joining? What did you think the project was before you joined? Were you a part-of-the-whole? To first player: Did you choose a project that allowed for others to become a part-of-the-whole?

Points of Observation:
    1. Warm-up for this game is the traditional game **New York**.

2. Play this game with your group until a flow of energy and connection between players becomes apparent.

3. Players reluctant to take a part for fear of being wrong about what they see as the activity can be comforted in the Evaluation period to find that many players joined in with quite different ideas.

4. Variation: Have teams choose two first players who secretly decide on a group project. All other rules remain the same. This variation came out of one group's inability to pick a first player, as no player wanted the responsibility of choosing a project. By splitting the responsibility between two players, the fear of being wrong was dissipated.

#2 PART OF A WHOLE OCCUPATION (**Who**)
(Warm-Up: **New York**)

Focus: on showing a profession through an activity.

Description: Teams of five to ten players choose a first player who secretly decides on a profession and begins an activity related to it. As the nature of the profession becomes apparent, other players freely join in, one at a time, and take a related part in the profession, For Example, first player is a surgeon; other players become nurse, patient, anesthetist, intern, etc.

Side Coaching: **Show us! Don't tell! Let your activity show us! Don't tell! Avoid dialogue! Other players, take time to see before joining! Join the activity as a definite character! Take a risk! Take a risk! Play the game!**

Evaluation: To audience: What was the profession? Did players show us through the activity or tell us with dialogue? To players: Were you sharing the different activities within the same profession or were you all doing the same thing? What did each of you think the profession was before you joined in? Were you Part-of-the-Whole? Did the first player choose a profession that allowed others a part?

Point of Observation:

The emphasis of this game is on relating through activity. Character is to come out through activity, rather than from dialogue which could become just telling who they are.

#3 PART OF A WHOLE RELATIONSHIP
(Warm-Up: **New York**)

Focus: on showing relationship through the activity.

Description: Teams of five to ten players agree on a first and second player. First player begins a simple activity of a general nature. He does not know **Who** he is. Second player, off-stage, decides **Who** they both are, joins the first player on stage, and using the general activity as a springboard, must *Show* the first player who they both are. When first player discovers the relationship, other players, one by one, decide on a related character and join on-stage players in the general activity. On-stage players must wait to find out who new players are through activity. For example, first player hanging drapes; second player decides to be the wife to first player and shows him that through the activity of hanging drapes. Other players may be the couple's children, neighbors, minister, etc..

Side Coaching: **Show! Don't tell! Stay with the activities! No guessing! No need to rush! Let who you are be discovered through the activity! When you know who you are, show us through playing! Other players, wait till the 1st player knows who they are before joining in! When you enter, let other players discover who you are through activities! Show! Don't tell!**

Evaluation: To audience: Who were the players? What were their relationships? Did players show who they were through activities or tell us with dialogue? To on-stage players: Do you agree?

Points of Observation:

1. This game will bring forth first signs of a scene emerging from the *focus*, as well as first signs of relationship rather than mere simultaneous activity.

2. Let the players enjoy the game even if the stage is somewhat chaotic with the large group of 'characters' in the scene. This childlike stage behavior releases pleasure and excitement and is essential to the social growth of the group. Refrain (no matter how tempted) from trying to get an orderly scene. Subsequent games will slowly clear disorder from scenes.

3. Variation: Limit teams to two players and play as above.

ADD A PART

Focus: on placing, finding or creating a part of an object in space.

Description: Large team. First player decides on a large object or an object with many parts, enters the playing area or stage and places or creates a part of it out of space and then leaves the stage. As the nature of the object becomes apparent, one by one, other players on the team go on stage, add another part and leave the stage. Game continues until all players have had a turn and the object is complete. For Example, Player #1 finds or uses a steering wheel; Player #2 places a seat, Player #3 adds a door to the car, etc.

Side Coaching: **Show us the object! Don't tell! Let us see what you see! Other players, see the WHOLE through the part left on stage! Find another part! Keep it in the space! Out of the head! Give each part its place in space!**

Evaluation: To audience: What was the object? Was it in players' head or in the space? Did the first player pick an object that everyone could add to? To players: Was your part in the space or in your head? To each player: What did you think the whole object was when you were adding your part? (The final object may change as more parts are added.)

Point of Observation:

This game is similar to **Part of a Whole Object** but in this game the player does not become *part* or fill the space with his body, but rather leaves a part of a large space object in the stage space.

PART OF A WHOLE OBJECT[1]

Focus: on being part of a larger object.

Description: Large teams. First player chooses a large object with many parts, goes on stage and becomes a part of it, using his or her whole body. As soon as the nature of the object becomes clear to another player, that player joins in as another part. Play continues until all players are participating and working together to form the complete ob-

---

[1] **Part of a Whole Object** has been imitated by many groups and is often called **The Machine**. Spolin felt that the imitation is limited and limiting, leading the players into conceptualizing. **Part of a Whole Object** can be many things, indeed!

ject. Players may assume movements, sounds, or positions to help complete the whole. For Example, a train with players becoming pistons, wheels, engine, whistle, semaphore; a statue grouping; bouquet of flowers; monster; an abstraction.

Side Coaching: **Show us! Don't tell! Use your whole body to become your part! Other players, take a risk! Take another part of the object!**

Evaluation: To audience: Did players work together on the whole? What was the whole object? To second player: What was Player #1 part of? What did you think before you joined in? (Ask all players what they thought the object was.) Did the first player choose an object that allowed others to join as parts of a whole?

Points of Observation:

1. This game is useful both before, or as an ending to, a session as it generates a great deal of spontaneity and fun, with players often straying from the original 'idea' of the first player, resulting in fanciful abstractions.

2. Leader should use Side Coaching to help single players become part of this larger community. A player who is afraid of being isolated may enter the playing without realizing what whole object is in the process of being formed. Another player may not participate because of the fear of being wrong. Questioning in Evaluation about what each player thought the whole object was before it was entered will help ease many fears of this nature.

3. This game is most useful for performance in many stories, with players becoming giants, monsters, etc. as called for in the story.

RELAY WHERE DEMONSTRATION

Leader: Before beginning **Relay Where**, give this short demonstration. Place a chair in the playing area. Point out to your group (what they already know) that the chair, being solid (lift it up), visible (turn it around), of a particular substance (knock on it), and concrete (sit on it), requires that we pay attention to it. We *see* it. It can be sat upon. We cannot walk through it. Show your group through the above and variations on the above that the chair, being visible and of solid material, takes up space.

After demonstration of the *visable*, concrete object in space, give a demonstration of the *invisable* - - the use of **Space Objects**. In most instances space objects will be used in theater games and in Story Theater performances. Any object needed or required by a player will be brought into existence through space or, to say this in reverse, we will bring **Space** into existence for viewing, through the object.

Demonstrate: Walk to a desk (made of space). Open a drawer in the desk, take a pencil (space), and write something on the desk top. Move to a window (space), open it. Set a bowl of flowers (space) on a table top (space). Etc., etc., etc. Ask the group: Was the object in the space or in my head?

If you do not care to give the demonstration, ask two students: Student one to set up an object (a desk) and student two to use it. Ask the group: Was the desk, et al., in the head or in the space?

If the group has had some work on **Play Ball**, **Tug of War**, **Jump Rope**, etc., this point of **In the Head or in the Space** will be easily grasped by the youngest of players.

It is necessary in theater games workshops to use chairs or benches for such things as couches, beds and chairs themselves. Until man has learned to levitate, something solid will be needed to sit upon. Suggest beds be but one chair and not a row of chairs. Demonstrate: The one chair is the support. Simply sit on the chair, bring your feet over as if reclining on a bed and let the feet fall into a natural position. Turn on a bed light (space), pull the covers (space) over you, etc.. The above, with a few additional demonstrations, is both amusing to the students and quickly makes it clear the difference between real (concrete/visible) objects and space objects (the invisible, which we attempt to make visible).

RELAY WHERE #1

Focus: to create a whole **Where** with space objects.

Description: Large teams of players, agree on first player. Without planning ahead and trying to keep a blank mind, the first player enters the stage and finds or places an object in the space. This object will become part of a **Where** (a place or setting, preferably indoors at first). When the first player has left the stage, each successive player enters the stage, places or finds another object in the **Where**, and before leaving uses or makes contact with every other object already placed by other players in the **Where**. For example, first player uses a refrigerator, second a stove, third a sink, fourth a table, fifth a window, etc., etc. The final **Where** is a kitchen.

Side Coaching: **Find the object in the space! Keep it out of your head and in the space! Use all the objects in the WHERE! Use your whole body! Find your part of the WHERE and use it!**

Evaluation: To audience: Where were the players' objects? Were the objects in players' heads? Or in space? Did all the players use all previous players' objects? To players: Was your object in your head or in the space? **Where** were you?

Points of Observation:

1. If players see fellow players' objects appear in space and witness the progress of the evolving **Where**, finding objects in space will happen spontaneously without preplanning, by the simple act of contacting or using the objects which have already become visible.

2. This game is particularly useful in developing skill with space objects.

RELAY WHERE #2

Focus: To define or build a chosen **Where** with space objects.

Description: Large teams of players each agree on a specific **Where**. First player enters the stage, finds an object in the space which will become part of the chosen **Where** and leaves the stage. Each successive player uses or makes some physical contact with all objects put in the space by preceding players, adds another space object and leaves the playing area.

Side Coaching: **Find the object in the space! Let your full body help you! Keep the objects in the space and out of your head! Give every object its place in space! Bring the object into existence through space! Use all the objects! Stay in the same WHERE! Feel your object's weight! Its texture! Its size! Use it!**

Evaluation: To audience: **Where** were the players and what objects did players put in the **Where**? Were the objects in players' heads or in the space? Ask players the same questions. Do players and audience agree?

Point of Observation:

Repeat this game again when your groups have chosen stories for performance. Have players build the various settings needed out of space objects and go through the story keeping the objects in the space and out of their heads.

D. Traditional Games

WHO STARTED THE MOTION?

Description: The full group stands in a circle. One player is sent from the room while another player is selected to be the leader who starts the motion which everyone in the circle reflects. The full body movements initiated by this player can be changed at any time and the whole group must reflect these motions. The outside player having been called back, stands in the center of the circle and is given three chances to say who started the motion. When the center player discovers the leader (or has made three wrong calls), the leader player then leaves the room (becoming 'it') and a new player is chosen to start the motion. Play the game until nearly everyone has had a turn starting the motion.

Side Coaching: Coach for changes, and for reflecting the player opposite so as not to give the leader's identity away.

Point of Observation:

This traditional game spontaneously introduces players to reflection of each other's movements and is a good warm-up for the theater game **Mirror.**

PUSSY WANTS A CORNER

Description: Full group stands around the perimeter of the playing space, except for one player (the pussy), who stands in the middle. The spot where each player stands is a 'corner'. Player who is 'it' approaches any player and says, "Pussy wants a corner!" The reply to this is "See my next door neighbor." Pussy continues this dialogue with other players in turn, while trying to jump into a corner vacated by fellow players, whose business it is to dare Pussy while trading places with each other, without Pussy pouncing upon a corner. The odd player out in such a case, is 'it'.

Point of Observation:
Players of all ages enjoy playing this excellent group warm-up.

NEW YORK

Description: The players count off into two teams of equal size and stand on parallel goals twenty or more feet apart. The first team huddles, coming to a decision on a trade or occupation to be shown, and then advances toward the other team while the following dialogue takes place:

First team: Here we come!
Second team: Where from?
First team: New York!
Second team: What's your trade?
First team: Lemonade!
Second team: Show us some! (If you're not afraid!)

Coming as near to the second team as they dare, the first team's players, each in his or her own way, show their trade or occupation. Players on the second team try to identify the occupation by calling it out at first sight. If wrong, first team goes on showing; second team calling out. When someone calls out the correct trade, the first team must run back to its goal with the second team in hot pursuit. Those who are tagged must join their pursuers' side.

Now the second team chooses a trade and dialogue is repeated, followed by showing the trade as before. Both sides have the same number of turns and the team having the largest number of players at the end wins.

Variations: Variations of this game can be played showing animals, flowers, trees, objects, foods, etc., instead of trades.

SECOND SECTION OF THEATER GAMES FOR STORY THEATER

A. Verbal Agility Series

MIRROR SOUND

Focus: on mirroring your partner's sounds.

Description: Teams of two players sit facing each other. One player is the initiator and makes sounds; the other is the reflector and mirrors the sounds. When 'Change!' is called, roles are reversed. The reflector becomes the initiator; and the new reflector mirrors his/her sounds. Changeovers must be made with no stop in the flow of sound. Teams gather in different spots around the room and play simultaneously as all teams are side coached at once.

Side Coaching: **No pause! Notice your body/physical feeling as you mirror your partner's sound! Change the mirror! Keep the sound going! Reflect the sound! Change! Change!**

Points of Observation:

1. Players communicate orally but nonverbally. Sounds can be loud or soft, humming or shouting. Variety is desirable.

2. In both classical and jazz music, one hears theme or rhythm played by one instrument and then repeated with variations by others.

3. The next time you present this exercise, try dividing the group into teams of three. The third player side coaches the other two. When you call 'New Side Coach!' the role of Side Coach goes to another player. All teams play simultaneously.

MIRROR SPEECH

Focus: on mirroring/reflecting another player's words out loud.

Description: Teams of two players face each other and choose a subject to discuss. One player is the initiator and starts the conversation. The other player is the reflector and mirrors *out loud* the words of the initiator *at the exact same moment*. After a time, **'Change!'** is called and roles are reversed. Changeovers must take place with *no stop* in the flow of words. After a time, call **'Follow the follower!'** Players will follow the follower in speech, thinking and saying the same words simultaneously and without conscious effort.

Side Coaching: **Reflector! Stay on the same word! Reflect what you hear! Reflect the question! Don't answer it! Share your voice! Change the reflector! Keep the flow of words between you! Stay on the same word! Change! Change!** When players are speaking as one voice, without time lag: **You are on your own! Follow the follower! Don't initiate! Follow the follower!**

Evaluation: To audience: Did onstage players stay on the same word at the same time? To players: Did you know when you initiated speech and when you reflected speech? Did you know when you were following the follower? To all players: What is the difference between repeating speech and reflecting speech?

Points of Observation:

1. If a question is asked, coach reflector to *reflect*, not answer it. Coach initiators to avoid questions.

2. The whole body, the senses, must feel the difference between repetition and reflection of the words of the other player before 'follow the follower' can take place. When true reflection takes place, the time lapse between initiator and reflector becomes very short, near nothing. In a sense, players connect with one another on the same word and become one mind, open to each other. Following the follower verbally creates dialogue.

3. If time is limited, teams of three (one being Side Coach) can play simultaneously in different areas of the room.

4. This game can also be played silently. See **Mirror/Follow the Follower**, *Improvisation for the Theater*, p. 61.

VOWELS AND CONSONANTS

Focus: on seeing the vowels or consonants in a word as it is spoken.

Description: Teams of two. Even number of players in a circle. Each player forms a team with the player opposite and quietly converses on any subject agreed upon between them. For six players, there will be three separate conversations. As Side Coached, players are to *see* either the vowels or consonants in the words they speak without putting emphasis on them or changing speech patterns.

Side Coaching: In four parts:

Part 1: **Vowels! See the vowels in your words! Consonants! See the consonants in your words! Vowels! Consonants! Don't accent them! See the vowels! Consonants! Vowels! Keep talking normally!**

Part 2: **Move back from each other! Make the circle larger! Vowels! Speak quietly! Move back more! Consonants! Keep talking! Vowels! Make the circle larger! Consonants! Speak quietly! Vowels! Make the circle as large as you can! Speak quietly! Vowels! Softer!**

Part 3: **Move in closer! Vowels! Speak more softly yet! Closer! Consonants! Quietly! Vowels! Move in more! Keep talking! Softer! Consonants! Quietly!**

Part 4: **Close your eyes! Keep talking! Vowels! Consonants! Quietly! Move in to your original small circle! Keep talking! Vowels! Very, very quietly! Very, very softly! Consonants!**

Evaluation: To players: What happened when you were conversing from long distance? When you had your eyes closed? When you were speaking softly? Did the cross conversations bother you? Did you find you were able to keep up your conversation?

Points of Observation:

1. Wait until players are physiologically attentive to their partners in each conversation, before coaching them to begin moving out.

2. Players are not to raise their voices as they put distance between them. Players have been able to converse quietly from as far away as 40 feet without raising their voices.

3. The coach to 'Close eyes!' opens players to the fact that they are not lip reading. Their whole body from head to toe is involved with the spoken word.

4. When players have returned to their original tight circle, have them continue in conversation with their eyes closed for a few minutes.

5. When using this game in workshop after the story or stories for performance have been chosen, players are to *see* the vowels and consonants in their dialogue as they tell the story to each other.

EXTENDED SOUND

Focus: on keeping the sound in space between players and letting it land on fellow player.

PART ONE:
Description: All players stand in the space at a distance from each other. One player sends a sound (not a word) to another player and lets it land. This other player then also sends a sound to a fellow player. All players send sounds in turn, attentive to the side coaching until each has contacted all or most of the other players.
Side Coaching: **No words! Keep the sound between you! Keep the body upright! Send forth the souuuuund! Keep the sound in the space! Let the sound land! Extend the sound! Send the sound in sloooow motion! Speed up the sound! Speed it up as fast as you can! Normal speed! Keep the space between you! Extend the sou- uuuund! Give and take!**

PART TWO:
Players are coached to focus on the sound as above, but this time to send a *word* and to let it land on fellow player.

PART THREE:
Players now send a sentence, keeping the focus.
Evaluation: Players, did you keep the sound in the space between you? Did the sound land? Players, did you physically extend the sound? Did you give and take?
Point of Observation:
This game shows that sound (dialogue) occupies space. Extending sound into space and letting it land on a fellow player brings about communication in the theater.

BUILDING A STORY

Focus: on staying with the words of the story; on making one voice/one story.

Description: Four or more players in a line facing the side coach, or entire group in a circle with the side coach. Coach points to one player to start any story he or she wishes. Players are chosen at random to continue the story. Players are not to repeat the last word or words of the previous player. (Optional rule, to be used only if necessary: Players caught starting with last word of previous player are out of the game.)

Side Coaching: In this game Side Coaching, which consists of choosing players at random to continue the story, will fall into four parts:

Part One: **At first allow players to finish a phrase or thought before moving on to another player.**

Part Two: **Players tell their story in slow motion. Coach, now begin to catch players off-guard in the middle of a sentence, phrase or thought. Watch for, point out or exclude players caught starting with the last word of previous player.**

Part Three: **Return to normal speed. Continue to catch players off-guard in mid-sentence, etc. If the exclusion rule is not used and players are caught repeating a word, either go on with the story or start a new one.**

Part Four: **Speed up the changes from one player to another. Story should continue until it is as if one voice were speaking.**

Part Five: **Coach players to PHYSICALIZE, to get up on their feet and *show* the beat of the story they are telling.**

*During the stops in the story when a player has been caught repeating the last word of previous player, you may wish to add coaches, i.e. Keep the story going! Stay with the word! Stay with your fellow players! No preplanning!

Evaluation: Did the story become as one story told by one voice? Were players caught up in the idea of where they thought the story should go, or did they stay with the words as the story evolved?

Points of Observation:

1. Catching players off-guard keeps individual playing energy high and prevents preplanning which fragments and alienates players. Point to the player least expecting it. Spontaneity results only when the players stay with the moment of the story being told.

2. Too many players starting with "and" is an indication to the side coach that he/she is not catching players off-guard and not tripping players into allowing the story to support them.

3. When players have chosen a story for performance, this game can be used in rehearsal to tell that story.

4. Another way to play this game is to first have each player contribute one word at a time to the building of the story. Then go to one sentence at a time, then one phrase, then pausing in mid-thought, and finally to physicalizing the telling.

5. The coach may tape-record the story and replay it for evaluation

SINGING DIALOGUE

Focus: on singing instead of speaking.

Description: Teams of two or more players, agree on **Where, Who** and **What** and begin. All dialogue is to be sung.

Side Coaching: **Full body singing! Share with the audience!**

Evaluation: To audience: Did players explore all the areas into which singing might go?

Points of Observation:

1. Good singing voices are not necessary for this game. Just as we had extended movement of the body in space object games, this game is an exercise in the extension of sound.

2. If a pianist is available, he or she can follow the group and improvise melodies as they go along.

3. When players have chosen stories for performance, this game, using the story as a springboard, can be useful in helping players out of rigid, tense-throated speech patterns.

RELATING INCIDENT WITH COLOR

Focus: on seeing the colors in a story as it is being told.

Description: Teams of two players. Player A tells Player B a simple story. Player B is to listen and see the incident in full color at the moment of listening to it. Player B repeats the story to Player A, adding only the colors he/she has seen while listening. Then reverse and have B tell A a story which he repeats to B adding colors only. For Example: *A narrates*: I was walking down the street; and there seemed to be a car accident. There was a group of people around the car. I wanted to see what had happened, so I used my hands to push through the crowds. *B*

repeats it with color: I was walking along the gray street and there
seemed to be an accident involving a green and black car. There was a
group of people wearing pink and blue dresses and dark suits around the
car. I used my flesh-colored hands with the gold ring to push through
the crowd of blond and black-haired men and woman.

Side Coaching: (only if needed) **See your fellow player! Let the
other see you! Don't wait to add color! See color as you hear the
story! Talk directly to one another! Share your voice!**

Evaluation: To players: How much color did you see as your partner was telling you the story? Did you see the incident clearly? To audience: Could more color have been added?

Points of Observation:

1. Players are not to embellish the retelling of the story except
to add color. See Example above.

2. The leader may have to stress eye-contact to the players who,
to concentrate on color, turn away from the speaker while listening.

3. This game is a warm-up to **Verbalizing the Where.**

4. There are many variations of this game, in which players add
sounds, shapes and textures to a story.

5. When working with a story or fable for performance, this
game has obvious advantages that lend themselves to workshop sessions.

VERBALIZING THE WHERE (in Two Parts)
(Warm-Up: **Relating an Incident**)

PART ONE:

Focus: on verbalizing the **Where** and every action within it in the present tense.

Description: Teams of two or more players agree on **Where, Who** and
What. Sitting in chairs, players are to verbally describe/externalize/ob-
jectify the physical **Where** and everything within it, including fellow
player and action, **Who** and **What**. Players narrate for themselves, not
other players. Dialogue may be entered into if it appears out of the theatrical structure, but all verbalization is to be in the present tense. For
Example: Player #1: **Where** - kitchen, **Who**- mother, **What** - finding a
recipe. Player #2: **Where** - kitchen, **Who**- son, **What** - coming in hungry. Player #1 verbalizes: I tie my checkered apron around my thick waist

and reach for the red-and-white, cloth-covered cookbook on the table. I sit down at the table and open the book. I turn to the section on cookies and thumb through the smooth, shiny, white pages, looking for a recipe. "Hmmm, sugar cookies - - that sounds pretty good." I ponder over it a minute and then decide to look further. Player #2 verbalizes: I open the screen door and run into the kitchen. Darn it, I let the door slam again! "Hey, Mom, I'm hungry. What's for dinner?" (and so on).

Side Coaching: **Verbalize that object! Verbalize the noises around you! Keep it in present time! Use dialogue when it appears! Verbalize the way your hand feels on the chair! Verbalize the smells! Keep it external/objective/out of your head!**

Evaluation: To audience: Did player verbalize externally or was the player emotionally in his/her head? To players: Do you agree with audience? Were there more areas that you could have verbalized? Parts of the **Where?** Action?

Points of Observation:

1. This game can aid in breaking players of subjectivity in their work and help you see the progress of players in learning to objectify and externalize the stage space.

2. If players persist in making this a game of ruminating, subjective thinking and emotional response to the objects and action and themselves in their setting, drop this game and return to simple "Space Object" games and **Relating an Incident**.

3. When the story for performance has been selected, use the story as the **Where Who** and **What** to base the game of **Verbalizing the Where** on.

4. With the same players, go right on to Part Two.

PART TWO:

Focus: While playing a given **Where, Who** and **What**, to verbalize the **Where** and every action within it in the present tense.

Description: Same two players repeat the same **Where, Who** and **What,** as they did in Part One, but rather than remaining seated are to move around the stage as called for in Part One, verbalizing the **Where**, and every action within it and entering dialogue as it appears. Again, all verbalizing is done in the present tense.

Side Coaching: **Verbalize that object! Verbalize the noises around you! Keep it in present time! Keep it external/objective!**

Enter dialogue only when it appears! Verbalize the way your hand feels on that chair! Verbalize smells!

Evaluation: To audience: Did verbalization help to bring players into the stage space, or were players in their own heads? To players: Do you agree with audience?

Points of Observation:

    1. Leaders are cautioned that this game be given only when your group has become objective in its work. Coach players to avoid narration that deals subjectively with parts of the **Where** or their actions within it. See Example in **Verbalizing the Where, Part One**.

    2. At the leader's discretion, the number of players can be increased or decreased for this game. Be sure to guide players away from ruminating about the **Where** and their subjective place within it.

    3. Once again, use this game with a story or stories chosen for performance.

B. Vocal/Technical Series

ECHO

Focus: on diminishing the sound of a given word.

Description: 2 large teams. Players on a team stand one behind the other forming a column. The two columns face each other across a room or the stage as though they were about to play Tug of War (see diagram below). First player in Column #1 calls out a word or phrase. Starting with the first player in Column #2 across the room, the word or phrase is repeated in turn by each succeeding player in Column #2 without pause. Each player is to pick up the word or phrase and diminish the sound so that the word finally fades away at the end of the line. First player in #2 Column then calls out a word or phrase for Column #1 to echo and the game continues back and forth between columns as outlined above.

Side Coaching: **Let the sound flow through each of you! Let sound slowly fade as it passes through you! Each column is one body - - the Echo!**

Evaluation: To audience: Did each succeeding player pick up the word without pause? Did the sound flow as one echo?

Point of Observation:

For clarification, below is a diagram of columns and positions for playing:

COLUMN 1   COLUMN 2
+++++++++   +++++++++
987654321   123456789

CALLING FROM LONG DISTANCES

Focus: on establishing long distances on stage between players through sound alone.

Description: Teams of four or more players agree on **Where, Who** and **What. Where** must be a setting in which players are separated by long distances.

Side Coaching: **Throw the sound a long distance into the space between you! Extend the sound! Use your whole body from the tips of your toes to the top of your head! Open throats!**

Evaluation: To audience: How far away were players from one another? **Where** were they? Did they tell you or show you? Was the distance in their heads or in the Space? To players: Was the distance between you in the Space, or in your heads?

Point of Observation:

Inasmuch as the actual space between players may be but a few feet, calling from long distances is more than shouting. If it is possible to get outdoors, let players work on actually calling from long distances to see what they will be establishing on stage.

WHISPER/SHOUT

Focus: on releasing throat muscles.

Description: Teams of two or more players agree on **Where, Who** and **What.** They are to play three times on the same structure: #1 whispering; #2 shouting; #3 in normal voice. Time limit: no more than fifteen minutes total.

Side Coaching:

Part #1: **Share your whisper with the audience! Full body whisper! Released throat! Extend your whisper! Open your throat!**

Part #2: **Shout with your whole body! Released throat! Put the sound into the full distance between you! Heighten your shouting!**

Part #3: **Normal voice! Released throat!**

Evaluation: To audience: Were players' voices more resonant in normal speech after **Whisper/Shout?** To players: Were you able to release your throat muscles/open your throats better after **Whisper/Shout?**

Points of Observation:

1. A variation of this game is to have the team choose a setting where whispering, shouting and normal speech can be integrated into one scene. Example: **Where,** jail cell; **Who,** prisoners; **What,** planning a break.

2. While this game can be used directly for what is commonly called 'projection' on stage, it also is an experience in physiological harmony and connection with fellow players within a playing space and thus can be used for its own sake.

3. Listen carefully for open throats. Tension means the problem has not been solved. For the third part of the game, cue the audience to also listen for released throats.

STAGE WHISPER
(Warm-Up: **Calling From Long Distances**; **Whisper/Shout**)

Focus: on sharing stage whisper with the audience.

Description: All members of the workshop should try using **Stage Whisper** with one another before counting off into teams. Teams of two or more players agree on **Where, Who** and **What** in which the players are *forced* to whisper to one another. For Example: thieves caught in a clothes closet, lovers quarrel in a church pew, quarreling weekend guests in a bedroom next to their host's room.

Side Coaching: **Use your whole body! Open your throat! More energy! Not a whisper - - a stage whisper! Share your stage whispers with the audience!**

Evaluation: To audience: Did players talk low or did they use a **Stage Whisper**? To players: Did you talk low, or did you use a stage whisper?

Points of Observation:

1. A stage whisper is not a whisper, for it must be shared with an audience, and in a sense is "acting out" a whisper. **Stage Whisper** is closely related to **Whisper/Shout** and **Calling From Long Distances** for it necessitates the same physiological response, open throat, and body support.

2, As this game requires a great deal of physical energy to solve the problem of stage-whispering, the released energy never fails (if players are truly stage whispering) to bring alive many amusing situations.

VOCAL SOUND EFFECTS #1

Focus: on making any sound effect vocally.

Equipment: microphone attached to a public address system.

Description: Full group. Players, in turn, are to make vocal sound effects using a microphone. As playing this game will lead to the ability to bring an environment (**Where**) into the stage space through sound effects alone, leader can encourage fearful players by asking for sounds of particular settings, i.e., forest, haunted house, farm, stormy day, etc. The game can be played by passing the microphone from player to player, by asking for volunteers or by leader suggestion.

Side Coaching: (only as needed) **Explore and heighten that sound! Try a mouse sound! Try some wind blowing! Rain! Bombs falling! Squeaky door!**

Evaluation: (after various sounds) Would anyone like to try that same sound? Is there another possible sound for rain (or whatever has been done)?

Points of Observation:

1. For orientation, it might be well for the leader to play around with a few sounds via the mike to help the group get started. Invariably, however, one or more players will have a natural skill in making sounds and can assist the hesitant.

2. When working with a microphone it is important to protect the delicate head from moisture by covering it with a thin piece of foam and/or a piece of cloth.

3. Paper tubes (toilet tissue center) might be introduced here for use with the microphone to produce echo chamber effects. A straw in a glass of water for bubbling streams and a piece of cellophane to crackle for fire are also useful. Have your group bring in other useful sound effects articles to use with the microphone.

VOCAL SOUND EFFECTS #2
(Warm-Up: **Vocal Sound Effects #1**)

Focus: on bringing the chosen **Where** into the space through and with vocal sounds.

Equipment: a microphone attached to a public address system.

Description: Teams of five or six players gather around the microphone, and using sound as part-of-a-whole, are to create an environment (**Where**) with sound effects alone. This game is played usually with the players on stage, but as the group becomes adept at it, you may want to pull the curtain or have a blank stage.

Side Coaching: **Sound is your fellow player! Bring the Where into the space! Give the sounds their place in space! Bring the environment into the space! The sound is part-of-the-whole!**

Evaluation: To audience: **Where** was it? Was the **Where** in space or in the players' heads? To players: Do you agree with the audience? To individuals: Were you part-of-the-whole?

Points of Observation:

1. A tape recorder adds to the awakening of the players, for when teams hear the playback of their created environment, great excitement and stimulation results as, intuitively, individual players recognize their contribution to the whole (part-of-the-whole).

2. This exercise, when used with the group's chosen story for story theater performance, can develop skills in sound effects to such an extent that mechanical sound effects can be minimized or avoided altogether.

VOCAL SOUND EFFECTS #3
(Warm-Up: **Mirror; Vocal Sound Effects** #1 and #2.)
Note: For this game to be effective, 'Follow the Follower' should be clear to players, so playing **Mirror** is an important warm-up exercise.

Focus: on following the follower

Description: Teams of six players agree on **Where, Who** and **What.** Three players will be the on-stage players, and three players gathered around a standing microphone (attached to a sound system) will produce all the sound effects vocally. On-stage players maintain their own dialogue. The scene will emerge as the sound effects and on-stage action connect through players 'following the follower'. On-stage players and sound effects players reverse positions and play the same **Where, Who** and **What** again.

Side Coaching: **Follow the follower! Don't initiate! Follow the initiator! Sound is your fellow player! Act! Don't react! Follow the follower! On-stage players, avoid anticipating sounds! Off-stage players, avoid anticipating movements! Don't initiate! Follow the initiator!**

Evaluation: To audience: Did players on and off-stage follow the follower? Did players on-stage react to the sound effects? Did sound effects react to players' movements on stage? To players: Do you agree with the audience?

Points of Observation:

1. Allow enough time, if possible, to have the full group experience both the on and off-stage player positions.

2. This game is very close to and can be used as a Warmup to **Dubbing.**

3. In this exercise, to *act* is to be spontaneously confronted with the sound and to allow sound to freely enter the Space. To *react* is cerebral - - thus subjective. The on-stage player who interprets, even if but for a flash, is cheated of the moment of spontaneity.

C. Integration of On and Off Stage Activity Series

CHORAL READING # 1

Focus: For the chorus, on following the conductor. For on-stage players, on playing out the **Where, Who** and **What.** For the conductor, on keeping the connection between chorus and onstage players in constant progression.

Description: Large team agrees on **Where, Who** and **What** and divides itself into 1) on-stage players; 2) a conductor; 3) a choral group. The choral group stands or sits (on risers, if available) to one side of the stage. Group agrees on various sounds and effects needed for the chosen structure and the choral group is divided into parts like sections in an orchestra. (Example: sections for two lost children in a forest might be birds, wind, wild animals, echoes, hummers or singers, whistlers for mood, etc..) Before starting, give the conductor time to practice with his 'orchestra' - - cueing sections by pointing to them and heightening or lowering the intensity of sounds by raising or lowering his/her arms. On-stage players begin. Conductor leads choral group in supplying background effects and is the connection between on-stage players and the choral group.

Side Coaching: **Conductor, keep the choral sections moving! Follow the follower!**

Evaluation: If possible, record the group effort and let everyone hear the playback before following the usual lines of evaluation.

Points of Observation:

1. The conductor's part helps to do away with fragmentation. An intense involvement is required to keep an ensemble moving. Allow many or all players to have the experience of conducting. To make this possible, it may be necessary to change conductor's role during playing, i.e., the conductor joins the choral group and a new conductor steps forward out of the group as designated. This can be done without stopping the playing through Side Coaching.

2. This is another **Part-of-a-Whole** game and can be played with the group's chosen story in place of the **Where, Who** and **What**.

3. Leader may wish to incorporate **Choral Reading #2** into this game simply by Side Coaching: **No conductor! Choral group, follow the follower! On-stage players, follow the follower!** without stopping the flow of the game.

CHORAL READING #2
(Warm-Up: **Choral Reading # 1**)

Focus: on following the follower.

Description: Large teams of players agree on **Where, Who** and **What** and divide themselves into on-stage players and a choral group. The choral group plays on the side (or sides) of the stage, as agreed. Full team agrees on various sounds and effects needed for the chosen structure and then the choral group divides into sections - - each section responsible for a particular effect or sound. Without a conductor to co-ordinate or connect on-stage players and the choral group, players (both on-stage and choral) are to follow the follower.

Side Coaching: **You're on your own! Choral group, follow the follower! On-stage players, follow the follower! Don't initiate! Follow the initiator! Explore and heighten!**

Evaluation: If a recording has been made, play it back at this time before following the usual lines of evaluation.

DUBBING

Focus: on voice and body as separate players acting as one unit.

Description: Two or three players choose or ask for volunteers from the audience/players to be their Voices. The four or six players then become a team and agree on **Where, Who** and **What**. The Voice players gather, possibly around a microphone, in a position facing the on-stage players. Before starting the game, have each on-stage player listen to his or her Voice to familiarize Body with Voice. Off-stage Voices are to reflect the whole body picture and movements of the on-stage players, and the on-stage Body players are to reflect and be moved by the off-stage players in turn. These phenomena must occur simultaneously. The scene will appear during playing as the Bodies and Voices become one.

Side Coaching: **Follow the follower! On-stage players, keep your mouths moving as if speaking! Avoid anticipating what will be said! Off-stage players, avoid anticipating what will be done! Don't initiate! Follow the initiator! Become one voice/one body! On-stage players, keep your mouths moving! Avoid mouthing exact words! Follow the follower! Don't initiate! Follow the follower!**

Evaluation: Did Body and Voice become as one between the on-stage and off-stage players?

Points of Observation:

1. At first the players on-stage and off-stage will become one voice/body only in flashes, but as the connection grows between Voice

and Body, there is no lag between off and on-stage players, and a tremendous burst of power rises between and through players, uniting them in true relation.

2. If this connection does not take place and the voices simply follow on-stage players around shadowing action, play more **Mirror** and **Space Shaping** games until 'follow the follower' is experienced by all the players. Then return to **Dubbing.**

3. Remember, all Side Coaching comes out of what is emerging out of the playing. The Side Coach does not demand, but acts as a fellow player, exploring and heightening what is seen - - not what one wants to see.

D. Character/Technical

BOX FULL OF HATS

Focus: on selection and integration of costume pieces.

Note: A collection of costume pieces is required for this game. See the first Point of Observation below.

Description: Teams of two or more players. This game can be played in two ways: 1) as an added focus to another game in which players agree on **Where, Who** and **What** and choose costume pieces from the 'Box Full of Hats' to fit the scene; or 2) players pick costume pieces at random and then choose **Where, Who** and **What** based on their selections.

Side Coaching: (None needed for this game unless players get bogged down by costumes, whereupon introduction of other acting problems, such as **Gibberish, Slow Motion**, or **Whisper/Shout** is called for.)

Evaluation: To audience: Did the costume pieces help or hinder the scene? To players: Do you agree?

Points of Observation:

1. The 'Box Full of Hats' required for this game is simply a collection of as many costume pieces as you can readily collect or make, i.e. chef's hats, sailor caps, Indian headdresses, helmets, shawls, crowns, floppy hats, berets, scarves, blankets, sheets, capes, gloves, canes, eyeglasses, umbrellas, pipes, paper wings and tails for animals, etc.

2. At first the players will love the idea of costumes and will put them on indiscriminately, odd piece by odd piece, whether a scene requires them or not. With all the fun of 'playing house', work on the problem will sharpen players' sense of spontaneous costume selection for character.

COSTUME PIECE

Focus: on retaining the character qualities (attitudes) suggested by costume bits.

Description: A collection of costume pieces or bits (canes, hats, scarves, umbrellas, gloves, shawls, etc.) must be on hand. Each player on team of two or more is to select a piece from the collection and to assume character qualities (attitudes) suggested by this costume piece. Team then agrees on **Where, Who** and **What.**

Side Coaching: **Retain that quality! Let that attitude support you! Show! Don't tell! Use your full body to retain that attitude!**

Evaluation: To audience: Did players impose character on their costume piece, or did they let the costume piece determine their characters for them? To players: Do you agree with audience?

Point of Observation:

Use costumes with spontaneity in selection. To keep the game from bogging down into socio-drama, throw other acting problems at the players such as: **Gibberish, Slow Motion, Whisper/Shout**

STAGE PICTURE

Focus: on sharing the stage picture with the audience.

Description: Players move in and out and around each other until teacher/director calls out 'stage picture!' Instantly, players stop moving. If some part of each and every player is not visible to the audience, continue to side coach 'stage picture!' Players then instantaneously move, doing whatever will make a part of them visible. Many random formations appear as players bend knees, raise arms, duck heads in response.

Side Coaching: **Stage picture! Continue! Any part of you is all of you! Stage picture! Continue!**

VARIATION ONE:

Continuous moving stage picture. All players keep visible at all times while group stays in constant movement.

Side Coaching: **Stage picture! Stage picture!**

VARIATION TWO:

Following one player, players all move in and out and around one another. When coach calls one player by name, all other players follow this one player in space until 'Hold' or 'Stage picture' is side coached.

Side Coaching: Name one player. When movement has led to formation: **Stage picture!** Name another player. When movement has led to formation: **Stage picture!**

VARIATION THREE:

Divide group into two teams; one team observes and one team plays. The audience team infers a **Where/Who/What** from their positions as each stage picture appears.

Evaluation: For Variation Three: Audience, how did you reach your conclusions? Players, how does your sense of the stage picture match what the audience saw?

Point of Observation:

The recognition that any part of you is all of you is given by this game, which also carries the implicit message that visibility is essential to stage life.

ROCKING THE BOAT

Focus: on integration of rocking or *not* rocking the boat within the agreed structure.

Description: Large teams agree on **Where, Who** and **What.** The stage is to be thought of as a boat - - a rowboat or a canoe at sea. It is a visualization easily grasped. During the playing, when **Rock the Boat** is Side Coached, players are to deliberately rock the boat by creating a lot of excitement, movement or concentrated mutual interest. When **Avoid Rocking the Boat** is Side Coached, players must find a way to balance the stage picture. All work on the problem (rocking or not rocking the boat) must be integrated within the agreed upon **Where, Who** and

What. (Example: A park in which assorted people pursue various activities.)

Side Coaching: **Rock the boat! Avoid rocking the boat! Find a way to rock the boat! Find a way to avoid rocking the boat!**

Evaluation: To audience: Did players impose rocking the boat on the scene or was it integrated within the scene? Did players just separate to avoid rocking the boat? Or did they integrate it within the scene? To players: Do you agree?

Points of Observation:

1. **Rocking the Boat** encourages self-blocking and is a phrase developed to evaluate the stage picture. This phrase and the concept of the stage as a boat gives every player the responsibility of the total stage picture.

2. **You're rocking the boat!** called by the Side Coach in any game played from now on should be enough to remind players of this responsibility. This side coach should be given to the full group, rather than one player, for all will then become responsible for finding and solving the problem.

ANIMAL IMAGES

Focus: on making the body rhythm, body and facial expression and vocal sound (Part Two) of an animal your own.

Description: Teams of two to ten players. Players are to discuss the movement, rhythm, and actual physical characteristics of animals. The bone and facial structures are as important as the more obvious movement. Each player decides on what animal he/she will portray and takes on the exact physical qualities of his/her animal. Players then move around the stage or playing area as animals. Side Coaching will be given in five parts. Between parts, players are not to stop playing but are to allow the energy to flow from one part to the next.

Side Coaching:

Part 1: **Reshape the forehead! The nose! Concentrate on the spine! Concentrate on the tail! Your animal's walk! The back legs! Bring your animal into the space through your body!**

Part 2: When players are moving around the playing area and have captured some new body rhythms, coach for sound: **Give the** sound of your animal! Keep moving! Give the sound of your animal!

Part 3: When sound and body movements are integrated, side coach: **Become human! Stand upright! Keep your animal qualities! Keep your animal rhythms! Sound like your animal! Use a human voice with the animal sound! Keep moving!**

Part 4: When animal sounds and movements are integrated as human, side coach: **Move in and around each other! See one another! Hear one another! Move in and around each other! Keep your animal qualities in body and sound as humans!**

Part 5: When players are in relation through voice and movement, a structure (**Where, Who** and **What**) will begin to take shape. Leader must be fully open and attentive to the on-stage players so as to be able to perceive the **Where, Who** and **What** as it emerges within the stage space. Players should be so accustomed to side coaching by now, that the leader's contribution of **Who, Where** and **What** should not interrupt the flow between players and the problem. Not stopping to discuss the structure with players is important so as not to create a drop in the heightened energy this game generates. See Example in Points of Observation, below, for indications of Side Coaching in Part 5.

Evaluation: To audience: Did players integrate their animal qualities as humans in the given **Where, Who** and **What?** To players: Were your animal qualities in your head or in the Space?

Points of Observation:

1. If at any time, players lose their animal rhythms of body and voice, side coach players back to the original animal sound, movement and rhythm. When animal qualities are restored, side coach players back to come back to human.

2. In Part 3, players are not to sound like an animal talking, but like humans with the animal quality added.

3. During Parts 3 and 4, when players are achieving a new dimension in physical and vocal qualities, the leader will note character qualities and relationships emerging and faint suggestions of places (**Where**) appearing quite spontaneously.

4. The necessity to grasp a possible emergence of a **Where, Who** and **What** and to quickly share it without interrupting the playing is the moment of crisis for yourself, the leader, and the student body as well. It is the key to spontaneity and the creative challenge. Remember, in crisis, all of us - - body, mind and X area - - respond.

5. Example of Part 5 (in context, as actually done by 10 & 11 year olds at the Young Actors Company in Hollywood): four players - two boys and two girls. The girls physicalized a parrot and an owl, the boys a hippopotamus and a cat. In Part 3 (becoming human), the parrot transformed into a shrewish talkative woman; the owl into a wide-eyed young girl; the hippopotamus, a lumbering sullen man; and the cat into a shy and anxiety-ridden young boy. In Part 4 (moving in and around each other), the combination suggested an office - - perhaps a school office. In Part 5, without interrupting players' movements, leader quickly set up chairs, tables and indicated (in space) doors and windows.

Side Coaching: **WHERE! You are in the Assistant Principal's office! That's the desk and chair! A couple of side chairs over here! Here is the door to the inner office! Here is a window! WHO! Parrot, you are the Assistant Principal! Hippo, you are the parent father of the girl! Owl, you are a student, daughter of the hippo! Cat, you are another student! WHAT! The Assistant Principal is in charge of who gets into the inner office and the rest of you are waiting to get in to see her because of school problems!**

Note: The ensuing scene took about ten to fifteen minutes and was most delightful as each character kept the physical qualities of their chosen animals and developed definite attitudes and problems around these characters and towards one another.

6. While useful in getting character qualities for stage work or performance of fables for your group's story, Animal Images is equally pleasurable to play for its own sake.

LIGHTING EFFECTS #1

Focus: on making any lighting effect.

Equipment: A lighting system with dimmer board, colors, spots and filters.

Description: Full group. Players, in turn, are to make lighting effects at the board. As playing this game will lead to the ability to bring an environment (**Where**) into the stage space through lighting effects alone, leader can encourage fearful players to experiment with specific effects, i.e., stormy nights; dawn, etc..

Side Coaching: (only as needed) **Explore and heighten that mood!**

Evaluation: (after various effects) Would anyone else like to try that effect?

LIGHTING EFFECTS #2

Focus: on bringing the chosen **Where** into the stage space through and with lighting effects.

Equipment: a lighting board.
Description: Teams of five or six players gather around the lighting board, and using light as part-of-the-whole, are to create an environment (**Where**) with lighting effects alone.
Side Coaching: **Light is your fellow player! Bring the WHERE into the space! Bring the environment into the space! The light is part-of-the-whole!**
Evaluation: To audience: **Where** was it? Was the **Where** in the space or in the players' heads? To players: Do you agree with the audience? To individual players: Were you part-of-the-whole?

SOUND AND LIGHT TOGETHER #1
(Warm-Up: **Vocal Sound Effects #1, #2, #3; Lighting Effects #1, #2**)

Focus: on bringing a **Where** into the Space with sound and light only.

Equipment: Standing microphone hooked up to a sound system and a theatrical lighting board.
Description: Teams of six to ten players decide on a **Where**. Each team divides itself into sound effects players and lighting effects players. Each sub-team takes its position either behind the microphone or at the lighting board. Working together, sub-teams are to bring their chosen **Where** into the stage space with sound and lighting effects alone.
Side Coaching: **Sound and light are your fellow players! Bring your WHERE into the space! Give the sound and lighting their place in the space!**
Evaluation: To audience: What **Where** did players bring on stage? Was it in players' heads or in the space? To players: Did you explore all

areas into which sound and light could go? To each individual player: Were you part-of-the-whole?

Point of Observation:

This game is an excellent one to return to when the group has chosen its story for performance and technical effects players have been cast.

SOUND AND LIGHT TOGETHER #2
(Warm-Up: Sound and Light Together #1)

Focus: on following the follower.

Equipment: Standing mike and lighting board; sound system.

Description: Teams of ten or more players decide on **Where**, **Who** and **What** and divide into sub-teams of on-stage players, sound effects players, lighting effects players. During play, each sub-team takes its respective position around the microphone, at the lighting board, and on-stage. Working together, sub-teams are to play out their **Where**, **Who** and **What** by following the follower.

Side Coaching: **Act! Don't react! Follow the follower! Trust your fellow players! Don't initiate! Follow the initiator! Sub-teams, don't anticipate what other sub-teams are going to do! Follow the follower! Act! Don't react!**

Evaluation: To audience: Did sound effects players react to on-stage and lighting effects players or did they follow the follower? Did lighting effects players react to the other sub-teams? Did on-stage players follow the follower? To players: Were you following the follower?

Point of Observation:

For final run-throughs of the group's story for performance, this game has obvious use.

THIRD SECTION: PREPARING THE STORY FOR PERFORMANCE

A. FINDING THE STORY
 1. Teacher/director finds it.
 2. Full group finds and/or agrees on story.

B. STORY BECOMES GROUP SUPPORT
 1. Story is read aloud, or told
   a. by teacher/director
   b. by players taking turns
   c. by one player
   d. if time, try all three ways
 2. Group uses VOWELS AND CONSONANTS in reading story.
 3. Whole group tells chosen story playing BUILDING A STORY theater game.
 4. Group in pairs tell each other the story using MIRROR SPEECH game.
 5. Group in pairs use RELATING AN INCIDENT games to bring color and sound to story.

C. CASTING
 1. Onstage players are chosen
   a. teacher/director chooses
   b. or, depending on group, self casting.
 2. Technical (offstage) players are cast for
   a. sound effects
   b. set and shadow props
   c. lighting effects and projections

D. EDITING THE WRITTEN STORY FOR PERFORMANCE
 1. Divide group into onstage players and technical players.
 2. a. Onstage players read story, each player reading his or her lines. Group agreement on words left out.
   b. Technical players add notations on sound and light needs.
 3. Working script drawn up.

E. RUN-THROUGHS FOR PERFORMANCE
 1. Use Theater Games in Section Two for coaching Specific theatrical problems.

ALPHABETICAL LIST OF THEATER GAMES FOR STORY THEATER